Boys in Children's Literature and Popular Culture

Children's Literature and Culture
Jack Zipes, *Series Editor*

Children's Literature Comes of Age
Toward a New Aesthetic
by Maria Nikolajeva

Sparing the Child
Grief and the Unspeakable in Youth Literature About Nazism and the Holocaust
by Hamida Bosmajian

Rediscoveries in Children's Literature
by Suzanne Rahn

Inventing the Child
Culture, Ideology, and the Story of Childhood
by Joseph L. Zornado

Regendering the School Story
Sassy Sissies and Tattling Tomboys
by Beverly Lyon Clark

A Necessary Fantasy?
The Heroic Figure in Children's Popular Culture
edited by Dudley Jones and Tony Watkins

White Supremacy in Children's Literature
Characterizations of African Americans, 1830–1900
by Donnarae MacCann

Ways of Being Male
Representing Masculinities in Children's Literature and Film
by John Stephens

Retelling Stories, Framing Culture
Traditional Story and Metanarratives in Children's Literature
by John Stephens and Robyn McCallum

Pinocchio Goes Postmodern
Perils of a Puppet in the United States
by Richard Wunderlich and Thomas J. Morrissey

Little Women and the Feminist Imagination
Criticism, Controversy, Personal Essays
edited by Janice M. Alberghene and Beverly Lyon Clark

The Presence of the Past
Memory, Heritage, and Childhood in Postwar Britain
by Valerie Krips

The Case of Peter Rabbit
Changing Conditions of Literature for Children
by Margaret Mackey

The Feminine Subject in Children's Literature
by Christine Wilkie-Stibbs

Ideologies of Identity in Adolescent Fiction
by Robyn McCallum

Recycling Red Riding Hood
by Sandra Beckett

The Poetics of Childhood
by Roni Natov

Voices of the Other
Children's Literature and the Postcolonial Context
edited by Roderick McGillis

Narrating Africa
George Henty and the Fiction of Empire
by Mawuena Kossi Logan

Reimagining Shakespeare for Children and Young Adults
edited by Naomi J. Miller

Representing the Holocaust in Youth Literature
by Lydia Kokkola

Translating for Children
by Riitta Oittinen

Beatrix Potter
Writing in Code
by M. Daphne Kutzer

Children's Films
History, Ideology, Pedagogy, Theory
by Ian Wojcik-Andrews

Utopian and Dystopian Writing for Children and Young Adults
edited by Carrie Hintz and Elaine Ostry

Transcending Boundaries
Writing for a Dual Audience of Children and Adults
edited by Sandra L. Beckett

The Making of the Modern Child
Children's Literature and Childhood in the Late Eighteenth Century
by Andrew O'Malley

How Picturebooks Work
by Maria Nikolajeva and Carole Scott

Brown Gold
Milestones of African American Children's Picture Books, 1845–2002
by Michelle H. Martin

Russell Hoban/Forty Years
Essays on His Writing for Children
by Alida Allison

Apartheid and Racism in South African
Children's Literature
by Donnarae MacCann and Amadu Maddy

Empire's Children
Empire and Imperialism in Classic British Children's Books
by M. Daphne Kutzer

Constructing the Canon of Children's Literature
Beyond Library Walls and Ivory Towers
by Anne Lundin

Youth of Darkest England
Working-Class Children at the Heart of Victorian Empire
by Troy Boone

Ursula K. LeGuin Beyond Genre
Fiction for Children and Adults
by Mike Cadden

Twice-Told Children's Tales
edited by Betty Greenway

Diana Wynne Jones
The Fantastic Tradition and Children's Literature
by Farah Mendlesohn

Childhood and Children's Books in Early Modern Europe, 1550–1800
edited by Andrea Immel and Michael Witmore

Voracious Children
Who Eats Whom in Children's Literature
by Carolyn Daniel

National Character in South African Children's Literature
by Elwyn Jenkins

Myth, Symbol, and Meaning in Mary Poppins
The Governess as Provocateur
by Georgia Grilli

A Critical History of French Children's Literature
by Penny Brown

The Gothic in Children's Literature
Haunting the Borders
edited by Anna Jackson, Karen Coats, and Roderick McGillis

Reading Victorian Schoolrooms
Childhood and Education in Nineteenth-Century Fiction
by Elizabeth Gargano

Soon Come Home to This Island
West Indians in British Children's Literature
by Karen Sands-O'Connor

Boys in Children's Literature and Popular Culture
Masculinity, Abjection, and the Fictional Child
by Annette Wannamaker

Boys in Children's Literature and Popular Culture

Masculinity, Abjection, and the Fictional Child

Annette Wannamaker

Routledge
Taylor & Francis Group
New York   London

Routledge
Taylor & Francis Group
270 Madison Ave,
New York NY 10016

Routledge
Taylor & Francis Group
2 Park Square,
Milton Park, Abingdon,
Oxon, OX14 4RN

© 2008 by Taylor & Francis Group, LLC
Routledge is an imprint of Taylor & Francis Group, an Informa business

Transferred to Digital Printing 2009

International Standard Book Number-13: 978-0-415-97469-1 (Hardcover)

No part of this book may be reprinted, reproduced, transmitted, or utilized in any form by any electronic, mechanical, or other means, now known or hereafter invented, including photocopying, microfilming, and recording, or in any information storage or retrieval system, without written permission from the publishers.

Trademark Notice: Product or corporate names may be trademarks or registered trademarks, and are used only for identification and explanation without intent to infringe.

Library of Congress Cataloging-in-Publication Data

Wannamaker, Annette.
  Boys in children's literature and popular culture : masculinity, abjection, and the fictional child / by Annette Wannamaker.
      p. cm. -- (Children's literature and culture ; 46)
      Includes bibliographical references (p.   ) and index.
  ISBN 978-0-415-97469-1 (alk. paper)
  1. Children's stories, American--History and criticism. 2. Masculinity in literature. 3. Boys in literature. 4. Boys--Books and reading--United States. 5. Children's stories, English--History and criticism. I. Title.

PS374.C454W36 2007
813'.5409352341--dc22   2007002634

    ISBN10: 0-415-97469-0 (hbk)
    ISBN10: 0-415-87551-X (pbk)

    ISBN13: 978-0-415-97469-1 (hbk)
    ISBN13: 978-0-415-87551-6 (pbk)

Visit the Taylor & Francis Web site at
http://www.taylorandfrancis.com

and the Routledge Web site at
http://www.routledge.com

CONTENTS

Series Editor's Foreword		ix
Acknowledgments		xi
Prologue: The Rhetoric of the Current "Boy Crisis"		1
Introduction: Beyond Stereotypes and Role Models: The Abject and the American Boy		13
Chapter 1	Me Tarzan, You Other: The Evolution of an Icon	37
Chapter 2	Reading in the Gaps and Lacks: (De)Constructing Masculinity in Louis Sachar's *Holes*	67
Chapter 3	"The Battle of the Bionic Booger Boy," Bodily Borders, and B.A.D. Boys: Pleasure and Abjection in the Captain Underpants Series	85
Chapter 4	And Majin Buu Said, "I'll Eat You Up!": Consuming Japanese Cultural Imports	103
Chapter 5	Men in Cloaks and High-Heeled Boots, Men Wielding Pink Umbrellas: Witchy Masculinities in the Harry Potter Novels	121
Conclusion: Marking Masculinity		147
Notes		153
Bibliography		163
Index		173

SERIES EDITOR'S FOREWORD

Dedicated to furthering original research in children's literature and culture, the Children's Literature and Culture series includes monographs on individual authors and illustrators, historical examinations of different periods, literary analyses of genres, and comparative studies on literature and the mass media. The series is international in scope and is intended to encourage innovative research in children's literature with a focus on interdisciplinary methodology.

Children's literature and culture are understood in the broadest sense of the term *children* to encompass the period of childhood up through adolescence. Owing to the fact that the notion of childhood has changed so much since the origination of children's literature, this Routledge series is particularly concerned with transformations in children's culture and how they have affected the representation and socialization of children. Although the emphasis of the series is on children's literature, all types of studies that deal with children's radio, film, television, and art are included in an endeavor to grasp the aesthetics and values of children's culture. Not only have there been momentous changes in children's culture in the past fifty years but there also have been radical shifts in the scholarship that deals with these changes. In this regard the goal of the Children's Literature and Culture series is to enhance research in this field and, at the same time, point to new directions that bring together the best scholarly work throughout the world.

Jack Zipes

ACKNOWLEDGMENTS

I am grateful to Eastern Michigan University for providing generous institutional support to complete this project. A Provost's New Faculty Research Award supplied valuable release time, and a grant from the Josephine Nevins Keal Development Fund helped to pay for a copy editor for this project.

I also want to thank the journals *Children's Literature in Education* and *The Looking Glass* for allowing me to reprint essays. The chapter titled "Reading in the Gaps and Lacks: (De)Constructing Masculinity in Louis Sachar's *Holes*," initially was published as an article in *Children's Literature in Education* (Vol. 37, no. 1, March 2006, 15–33). The chapter titled "Men in Cloaks and High-Heeled Boots, Men Wielding Pink Umbrellas: Witchy Masculinities in the Harry Potter Novels" initially was published in *The Looking Glass: Alice's Academy* (Vol. 10, no. 1, January 2006, http://www.the-looking-glass.net/v10i1/alice4.html).

When I attended my first Children's Literature Association conference in June 2005, several people said to me, "This is a friendly group; you'll like it here." They were not exaggerating. Colleagues in the children's literature community have been more welcoming and giving than I could ever have imagined. Although I've only briefly known them, several colleagues at institutions other than my own graciously have given of their time to read drafts of chapters, to share their expert advice, and to serve as mentors. I am grateful to Karen Coats for reading a draft of a chapter and for helping me to work through some difficult theoretical concepts I would not have been able to navigate without a guide and to Michele Fry for sharing her expertise on Harry Potter and for her editing advice. I especially want to thank Kenneth Kidd, who read drafts of several chapters, offered words of encouragement at several stages of this project, and whose own work on masculinity and children's literature significantly influenced my thinking on this subject. Finally, I want to thank all the members of Child_Lit: Theory and Criticism of Children's Literature Listserv, a sort of collective oracle I go to when I am stumped and need sage advice.

At a local level I am fortunate to work in an English department that is truly a community. I could not have completed this project without the support of my friends and colleagues in the Eastern Michigan University Department of English Language and Literature. I want to thank my past and present department heads, Russ Larson and Laura George, who have been supportive of the Children's Literature Program and of the scholarship and teaching of its individual faculty members. I want to thank members of the Literature Faculty Writing Group, who read and offered advice on several chapters: Lori Burlingame, Abby Coykendall, Joe Csicsila, Charles Cunningham, Craig Dionne, Laura George, Robin Lucy, Andrea Kaston-Tange, Jim Knapp, and Christine Neufeld. I also want to thank them for sharing their excellent work with me over the past five years and for creating a vibrant group to support the scholarship of junior faculty. Also I am grateful to two of my colleagues in our English Education Program, Cathy Fleischer and Becky Sipe, who generously lent books, forwarded articles, and shared their expertise about boys, literacy, and education. Other colleagues, Martin Shichtman, Elisabeth Däumer, and Linda Adler-Kassner, offered advice about writing an academic book and have helped me to feel less isolated during the process. I also want to thank Barry Hall for copyediting my manuscript and for helping me to make and keep writing deadlines.

This project would not have been successful without the expert help of the librarians at EMU's Halle Library. I thank our children's literature librarian Margaret Best for helping me to navigate online databases. I also want to thank librarian and fellow scholar Walter Hogan for reading a draft of a chapter, offering writing advice, and looking out for research I might otherwise have missed.

I especially want to thank my colleagues in the EMU Children's Literature Program who have been the best senior faculty one could hope for. I am grateful to Ian Wojcik-Andrews and Sheila Most, not only for their support and encouragement of this project but also for being mentors, confidants, role models, and pioneers in the field of children's literature.

I am indebted to my friends for their patience, love, and support. I want to thank the owner and staff at Bombadill's Coffee House in Ypsilanti, Michigan, especially Peter Rinehart and Ross Anderson, for providing a warm and friendly writing space and for never once tossing me out, even when I sat for five hours with an empty coffee cup on my table. I thank Roberta Wojcik-Andrews for making exceptional cosmopolitans and Rachel Dewees for enduring hours of shoptalk at her dinner table. I thank Annette Saddik (my son's fairy godmother) for teaching me how to navigate the difficult terrain of academic publishing. I thank Mary Thompson for all the help she has given me over the years working through feminist theory and masculinity studies. And I thank Laura Moyer for helping me through various versions of writer's block and crises of confidence for more than twenty years.

Finally, I want to thank my family. My parents, Bill and Irmgard Wannamaker, have supported my journey all along the way. I especially thank my husband, colleague, and best friend, Steven D. Krause, whose love, understanding, and unfailing support make everything possible. And, last, I thank my son, Will, for introducing me to the wonderful world of boys and boy culture and for being my muse.

PROLOGUE
The Rhetoric of the Current "Boy Crisis"

When we first began working with and speaking about boys, a large part of our task was to convince skeptical parents and educators of a truth we knew from our years of experience as therapists: that boys suffer deeply as a result of the destructive emotional training our culture imposes upon them, that many of them are in crisis, and that all of them need help.

—**Kindlon and Thompson (1999: 5)**

American boys face genuine problems that cannot be addressed by constructing new versions of manhood. They do not need to be "rescued" from their masculinity.

—**Sommers (2000: 15)**

Philippe Aries taught us not only that childhood has a history but that there may have been a period before childhood existed. James Kincaid tells us that "what the child *is* matters less than what we *think* it is." Jacqueline Rose suggests that behind the category of children's fiction, there exists only a fictional child—a projection of adult desire.

—**Jenkins (1998b: 23)**

If what we, in the contemporary United States, *think* about boys matters more than what boys actually *are*, then our boys are in big trouble because they are, at least within popular discourse, in the midst of a crisis. Who is the "fictional child," the troubled boy, being constructed within the discourse of the current boy crisis? American boys are currently the center of a debate—they are the objects of scrutiny—over which political and cultural battles are being waged by educators, politicians, psychologists, and other experts. Girls are also implicated in the debates about the boy crisis because they are what the boys in crisis are being compared against. According to recent research, which is gaining increased attention in the mainstream media, boys are more likely than girls to drop out of high school and less likely to attend college.[1] Boys are less likely than girls to read books and more likely to be diagnosed with attention deficit disorder or attention deficit/hyperactivity disorder. They are more likely to commit suicide, to commit violent crimes, and to end up in juvenile detention facilities or jail. They are less likely to take advanced placement high school English and more likely to be placed in remedial classes and be diagnosed with learning disabilities.[2] After learning about recent studies citing declining levels of literacy for boys and other problems that American boys may be facing, U.S. first lady Laura Bush made boys a major focus of her agenda. "I think we need to pay more attention to boys," she said in an interview in 2005 with *Parade* magazine. "I think we've paid a lot of attention to girls for the last 30 years, and we have this idea in the United States that boys can take care of themselves" (Winik 2005). She says that boys are being neglected and need more attention because "they're the ones who are in trouble, who have been adjudicated, who can't read, who are not doing well in school and drop out in frustration and embarrassment. A lot of times they're the ones with the drug and alcohol problems" (Winik 2005).

As is the case with most public crises, the causes of, implications of, and solutions for this particular crisis vary depending on the political bent of the experts raising the alarms. For example, in their book *Raising Cain: Protecting the Emotional Life of Boys,* child psychologists Dan Kindlon and Michael Thompson claim that dominant constructions of masculinity that require boys to be stoic and unemotional damage boys' emotional health. They argue that boys (the men they will become and the girls and women with whom they will interact) would benefit if we taught them to "honor and value their emotional lives" (Kindlon and Thompson 1999: 20), if we broadened our definitions of masculinity to allow boys to identify and express their emotions, and if we helped them to develop empathy. Conversely, conservative pundit Christina Hoff Sommers argues the opposite in her book *The War Against Boys: How Misguided Feminism Is Harming Our Young Men:* "American boys face genuine problems that cannot be addressed by constructing new versions of manhood. They do not need to be 'rescued' from their masculinity" (Sommers 2000: 15). Sommers argues instead that a return to single-sex education and traditional value-based schooling will benefit our boys, who supposedly are being sissified by feminist educators. Ultimately, she argues, "boys badly need moral education and discipline" (p. 65), not feminizing.

Henry Jenkins and other cultural critics have argued that childhood is socially constructed within public discourse and often becomes a signifier in larger political battles. Childhood becomes an empty vessel of a word; it is heavy with contradictions that can carry multiple meanings, and within public discourse it can signify our hope for the future, or nostalgia, or innocence, or fear. Therefore, if public discourse about childhood is a blank slate onto which we write our cultural anxieties, what are we to make of the recent fixation with boys in the United States? What fears and desires are we projecting onto our boys, and why? What is at stake, politically, in claiming that boys are in crisis, and in the causes and solutions we offer for the crisis? Furthermore, if, as Jenkins argues, "our beliefs about childhood have some impact on our treatment of children" (Jenkins 1998b: 21), then what impact is this so-called crisis having on boys, who are the subject being debated, the objects being scrutinized, the innocent children being rescued, and the dangerous youth being brought under control?

I begin my discussion of boys in contemporary children's and adolescent literature within the context of the current boy crisis not because I wish to enter into the current debates about boys in crisis but because such public discourse makes its way into the texts we write for our children and also affects the ways we read and understand those texts. For example, in *Life Is Tough: Guys, Growing Up, and Young Adult Literature,* librarian Rachelle Lasky Bilz compiled a bibliography of books meant to help teenage boys navigate the difficulties of being adolescent males. Her list of recommended books and the discussions of these clearly reflect some of the current conclusions reached by psychologists and sociologists that boys suffer from having to conform to hegemonic versions of masculinity. Good books, she argues, can counteract the "tough guy demeanor reinforced in music videos, video games, movies, and sports heroes" (Bilz 2004: xii). She encourages teachers to find books that portray boys who are positive role models, that show boy readers examples of adult male mentors, and that work as bibliotherapy for boys coping with difficulties. She argues, for example, that young adult novels such as E.R. Frank's *America,* Robert Cormier's *Tenderness,* and Walter Dean Meyers's *Scorpions* are texts where "a young man with a proclivity for violence could find characters to empathize with, realize the effects of brutality on victims, see that help is available for troubled teens, and perhaps find the courage to ask for help himself" (p. 86).

On the other hand, some conservatives argue that schools need to give boys more traditional books that provide them with the adventurous tales of heroes, not the dilemmas of sensitive boys. For example, in a column they wrote for the *Washington Post,* Mark Bauerline and Sandra Stotsky, who both served on the steering committee for the new reading assessment framework of the National Assessment of Educational Progress, argue that adolescent problem novels, such as the ones Bilz recommends, are a problem. Stotsky and Bauerline even go so far as to blame them for boys' declining levels of literacy. They argue that teachers are not teaching the classics and are instead requiring boys to read young adult literature, which they define as

> easy-to-read, short novels about teen-agers and problems such as drug addiction, teenage pregnancy, alcoholism, domestic violence, divorced parents and bullying. Older literary fare has also been replaced by something called "culturally relevant" literature—texts that appeal to students' ethnic group identification on the assumption that sharing the leading character's ethnicity will motivate them to read. (Bauerline and Stotsky 2005: A15)

Implicit in their argument are assumptions similar to Sommers's that boys are being harmed by misguided liberal educators who have abandoned traditional literature (and the values contained therein) in favor of texts meant to offer children representations of a variety of cultures, ethnicities, races, genders, sexual orientations, and experiences. Boys, they argue, are turned off by such politically correct fare and instead prefer "adventure tales, war, sports and historical nonfiction"—in other words, traditional stories about (white, heterosexual) boys and men engaged in (white, heterosexual) heroic activities that do not, apparently, involve talking about feelings, being sensitive to others, or being tolerant of difference.[3]

In both cases, the boys we are so worried about helping to become more literate actually become a blank slate for adult fears and desires. The books we claim will most benefit our boys are those books that reinforce whichever version of masculinity we most value. Jenkins points out, "Often, in our rhetoric, the child embodies change, its threat and its potential. The child, both literally and metaphorically, is always in the process of becoming something else" (1998b: 5). For both conservatives and liberals, then, debates about boys' declining literacy levels and other perceived problems ultimately represent anxieties about the future or an opportunity to shape the future. Furthermore, these current debates about boys are often shaped by current attitudes about gender, what we think proper boys and girls *should* ideally be. The current fixation on boys is also clearly a reaction to recent progress feminists have made and our hopes or uncertainties about the future direction of accepted gender roles in the United States.

Also evident in these debates are the authors' assumptions about the nature of gendered behavior: those who see gender as being socially constructed argue that boys can be taught and guided to perform their gender in less hegemonic ways, and those who see gender as biologically determined often argue that misguided parents and educators should just "let boys be boys." For example, Sommers often scoffs at scholars who discuss gender as being constructed and argues that such liberal ideas have influenced America's educational system to the extent that "resocializing boys in the direction of femininity is now high on the educational agenda of many educators, women's institutions, and government officials" (Sommers 2000: 74). She lists in her book several examples of cases where boys were penalized simply for being "normal" boys because they are prohibited from engaging in rough-and-tumble play, running, jumping, wrestling, and play fighting with toy weapons. Boys, according to Sommers, are under siege by schools bent on wiping out their natural and normal boyishness. She claims that "many educators regard the normal play of little boys with disapproval and some ban it outright" (p. 95). Defenseless "little boys" here (they are "young men" in the title of the book) are constructed as the innocent victims of bullying feminists. Educators, who either are liberal feminists or are under the influence of liberal feminists, are supposedly conspiring to valorize girls and to emasculate helpless boys.

Several scholars have recently argued that a danger of the "boy crisis" debates is that they are increasingly becoming politicized (were they ever *not* politicized?), pitting conservatives against liberals, politicians against educators, and boys against girls. For example, Thomas Newkirk characterizes the debate as being separated along ideological lines, "with liberal feminists the advocates for girls and members of the educational Right the advocates for boys" (Newkirk 2002: 21). Moreover, Michael Kimmel writes that quite a few "experts" on boys are less concerned about the welfare of our boys and more concerned with "using boys as a foil with which to critique feminism" (Kimmel 2004: xi). It is no surprise, then, when Newkirk acknowledges that "attempts to raise the issue of boys' difficulties are often received skeptically by many feminists who have worked so hard to expose the bias against girls" (p. 29). Indeed, some conservatives such as Sommers have even used the so-called boy crisis as a way to challenge programs for girls such as Title IX and the Women's Educational Equity Act, which they claim are giving girls an unfair advantage over boys. Mrs. Bush, for example, echoes the Right's interpretation of the current boy crisis when she says, "I think we've paid a lot of attention to girls for the last 30 years," whereas boys have been neglected (Winik 2005). Within this context many feminists are suspicious of claims about "boys in crisis" because they fear that the crisis is simply being fabricated as part of a backlash against the progress that women and girls have been making, as Mrs. Bush points out, over the past thirty years. For example, is it a crisis that women are getting about 55 percent of the undergraduate degrees awarded in the United States when men still are making significantly more money than women in the workforce?

As a feminist I share these concerns, and, as the mother of a boy, I worry about discourse that pits boys against girls in ways that cannot possibly be beneficial for children of either gender. Furthermore, I am not heartened by the political Right's recent concern for the welfare of boys or the motives behind this concern. When Sommers titled one of her book chapters "Save the Males," she was not being ironic. Kenneth Kidd, in his book *Making American Boys: Boyology and the Feral Tale*, insightfully works through some of the complexities and contradictions in the rhetoric of the current boy crisis by pointing out:

> The boys' movement is imagined variously as a pioneering defense of boyhood, as a rejoinder to an exaggerated girl crisis, and as a parallel crisis that also demands attention. The rhetoric of the boy crisis is at once sexist and indebted to feminism; it also echoes the language of civil rights while ignoring racial and class biases of our culture. That the new boyology should function as a referendum on feminism and indeed all of the social reforms of the last thirty-plus years isn't surprising, as boyology is at heart a conservative American ideology of masculine self-making. (Kidd 2004: 170)

Furthermore, Kidd, Kimmel, and other scholars have also pointed out that much of the recent research about boys has focused predominantly on white, middle-class, heterosexual boys, thus ignoring or marginalizing boys who do not fit into these dominant categories.[4]

There is also quite a bit of evidence to suggest that many boys are not in crisis at all and that we are not focusing our attention on the right populations of boys. Caryl Rivers and Rosalind Chait Barnett put it quite well in a *Washington Post* column titled "The Myth of 'The Boy Crisis'": "The boy crisis we're hearing about is largely a manufactured one, the product of both a backlash against the women's movement and the media's penchant for continuously churning out news about the latest dire threat to the nation" (Rivers and Barnett 2006: B01). They point to recent research that calls into question many of the assumptions fueling alarms about boys. For example, they argue that there is not a great enough gap between boys' and girls' brains or verbal skills to warrant significant differences in learning styles or reading ability:

> In 2005, University of Wisconsin psychologist Janet Hyde synthesized data from 165 studies on verbal ability and gender. They revealed a female superiority so slight as to be meaningless. And psychologist Diane Halpern of Claremont McKenna College looked at many studies of verbal and math abilities and found that, overall, the gender differences were remarkably small. This research casts doubt on the idea, championed by author Michael Gurian ("The Wonder of Boys") and others, that boys' and girls' brains are so different that they must be taught in very different ways. Although there are indeed some structural differences in the brains of men and women, we don't know what they mean. Perhaps very little. In the 19th century, scientists thought that the greater size of the male brain meant that men were a lot smarter. We now know how off the mark that was. (Rivers and Barnett 2006: B01)

The real crisis, Rivers and Barnett argue, is not one of gender but one based on differences of race and economic class. They argue that when one breaks down statistics about boys based on categories such as race and socioeconomic class, "it becomes clear that if there is a crisis, it's among inner-city and rural boys. White suburban boys aren't significantly touched by it" (Rivers and Barnett 2006).[5] Indeed, among whites, college freshmen are 51 percent female and 49 percent male, and in Ivy League colleges women are still outnumbered by men—hardly a crisis. They report, "Although poor and working-class boys lag behind girls in reading when they get to middle school, boys in the wealthiest schools do not fall behind, either in middle school or in high school." The real crises among boys appear when differences in income and race are accounted for. They write, "Among blacks, for every 100 males who graduate, 139 females do. Florida's graduation rates among all students show a striking picture of race and class: 81 percent for Asians, 60 percent for whites, 48 percent for Hispanics and 46 percent for blacks." It is ironic that white, middle-class, suburban boys have been the ones that we have been most worried about saving, the ones whose photos fill the covers of books and magazines about the crisis.

Of course, public debates about the boy crisis may smooth over differences among boys precisely because boys are being used as blank slates in public discourse—they are standing in for something else. The overwhelming focus on white boys in crisis is more about adult anxieties in regard to shifting gender roles, or even reflects shifts in power relations among races and classes, than it is a concern for the welfare of all boys. Ensuring the superiority of white, middle-class, heterosexual boys against an imagined threat of feminizing U.S. schools may be a way of working to maintain older power structures based on gender, race, and class.

Because much of the discourse about which texts boys should or should not read has been influenced by discourse about the boy crisis, it is important to reframe a discussion about boys and books within critiques that complicate this so-called crisis. It is also significant that the popular texts I've studied for this project are, for the most part, texts about straight, white, middle-class boys struggling with hegemonic masculinity—the fictional boy at the center of these texts is also the straight, white, middle-class boy at the center of public debates. Gay boys, poor boys, and minority boys are often invisible in popular texts or, worse, are presented as the Other against which a protagonist's subjectivity is defined. This doesn't mean, however, that white, middle-class, heterosexual boys are the only ones reading, viewing, and consuming these texts or being affected by them. Quite the contrary, minority boys, poor boys, and gay boys must still develop what W.E.B. DuBois described as a double-consciousness—they learn to view themselves through dominant versions of masculinity, and other ways of being male are defined and filtered through this lens. In other words, they see themselves through the eyes of a dominant culture created by popular texts as different, as on the margins, or as Other.

Finally, because some researchers and authors writing about the boy crisis automatically assume that there is something wrong with all boys that needs fixing, or that gender is solely biologically determined, or that boys are blank slates helpless before the influences of culture, they often ignore the "ways boys resist succumbing to negative stereotypes and actively seek out ways to thrive in the midst of great challenges" (Way and Chu 2004: 2). In other words, the rhetoric of the current boy crisis quite often ignores the complexities of subjectivity formation and the nuances of gendered identity that is negotiated by subjects, not merely imposed by either culture or nature. Of course, public debates may simplify issues of subjectivity precisely because boys are being used as blank slates in public discourse.

Furthermore, alarmist reports about the current dire status of American boys ignore a long history of complaints periodically made about "today's youth." Historians point to a series of crises about "those darn young people," who just aren't measuring up to current standards or, more accurate, measuring up to nostalgic views of the young people we romantically believe we once were. Even the ancient Greek rhetorician Isocrates lamented the state of "those punk kids" when in 353 B.C.E. he wrote in "Antidosis," "The most promising of our young men are wasting their youth in drinking bouts, in parties, in soft living and childish folly. ... You see some of them chilling their wine at the Nine Fountains; others, drinking in the taverns; others tossing dice in gambling dens; and many, hanging about the training schools of the flute girls" (p. 53). In his book *Youth Media* (2004), Bill Osgerby points out that since the late nineteenth century we have experienced quite a few panics about boys, and several of these have cited the media's influence over impressionable youth as a major factor in delinquency. During the Victorian era in Britain, "penny gaff" theaters and "penny dreadful" novels supposedly corrupted young men, and in the 1920s and 1930s gangster films supposedly led impressionable young men into a "career of crime through depicting mobsters as glamorous and exciting" (p. 66). In the 1950s in the United States, comic books were blamed for "juvenile depravity," and "concerns about rising levels of juvenile crime prompted the appointment of a Senate Subcommittee to investigate the causes of delinquency" (p. 66). As a result, in 1954 makers of comic books agreed to adhere to a "self-regulatory Comics Code" (p. 67), just as in 1990 the record industry agreed to include "parental advisory" notices on albums after rap music came under fire as the latest corrupting influence on our youth. Violent video games currently seem to be taking the blame for juvenile delinquency. Legislators around the country have proposed laws to restrict the sale of violent games such as "Grand Theft Auto." Research tells us that "a steady diet of mature-content, violent, video games alone is unlikely to influence a child to commit violent, anti-social crimes. For that, researchers agree, there needs to be a host of other risk factors, including parents who are uninvolved or negligent, genetic influences, and negative social and environmental factors such as poverty and neighborhood violence" (Melnz 2003: H1). Because those other risk factors, such as poverty and neglect, would require significant changes in U.S. culture and policy that many are not willing to make, video games (used mostly by boys, teenagers, and young men) become an easy target. Newkirk and other education theorists studying boys and literacy point out that the very texts that boys most enjoy are those texts most often targeted for being low-brow, commercial, violent, and potentially dangerous for the impressionable or delinquent boys who watch and consume them.

Therefore, although this book is not focused entirely on the current boy crisis, it must necessarily be written conscious of the fact that any discussion of the texts boys are reading (or should or shouldn't be reading) exists within the context of the current boy crisis that is framing much of the discourse about boys, books, and popular culture. Texts that are read, viewed, or consumed by boys are currently under scrutiny because of this crisis, and as a result the ways our culture defines boyhood within these texts also are being scrutinized. For example, some claim that boys need to read texts that offer positive male role models. Others, who worry about boys' lower levels of literacy, argue that we just need to give boys books they will enjoy. What are teachers, parents, and scholars of children's literature to make of these recent studies and debates? If, as several recent studies conclude, boys do not read books with girl protagonists but girls are able to identify with both females and males, should teachers assign only books with boy characters in them to encourage increased reading among boys? On the other hand, shouldn't girls have a steady diet of books with strong female characters? Should teachers create separate reading lists for girls and boys? Can't boys also benefit by reading about strong female characters? And how does one define a "strong character" or a "good role model"? Is she or he stereotypically feminine or masculine, or do strong characters break gender molds? Should the gender of a character or the genre of a book even be the main criteria used for deciding which books to teach and to study? Finally, should questions of gender supersede questions of literary merit, development of aesthetic appreciation, cultural literacy, or the pleasures of reading a good book?

These are some of the questions I explore in this book. I am most invested in studying contemporary texts written for children and adolescents as cultural artifacts that can make visible the ways we construct gender, specifically the ways we construct gendered children within cultural discourse. Who is the "fictional boy" implied in the texts that adults write for boys? In more than a few contemporary texts written for boys, masculinity is—not always but quite often—portrayed in complicated, contradictory, often paradoxical ways that highlight the difficult negotiations boys are making as they develop gendered identities within, against, or on the margins of current cultural constructions of masculinity. Cultural anxieties about gender identity that are expressed publicly through debates about the current boy crisis are also expressed in literary texts for our children and adolescents and in some of the criticism written about these texts. Furthermore, some of the texts that boys choose to read assume that boy readers are aware of, affected by, and capable of affecting the current debates of which they are the Object.

INTRODUCTION
Beyond Stereotypes and Role Models: The Abject and the American Boy

> One thing that an elite education teaches us is how to construct a hierarchical map of reading; it helps develop a "taste" for the serious and a "distaste" for the vulgar ("popular" in its original meaning). It is also a map that places most of the genres boys love near the bottom.
>
> —**Newkirk (2002: 79)**

> The book [Robert Westall's *Futuretrack 5*] will appeal greatly to teenage boys, which is the best reason for not buying it.
>
> —**Quoted in Hollindale (1988: 10)**

When we assume that any text that might genuinely appeal to a teenage boy is not worth reading, it is clear that issues of taste or of literary merit are inextricably linked to issues of gender, childhood, and the study of texts written for children. Many of the books and articles making recommendations for the sorts of books boys should be reading seem to assume that boys are not capable of making wise choices and must be guided toward texts that are more literary, less offensive, less violent, less vulgar, and less stereotypically masculine. Why is there such a disconnect between those popular texts that boys prefer and those texts many adults wish they would prefer? To understand this disconnect, we need to move discussions about boys and books beyond prescriptions that promote texts with positive role models or that admonish boys to avoid texts with stereotypical portrayals of characters and into spaces that acknowledge the complex intersections between masculinity and childhood within the context of contemporary culture.

As I explain in the prologue, because there is such public concern about boys in crisis, the texts that boys read or do not read or should or should not read have come under increased scrutiny in both academic and mainstream publications. Within the context of the current boy crisis, some critics are looking for texts to blame for boys' real or perceived problems or texts that hold a promise of a cure. But opinions about which texts are which are often in direct opposition and often reflect different investments that adults have in the maintenance of or disruption of traditional gender roles and different perceptions about the relative importance of literary merit and adherence to a canon of classic literature in developing literacy. Bilz, for instance, encourages teachers to find young adult novels that portray boys who are positive, nonstereotypical role models that show boy readers examples of adult male mentors and that work as bibliotherapy for older boys coping with the difficulties of growing up. Her recommendations assume that boys are harmed by hegemonic depictions of masculinity that constrain boys and do not allow them a broad range of emotions or ways of expressing them. Bauerline and Stotsky, on the other hand, blame such young adult literature (which they label "problem novels") for boys' declining levels of literacy. Boys would enjoy reading more, they argue, if they were assigned to read classic works that depict the more traditional versions of masculinity that boys crave and that are supposedly being denied them by a feminized and feminizing education system.

Other books offering textual remedies for boys' ills reveal in their reading lists commitments to different sides of the nature–nurture debate. William Brozo's book *To Be a Boy, To Be a Reader: Engaging Teen and Preteen Boys in Active Literacy* works to compile a list of books boys should be reading because they feature positive male role models that can help to counter the negative images boys come across in popular culture. "Popular media has contributed to the stereotypical construction of males as one-dimensional, incapable of self-reflection, and physically and psychologically oppressive. Exposing adolescent boys to quality literature filled with a variety of positive male archetypes can only help to provide them with realistic and in-depth images of what it means to be a man" (Brozo 2002: 6). In *What Stories Does My Son Need? A Guide to Books and Movies That Build Character in Boys*, Michael Gurian and Terry Trueman similarly argue that boys need texts that will contribute to a moral education. They argue, "We must finally admit that the majority of media-created stories are at best amoral" (Gurian and Trueman 2000: 7). According to Gurian and Trueman, young males, left to their own testosterone-fueled biological urges, "gravitate toward media that stimulate them to hunt and kill, as boys a thousand years ago had a special relationship with hunting and war itself. This is built into boys, to a great extent, and is enhanced by our highly violent and sex-charged culture" (p. 6). Therefore, they write that adults need to help boys to navigate the morally ambiguous terrain of popular culture and work to steer boys toward texts that are both exciting and that teach moral behavior.

These are only a few of the varied, often conflicting arguments for the sorts of texts that boys should be reading and should not be reading. For the most part, these arguments, regardless of the critical lens used or the political agenda guiding them, all share a common mission: to offer antidotes to the negative images of masculinity supposedly portrayed in popular American culture and supposedly remedied by literature of quality. I don't disagree with some of these arguments. Boys should be reading texts that they enjoy and that encourage literacy. Boys should be reading texts that feature a wide array of characters that represent various ethnicities, races, nationalities, sexualities, and, most important, a wide range of ways of being male. They should be reading texts that feature female protagonists. They should be reading rich and varied literary works from a range of periods and genres. They should be reading texts featuring males who are nonviolent, sensitive, tolerant, and wise, not only those depicting males who are violent, stoic, and individualistic.

However, there is a wide gap between what many well-meaning adults (parents, educators, psychologists, political pundits, and scholars) think boys *should* be reading and the texts they actually *are* reading. The major researchers currently studying boys and reading—Thomas Newkirk, Bruce Pirie, Michael Smith, and Jeffrey Wilhelm—all agree that, despite dire reports of illiterate boys, many boys are reading a wide variety of texts, just not the texts that most adults would count as being literary. Although they all argue that there is no monolithic American boy and that there are more differences among various boys than similarities, there are conclusions to be drawn about the reading habits of boys and the ways these are not always acknowledged or validated by educators. Newkirk writes, "Boys' traditional favorites—information books, humor, science fiction, action stories—are often treated as subliterature, something that a reader should move beyond as he moves toward realistic fiction with thematic weight" (Newkirk 2002: 70). In his book *Teenage Boys and High School English,* Bruce Pirie observes teachers valuing the conventions of realistic fiction, with its emphasis on character development, emotions, and relationships. Furthermore, many teachers reinforce this emphasis in the ways that they talk about literary texts in their classrooms and in the ways they expect students to interact with texts. But boys, he argues, "don't automatically recognize all the 'rules' of the literary games they're expected to play" (Pirie 2002: 71), and they often see reading as a feminine activity because it involves "emotion talk." Smith and Wilhelm compiled recent data about gender and reading preferences that mirror the conclusions reached by Newkirk and Pirie. On the basis of a variety of studies, they conclude that boys and girls have different reading habits and that boys are more inclined than girls to read informational texts, magazine articles, newspapers, graphic novels, comic books, electronic texts, humor, science fiction, fantasy, books about hobbies and sports, and series books or texts that need to be collected. Boys, they conclude, are less likely than girls to read books with female protagonists, poetry, or realistic fiction (Smith and Wilhelm 2002: 11). All of these researchers, invested in helping boys to become more literate, advocate working with boys using methods and texts that appeal to their literary tastes and ways of interacting with texts.

On the basis of this research, my exploration in this book of some of the texts that are popular with boys in the contemporary United States includes Disney films, television programs, video games, manga, anime, comic books, adventure stories, and novels that are sometimes less than literary—mostly texts that have been largely ignored by literary scholars.[1] Indeed—and I believe it is no coincidence—most of the texts that boys enjoy are precisely those texts that most repulse many adults who want children to read literature of quality. Even when literary scholars disagree about what "literature of quality" might mean, most seem to agree that many boys are not reading it. This gap between adults and boy readers is evident in the American Library Association's "top ten" most censored lists, which feature a disproportionate number of books for and about boys; it is evident in the "should read" lists compiled by well-meaning adults in an effort to steer boys away from the influence of mass media; and it is evident in many boys' disdain for quality literature (at least as it has been defined for them as character-driven, realistic novels) as something that is feminine or feminizing, as something stuffy and bookish, and as something that should be avoided if one wants to be considered masculine.

Why is there such a disconnect between what adults believe boys should read and what boys actually are reading? What is it about these popular texts that so repulses many adults and so attracts many boys? Inherent in most prescriptive recommendations of quality texts for boys is an assumption that the fictional child, the fictional character depicted in a text, functions as part of a cultural artifact or ideological apparatus working to interpellate the child reader as a subject of ideology. I don't necessarily disagree with this general assumption but believe that subjectivity—the ever-evolving construction of the conscious and unconscious self in dialogue with culture(s)—is far more complex, contradictory, fluid, and multifaceted than most of these recommendations lead us to believe. We cannot simply prescribe a list of books that will cure boys of a perceived adherence to stereotypical gender roles for multiple reasons: because there is no monolithic "Boy" in our diverse American culture(s); because children are not blank slates that can be written upon; and because the gendered self—even the fictional self—is layered, continuously shifting, and determined through a dialogue with(in) culture(s), not solely through a top-down imposition of culture. "Ideology is not something which is transferred to children as if they were empty receptacles. It is something which they already possess, having drawn it from a mass of experiences far more powerful than literature" (Hollindale 1988: 17). Furthermore, Michael Messner writes that in the field of sociology the previous "top-down (adult-to-child) approach of socialization theories tended to ignore the extent to which children are active agents in the creation of their worlds—often in direct or partial opposition to values or 'roles' to which adult teachers or parents are attempting to socialize them" (Messner 2000: 765). This is why we cannot assume that simply enticing boys to read didactic texts advocating appropriate gender roles (whatever those might be) will significantly change children's behavior or attitudes about gender. We must instead consider fictional texts and our interactions with these within a larger cultural context that includes children's culture, consumer culture, dynamic subject formation, and the myriad influences with which boys interact.

For example, the fictional child depicted even in those books that make up the prescriptive should-read lists is more than just a transparent, easy-to-decipher depiction of a character (stereotypical, traditional, counterhegemonic, or role model) that a boy who is reading the text then uncritically emulates. The fictional boy portrayed in a text is the subject (or more accurate, the subject-in-becoming) interpellated by, but also simultaneously marginalized by, reading, resisting, and negotiating dominant ideology. The fictional boy is also the implied reader of a literary or cultural text, the boy who we, or the author, imagine that reader to be. The fictional boy is also constructed through public discussions about the boy crisis, or video games and violence, or stereotypical masculinity, or lower levels of literacy, or "those darned kids today." And, finally, many real boys are directly affected by all these manifestations of the fictional boy and must navigate cultural expectations imbued with these, but in ways that are difficult to predict, understand, or easily classify.

For instance, some critics claim that boys are attracted to popular texts that are amoral and violent or ones that work to maintain dominant versions of masculinity that reinforce cultural norms and the status quo. But is it that simple? Do all boys growing up in the United States in the twenty-first century simply want various versions of the hero monomyth that continuously reinforce the dominance of white, Western, heterosexual males over women and minorities? Do all boys simply want texts that define masculinity in narrow and confining ways? Are all boys complicitous agents in the maintenance of hegemonic masculinity, or, conversely, are they unwitting dupes of dominant ideology? Or can the relationship between boys and the popular texts that they read, watch, and consume be more complex than any of these? Indeed, perhaps adult reactions to texts enjoyed by boys and young men can tell us as much about the fictional boy being constructed through public discourse, about the ways boyhood currently is being conceived in the United States, as they do about the texts themselves.

Perry Nodelman notices this difference of interpretation between adult and boy readers and offers a practical explanation for the distance separating the reading preferences of children's literature scholars, teachers, and librarians and those of many boys. He writes that members of award committees and teachers often prefer those books with male protagonists that "are about boys seeing through the conventional constructions of masculinity, learning to be more sensitive or more loving or more openly imaginative or literate, or less caught up in the pleasures of aggressive bullying" (Nodelman 2002: 11). For instance, he puts books like Jerry Spinelli's *Wringer* (1997) and *Crash* (1996), Diana Wieler's *Bad Boy* (1989), Rich Wallace's *Wrestling Sturbridge* (1996), and Jack Gantos's *Jack's New Power* (1995) onto a list of titles about boys that are preferred by adults but not necessarily by most boys. He points out that this interest in alternative versions of masculinity in the field of children's literature is not surprising:

> Most of the students I teach, indeed, most adults interested in children's literature whether authors, editors, librarians, or teachers—are women. In our contemporary culture, anything to do with children remains what it traditionally was, primarily the domain of women. As a result, children's literature often tends to be a maternal sort of literature, even when produced by men following the conventions of the genre. It often admires the kinds of boys that mothers might most easily love—good, safe, nonrowdy

boys who do not break rules and cause maternal anxiety. (Nodelman 2002: 11)

Why would most boys be attracted to such literature? Nodelman's answer is that many of them often are not. Boys who are comfortable with the dominant versions of masculinity portrayed in popular culture are not the target audience for those books endorsed by experts in the field of children's literature, he argues. Instead, they are written for an audience of readers "with a vested interest in critiquing the assumptions about masculinity shared by large numbers of 'normal' boys" (p. 13). The readers for these sanctioned texts are "girls (and adult men and women who parent or who deal professionally with boys) who do not want to accept the supposed male right to power or testosterone-initiated aggression or lust. They are gay boys or potentially gay boys coming to terms with their sexuality. They are supposedly effeminate boys and the scholarly geeks and imaginative freaks and other male outsiders" (p. 13). In addition to these groups, I would also include many minority boys whose lives often are not mirrored in the popular media and lower-class boys who also are often on the margins. Members of these groups need to see themselves represented in literature that challenges hegemonic masculinity, and it makes sense that they would be attracted to such literature. However, members of these groups also are exposed to (how can they avoid it?) those texts that are part of mainstream popular culture.

This trend also seems to be mirrored in texts by and for adults that interrogate masculinity. For example, in his prologue for a collection of essays titled *The Emergence of Man into the 21st Century*, Ed Madden explains that he and the other editors for the collection noticed patterns among the essays in those topics that were frequently discussed and observed that some topics were glaringly absent. "Many of the topics we expected to see—sports, adolescent heterosexuality (the sexual and social rites of passage), male bonding (as well as hazing and initiation rituals), courtship and marriage, that is, the normative narratives of manhood—either weren't showing up in the work, or were showing up in conflicted and complicated ways" (Madden 2002: xxix). He speculates that perhaps those people who are most conscious of the ways that dominant masculinity is constructed in our culture and those most invested in making it visible are perhaps those who have been most marginalized by it, not those who most easily conform. "I began to wonder if those most willing to write—or those most driven to tell their stories—were those who felt some sense of marginality, inadequacy, or difference" (p. xxix). This pattern emerged as a topic of discussion at the

2006 meeting of the American Men's Studies Association. In a panel discussion about the state of the field, many participants noted that masculinity is still something that, to a great extent, is not interrogated because most men still do not see a need to talk about being men. According to panelists at the conference, gender studies is still largely seen as the study of femininity, and many of the students who enroll in men's studies courses are often women, not men.

Like the adult readers of children's literature whom Nodelman describes, I was initially motivated to investigate and write about dominant versions of masculinity because I have often felt marginalized by these in several ways: as a girl growing up with a military man for a father and spending much of my girlhood living in the highly masculine spaces of military bases; as a woman in academia married to (and sometimes following) a male academic; and as a mother currently raising a son and working to learn about and to understand the culture of contemporary boys. As a literary critic and as a feminist, I have often found myself most drawn to those texts for and about boys and young men that depict alternative versions of masculinity or that expose dominant versions of masculinity as damaging constructs: Stephen Chbosky's *The Perks of Being a Wallflower* (1999), Robert Cormier's *The Chocolate War* (1974), Chris Crutcher's *Whale Talk* (2001) and *Staying Fat for Sarah Byrnes* (1994), Nancy Farmer's *House of the Scorpion* (2002), Brent Hartinger's *Geography Club* (2003), Francisco Jimenez's *The Circuit: Stories from the Life of a Migrant Child* (1997), Lois Lowry's *The Giver* (1993), Walter Dean Myers's *Bad Boy* (2001) and *Monster* (1999), Jerry Spinelli's *Maniac Magee* (1990), Virginia Walter and Katrina Roeckelein's *Making Up Megaboy* (1999), and a host of other quality books for young adults and children that, at their best, work to make visible and to subvert hegemonic masculinity. After all, those of us who are committed feminists often assume that if we can effectively argue that hegemonic masculinity damages boys and men as much as it damages girls and women, then we may be able to persuade more men and boys to embrace versions of masculinity that are not based on the oppression of women, gay men, minorities, and other "others." However, the fact of the matter is that dominant masculinity does not always damage all boys and indeed helps to maintain systems of power that benefit many boys and men, and even some girls and women. Before we can work to affect change, we need to more carefully work to understand the complex systems of power relations—of which cultural artifacts such as children's books and films are a part—that support and are supported by such dominant ideologies as hegemonic masculinity.

But what, precisely, is contemporary, hegemonic masculinity in the United States? Should we assume that it is what is most often portrayed in popular and commercial texts? And what are the "large numbers of 'normal' boys," to whom Nodelman refers, reading? If most of these boys are not reading the maternal, literary texts sanctioned in schools and praised by literary critics, are they only reading and consuming texts that promote the most stereotypical versions of dominant masculinity? Are they not reading anything at all? As I discussed earlier, some scholars in literacy and education argue that boys are doing plenty of reading, just not of texts that educators would count as being literature or even, in some cases, as being texts. In his insightful book *Misreading Masculinity: Boys, Literacy, and Popular Culture*, Newkirk argues that the gap between the literary preferences of adults and boys is caused by a "deep cultural anxiety about the socialization of boys" (Newkirk 2002: xvii). He writes that ever since the school shootings at Columbine, adult concerns have focused on "boys' perceived propensity to violence and aggression, triggered by suggestions in music lyrics, violent video games, and action movies" (p. xvii). Well-meaning adults have established no-violence policies in schools across the United States that prohibit violent writing or drawing and discourage students from reading violent texts. Furthermore, many see America's popular culture as both a cause and a symptom of "a contemporary crisis of declining moral values and academic standards" (pp. xvi–xvii), not as something that should be studied, taught in schools, or even consumed by boys and young men. In this climate, then, the texts that many boys enjoy are simply off the radar of many educators and scholars or are simply dismissed as so much garbage that boys should be discouraged from enjoying.

Newkirk, who describes himself as a defense attorney arguing on the behalf of lowbrow, popular texts that appeal to boys, claims that educators have defined literature and literacy in ways that are far too narrow:

> We have failed to support, or even allow, in our literacy programs the tastes, values, and learning styles of many boys. More specifically, we have discouraged, devalued, or even prohibited the genres of reading and writing that are most popular with boys, stories that include violence, parody, and bodily humor. (Newkirk 2002: xvi)

He argues that instead of turning up our noses at the scatological humor in the Captain Underpants series or cringing at the violence in the Spiderman comic books, instead of valuing only character-driven novels with sensitive protagonists who are role models for maternally sanctioned behavior, we need to work to better understand, appreciate, and analyze those texts that genuinely appeal to many boys. Although Newkirk's promotion of teaching everything that boys love to read, as long as it gets them reading, is excessive, we also should not automatically assume that all popular texts are inherently negative. Instead of simply dismissing such texts, we should work to carefully study and understand them. As Peter Hollindale wrote in his groundbreaking essay "Ideology and the Children's Book," "Our priority in the world of children's books should not be to promote ideology but to understand it, and find ways of helping others to understand it, including the children themselves" (Hollindale 1988: 10). Understanding and making visible the ways masculinity functions in popular, commercially successful texts is vital to beginning to understand the broad array of texts that make up children's culture, not just those texts of quality that we prefer children read.

In the field of children's literature, scholars have spent decades working to claim legitimacy for a field that still is not often taken seriously in the academy. They have worked and continue to work to claim a space in the literary canon for texts written for an audience of young readers. It is understandable that these scholars have worked to establish legitimacy for children's literature as a field of study by arguing that many children's texts are rich, complex literary works worthy of the same critical attention as texts written for an audience of adult readers. This quest for legitimacy, however, has had the unfortunate side effect of widening the gap between children and the academics studying the literature written for them. Jack Zipes writes, "Clearly the majority of children in the U.S. are not reading what the experts in children's literature are reading" (Zipes 2002: 35). He argues:

> Instead of irresponsibly arguing for a canon of preferred literary texts to which all children should be exposed, as William Bennett and Edward Hirsch, among others, have sought to do, we should assume the responsibility for all the different kinds of texts which we help to produce, promote, and disseminate and to which children are exposed. (Zipes 2002: 58)

Boys in Children's Literature and Popular Culture works to understand some of the popular, contemporary texts written and produced for boy readers and consumers. It assumes that we have a responsibility to work to understand even those popular or lowbrow texts from which critics of children's literature often try to distance themselves. This book is an attempt to carefully and closely read these texts with the same critical attention given to texts considered to be more literary.

By closely examining several popular texts that represent different genres and that are written for different age groups using various critical approaches, I attempt to understand the broad appeal of these texts and their role as cultural artifacts, which both affect and reflect contemporary culture. After all, those texts that are most popular with boys are those texts that may most influence this generation of boys. Although I do think that individual boys, boy culture, and masculinity are influenced by various cultural texts (among many other factors), I do not assume that popular, commercially successful texts are inherently negative, amoral, or the causes of illiteracy and violence among America's boys and young men. The relationship between texts and child readers is a complicated one. It is a relationship that moves beyond just the child and the text to include the adult author and publisher, the adult who is buying the text and mediating the text for the child or reading the text to the child, the corporations who market texts to children, and a children's culture that is formed not only by teachers, peers, and family members but also by mass media and public discourse about children. Children's texts are, most often, written by adults and reflect less children's real, lived experiences in the world and more an adult view of childhood or what childhood ought to be for an audience of imagined child readers. "Children's fiction," writes Jacqueline Rose, "draws in the child, it secures, places, and frames the child," and in doing so it often is more about adult "desires in the very act construing the child as the object of its speech" (Rose 1984: 2). It is also important to remember, however, that children are not blank slates acted upon by texts. Although children have less experience than adults in reading texts and in negotiating their place in the world, they are in fact readers, thinkers, and consumers, who are actively defining self and culture at the same time as these are being defined for them.

Because most concerns about the popular texts that boys (and girls) read focus on identity formation—What sort of man will the boy reader become?—the multilayered relationship between text, reader, and culture is the focus of this project. There seems to be an implicit assumption held by some of the critics cited earlier that children's identities are directly influenced by the texts they read, see, hear, and purchase. Indeed, much work discussing gender in children's literature focuses on depictions of gender that are described as being either "stereotypical" or "nontraditional," as if there is a clear line differentiating between the two that can easily be identified, and as if children will unproblematically adopt the behavior of literary characters. However, the formation of individual identity within a culture—and the role that stories play in this formation—is something scholars and theorists in a variety of fields are continuously debating and working to understand. For example, in the diverse field of cultural studies, proponents of the Frankfurt School might agree with the assumption that children are dupes of the media, whereas followers of Stuart Hall might see subversive and liberatory potential in some of the cultural practices of young people. I, critically, find myself somewhere between these two schools, and my analyses of texts in this book rely mostly on criticism that works to acknowledge the complex, contradictory, symbiotic relationship between various cultural forces and diverse child readers.

To move beyond a discussion of stereotypes and role models, I rely on the work done by literary theorists, cultural theorists, philosophers, educators, and gender theorists in the fields of women's and men's studies. Although Gurian argues, "Boys are testosterone-based (testosterone is the sex and aggression hormone) and often gravitate toward stimuli that appeal to this aggression-based hormonal system" (Gurian and Trueman 2000: 5), most scholars in the field of men's studies echo Simone de Beauvoir in varying degrees by claiming that men are made, not born. A major goal of masculinity studies is to make masculinity visible as a social construct that is, in varying degrees, created by society and, therefore, also alterable by society. Mei-Ying Wu, for example, characterizes the major goal of the men's studies movement as an attempt to "unmask the invisibility of masculinity or to destabilize the unifying discourse on masculinity" by challenging "commonsense" literary and cultural narratives that claim a naturalness for boys and men; for example, "boys will be boys" (Wu 2005: 8–9). Timothy Beneke, for example, argues that masculinity can be made quite visible as a social construction because masculinity must always be proved, over and again, often through public rituals. And if it must always be proved, then it is always being threatened, always in process, fluid and tenuous, and subject to change. Indeed, those moments in which we see identity categories such as race or gender as being most reified by culture and biology are actually those moments when these categories might be at their most tenuous. It may be, then, that those texts, such as *Tarzan* or *Dragon Ball Z*, that most vigorously perform exaggerated versions of masculinity may, ironically, be those texts that can be used to make dominant masculinity most visible as a social construct.

These sorts of theoretical discussions of masculinity in literary and cultural texts have been slow to reach the field of children's literature. In his introduction to the collection *Ways of Being Male*, one of the few texts to critically study masculinity in texts for children and adolescents, John Stephens writes:

The critical and analytical discourses relating to children's literature have seemed surprisingly slow to generate a body of discussion drawing conceptually on the discourses dealing with masculinities in literary and cultural theory more generally, while at the same time maintaining a clear grasp on the more specific ontological and social issues pertaining to textual representations created for the young, such as the thematic dominance within the literature of social issues and character development. (Stephens 2002: x)

The sort of criticism Stephens is calling for—one that accounts for the distinct characteristics of children's literature, while also acknowledging new developments in gender studies—requires juggling approaches that sometimes are conflicting and requires moving among different disciplines, each with varied critical lenses and different ways of knowing. However, it is necessary work needed to fill a gap in several fields. We need a critical language to discuss masculinity in popular texts for children and adolescents that moves beyond just valorizing the literary canon or labeling gender stereotypes or positive role models and that, instead, considers theories of reading, identity formation, children's culture, and gender that can help us to better understand the difficult negotiations individuals make (both consciously and subconsciously) as they form gendered identities and are interpellated as gendered subjects.

With the exception of works such as Kenneth Kidd's book *Making American Boys: Boyology and the Feral Tale* and Stephens's edited collection, much of the scholarly work about gender in children's literature has primarily focused on stereotypes or on women and girls. Although the study of women and girls as readers and as characters is necessary and important work, a continued focus solely on women and girls as the primary subjects of the study of gender in children's literature runs the risk of further naturalizing masculinity and of perpetuating the assumption that girls are gendered, whereas boys are just naturally boys. Tami Bereska, in her article "The Changing Boys' World in the 20th Century: Reality and 'Fiction,'" argues, "Relatively less is known about boys, their popular cultural products, and masculinity, than is known about girls—for many years, gender has been perceived as a female quality" (Bereska 2003: 159). When girls are gendered and boys just are, then boyhood takes on a universal quality—boyhood is the norm against which (abnormal) girlhood is measured. As long as masculinity is invisible, natural, and universal (boys will be boys), it remains rigidly defined and works to maintain, by naturalizing them, definitive borders that narrowly define dominant, acceptable versions of the masculine subject.

In the third edition of *The Pleasures of Children's Literature,* Nodelman and Reimer write, "Although considerable work has been done with sex-role stereotypes in children's literature, rethinking how the 'natural' is produced in texts for children is work that has yet to be done" (Nodelman and Reimer 2003: 242). Considering how the natural is produced, how social constructions are reified or made to seem like common sense, means working to understand subjectivity. Karen Coats's definition of subjectivity is a good place to begin a discussion of boys in children's texts because her work simultaneously acknowledges the complex interactions between self, text, and culture and does so within the context of children's literature and literary criticism about children's texts. Coats explains that she asks her students to consider the various meanings of the word *subject,* which has "resonances of both agency and subservience" (Coats 2004: 3). She writes, "Subjectivity, then, is more than identity—it is a movement between that which we control and that which controls us" (p. 5). To more fully understand the complexity of the subject, we need to "hold these contradictions in unresolved ambiguity" and conceive of the subject as "both active and passive; it has agency and responsibility, but at the same time it is bound by rules and laws outside itself and constrained by its own unconscious processes" (p. 3). An attempt to understand subjectivity, then, would need to consider not only the impact of culture(s) on individuals but also the ongoing processes involved in shaping subjectivity: in what way is "I" defined, what constitutes the "I," and how is gender integral to the formation of "I"?

Judith Butler argues that gender is a foundation of subjectivity and an aspect of subjectivity that illustrates the difficulty of attempting to differentiate between what we determine and what is already determined for us:

> For if gender is constructed, it is not necessarily constructed by an "I" or a "we" who stands before that construction in any spatial or temporal sense of "before." Indeed, it is unclear that there can be an "I" or a "we" who has not been submitted, subjected to gender, where gendering is, among other things, the differentiating relations by which speaking subjects come into being. Subjected to gender, but subjectivated by gender, the "I" neither precedes nor follows the process of this gendering, but emerges only within and as the matrix of gender relations themselves. (Butler 1993: 7)

Discussions of gender are integral to discussions of who we are, and gender is continuously and simultaneously constructed for us and by us as subjects in ways that make it very difficult to tell what is natural and what is constructed, what is imposed and what we determine. Furthermore, Butler argues that debates attempting to differentiate between what is socially constructed and what is natural "miss the point of deconstruction altogether" (p. 8). "Why is it that what is constructed is understood as an artificial and dispensable character? What are we to make of constructions without which we would not be able to think, to live, to make sense at all, those which have acquired for us a kind of necessity?" (p. xi). In other words, to say that gender is socially constructed does not mean that we can easily perform our gender in self-determined ways. Conversely, even though gender has already been defined for us in many ways before we were born, this does not mean that we have no power to alter those definitions. Finally, to say that gender is constructed does not make it any less real and does not mean that it doesn't affect the everyday experiences of living in a body that is gendered.

A discussion of gendered subjectivity also, then, must necessarily include a discussion of the body, the ways we inhabit the world and interact with the world in bodies, the ways culture acts on our bodies, and the ways bodies bound and define the self. Bodies are at once both natural and constructed, constricted by cultural norms that determine how we dress, how we move, and the spaces we are allowed to inhabit and to what degree. This is especially important to consider within those fields that study education, children's literature, and children's culture, where there have always been varied theories postulating that children are blank slates. In a fascinating discussion on Child_Lit: Theory and Criticism of Children's Literature Listserv, members debated for several days in late 2005 the degree to which children are or are not blank slates. Perry Nodelman explained quite eloquently why this cannot be:

> One part of an answer to that question is simply that children have bodies (or more accurately are bodies), and that means that to some extent they are already written upon, already to some extent written. The colour of their skin, the nature of their genitalia, the body type their genetics has provided them, the significance of the shape of their nose or lips or other parts of their bodies in terms of codes of beauty, the physical location and the cultural location of their body on the planet and all the social and economic implications of these simple matters of geographical placing—all of these and many other ways in which we humans ascribe differing

amounts of power to each other inevitably and unavoidably write themselves onto individual embodied humans and severely effect what more or different can be written by individuals or those who care for them. Whatever we choose to do or try to be, to have and be a body in an environment of other embodied beings and a history that gives significance to bodily differences (as human history always has) is to be already and always in history, in culture, in politics. (Nodelman 2005)

The arguments made by both Butler and Nodelman illustrate some of the complexities of being born into a body whose characteristics have already been defined for us. It is no wonder, then, that so much of children's literature that highlights gender also highlights the body and, more specifically, the ways the body is bounded. The popular texts that I examine for this project focus on the body in ways that test and then reaffirm bodily borders using literal and metaphorical depictions of the abject.

A number of gender theorists argue that the concept of abjection—the illegible, the indefinable, that which threatens the self, not because it is an Other but because it cannot even be defined as a whole other being—is primary to understanding subject formation. Indeed, Kristeva argues that abjection is a central focus of most literature:

On close inspection, all literature is probably a version of the apocalypse that seems to me rooted, no matter what its socio-historical conditions might be, on the fragile border (borderline cases) where identities (subject/object, etc.) do not exist or only barely so—double, fuzzy, heterogeneous, animal, metamorphosed, altered, abject. (Kristeva 1982: 207)

The dichotomies that fix subjectivity are defined through borders: the more rigidly defined the dichotomy—me–you, self–other, adult–child, male–female—the more solid (seeming) the borders. But those spaces, those moments where borders are being articulated through binaries, are also those sites where the abject appears as a threat because it challenges the fixity of the borders and unmasks them as porous, fluid, constructed, and illusory. The "I" must necessarily be defined against a "not I," but this "not I" is not always so neatly differentiated. Kristeva argues, "From its place of banishment, the abject does not cease challenging its master" (p. 2). These moments when borders are both challenged and reified and also always haunted by the challenge are those spaces where gendered subjectivity is being continuously constructed.

In the case of the popular children's texts discussed next, these are spaces filled with anxiety for both child and adult readers. A focus on abjection can make visible the ways "the limits of constructivism are exposed at those boundaries of bodily life where abjected or delegitimated bodies fail to count as 'bodies'" (Butler 1993: 15). In other words, a focus on abjection can highlight the ways that the "I" of dominant masculinity is often constructed against an abjected "not I" that is decidedly feminine or queer. Narratives focusing on the threat of the abject are a feature of many of the most popular texts for boys, which repeatedly perform the necessary rituals of subject formation in overtly grotesque ways: a monster threatens to engulf bodies; children are eaten; a body morphs into an animal or a machine or a turd; characters move in and out of the bodies of others; food is splattered, thrown, and worn; and characters vomit slugs and Sploosh and are themselves vomited by toilets and monsters. Over and over subjectivity is threatened in literal ways by blurring the distinctions between what is outside the body and what is inside, between what is "I" and what is "not I," between what is utterable and what is unintelligible.

Kristeva writes, "The abject has only one quality of the object—that of being opposed to *I*" (Kristeva 1982: 1) and attempting to define the abject "draws me toward the place where meaning collapses" (pp. 1–2). Because the abject is more ambiguous even than "not I," it is in a space beyond language and is difficult to describe and understand; in the process of attempting to describe abjection, it slips away from us and eludes language or representation. Kristeva (1982) writes, "Abjection is above all ambiguity" (p. 9), it is "what disturbs identity, system, order" (p. 4), and it "is the violence of mourning for an 'object' that has always already been lost" (p. 15) because "How can I be without a border?" (p. 4). The "I" needs a "not I," and even a "not other," to define itself and its place in the world, and this abject is often, initially, the mother. If this is so, is the child, then, not yet a subject, not yet fully defined as an "I"? Does the fictional child depicted in children's literature represent for adult readers "the violence of mourning for an 'object' that has always already been lost"? Kristeva uses the term *chora* to describe a stage when the child does not yet acknowledge boundaries between "I" and "not I," when the baby's identity spreads out into the world in ways that do not distinguish between self and other because the self is the world and the world is the self. A child must move beyond this initial phase before it can enter into language. Language use requires an acknowledgment of an Other that is distinct from self, and language requires binaries, a distinction between this and not this, between representable and unrepresentable.

Is the child, then, a subject, an object, a subject-in-becoming, or a fluid body that takes in and exudes the abject? Is the drooling, puking, pooping baby, that leakiest of bodies, only recently inside the body of the mother, consuming the body of the mother while attached to her breast, worthy of adoration or repulsion? Does the child, then, represent that space we no longer wish to inhabit or that space to which we impossibly long to return? As Lucy Rollin writes, many adults have repressed the "raging, craving inner child in the books we give our children—so deep is our need to protect ourselves from that image" (Rollin and West 1999: 79). Indeed, this adult need to protect ourselves may explain the gap between the reading preferences of adults and boys—boys who seem to figure out fairly early that many adults are easily repulsed by depictions of the abject and who take great pleasure in grossing out grown-ups. My questions, then, are as follows: Why are the grotesque and abject so overtly depicted in texts enjoyed mostly by boys? Are depictions of the abject directly connected to rigid definitions of hegemonic masculinity? Also, why do many adults simultaneously disapprove of grotesque, violent images of abjection in the texts boys enjoy, while also often winking at such texts, saying that "boys will be boys" and just "naturally" will be drawn to fart jokes, food fights, slime, and morphing monsters? Do we, as a culture, believe that such depictions are a necessary, though perhaps unpleasant, phase of subject formation for boys that they will pass through and then move beyond?

Furthermore, how are these perceptions of childhood as a phase we pass through on our (always incomplete) journey toward subjectivity depicted in children's literature, a body of texts written by adults for an imagined audience of children? Jacqueline Rose would argue that this is the impossibility of children's fiction and that the apostrophe in "children's" is misleading because the fiction does not belong to children, who are often objectified or idealized or colonized by it. "Sentimentality about childhood," writes Rose, "is the other side of guilt" (p. x). When we write for and about them, she asks, what do we do to our children? What do we do to the memory of the child we once were? Rose speaks of the "impossible relation between adult and child" (p. 1) and the space between these two that is, in many ways, uninhabitable and unrepresentable. So great is our need to separate ourselves from the child that we work to create the illusion for ourselves that one can finally, incontrovertibly become an adult. But Rose argues that Freud taught us that "there is no childhood which is simply over and done with" (p. 17); we only like to create the fiction that there is such a definitive boundary. We write coming-of-age stories that create a clear demarcation between the child subject-in-becoming and the adult he will one day become.

Rose writes, "Children are no threat to our identity because they are, so to speak, 'on their way' (the journey metaphor is a recurrent one). Their difference stands purely as the sign of just how far we have progressed" (p. 13). So, perhaps, those texts that are most threatening to adult readers, those texts from which we attempt to shield our children, are those texts that most remind us that the journey toward subjectivity is never truly complete. Is *The Chocolate War* (1974) so frequently challenged and censored because of its deliberate lack of closure, because of the ambiguous and incomplete identity development of the protagonist? Do we avert our eyes from the grotesque animation of many of the cartoons and films most popular with boys because it challenges the boundaries we have erected between "I" and "not I," between adult and child?

Rose writes of J.M. Barrie's *Peter Pan* (1904), "Precisely by touching on the most vulnerable point of identity, it always contains a potential terror" (p. xv). This "potential terror" and "most vulnerable point" is abjection. It is a threat to subjectivity because it makes visible the absence of a clear line between child and adult. If children's and adolescent literature that openly depicts images of abjection often repulses adults, why are images of abjection so prevalent and often so overt in popular texts for boys? Why do adults write such texts? Why do boys seem drawn to these texts? Is it because they understand that as children they represent to adults a form of the abject? Or is it because rigid definitions of masculinity rely on the abject for definition? And why boys and not girls? Perhaps it is because a boy is simultaneously seen as an Other (a colonized child) and a subject-in-becoming. Kidd argues that the image of the "wild boy" prevalent in much literature and public discourse about boys is essential to constructions of boyhood and manhood that have been dominant for more than a century: the idea of the white, middle-class, heterosexual "bad boy" who then grows into a good man is an image that depicts savagery, femininity, or otherness "as a stage to be suffered through and then surpassed" (Kidd 2004: 59). Becoming a subject, within this cultural narrative, then, means moving from one side of a dichotomy to another: child to adult, feminine to masculine, abject to object, object to subject. Furthermore, within this dominant coming-of-age narrative, women, gay men, and men of color can never, of course, fully gain access to subjectivity because they cannot transcend positions marked as Other. Contemporary popular literature for boys adheres to this dominant coming-of-age narrative in the ways that it often focuses on bodily humor, or the grotesque, or the morphing body, or the monstrous (m)Other. It often depicts in visceral, physical ways masculine subjectivity that is in the process of being formed, threatened, reinforced, and reperformed. In these texts, gender is at once fixed and tenuous. And, far from being part of the stereotypical–nontraditional binary that some critics hope to use to classify and monitor texts for young people, gender is often depicted in ways that are multifaceted, shifting, ambiguous, excessive, and discomfiting.

Of course, these negotiations with popular texts become even more complex for those boys who do not fit the mold of dominant masculinity because they are gay, or poor, or a member of a minority culture, each with different expectations for males, some of which may be seen as the abject or the Other against which dominant masculinity is compared. Stacey Lee writes, "Although there are a variety of masculinities within cultures, there is always a single hegemonic masculinity within a given culture or community" (Lee 2004: 14). Boys within minority cultures or subcultures must navigate both the dominant masculinity of their specific culture and the dominant masculinity portrayed in the mass media, and these are often at odds with one another. Coats explains that although subjectivity is contingent, shifting, and multifaceted, it is often portrayed in children's fiction in ways tied to dominant cultural understandings of subjectivity: "It is avowedly patriarchal and understands Whiteness and heterosexuality as sites of privilege and desire" (p. 7). For this reason, making dominant versions of masculinity depicted in popular texts visible as constructions and marking the ways these constructions are connected to class, race, ethnicity, and sexuality is necessary work that can benefit boys who see themselves as outside of dominant masculinity. "To the extent that white middle-class boys are not viewed as white or middle class but simply 'boys,' boys who are not white or middle class are regarded as 'other,' and their experiences tend to be marginalized or neglected altogether" (Way and Chu 2004: 1–2). This is most definitely the case with the most popular texts for boys, which almost exclusively depict white, heterosexual, middle-class boys as protagonists. It is also the case with most discussions about the current boy crisis. Kidd writes, "It's painfully obvious that the young subject of boyology is the middle-class white boy. There's no information in these [advice] books about how to live below the poverty line, or how to survive racism or homophobia or job de-skilling" (p. 184). What (or who) is abjected or othered in contemporary popular texts for boys to construct hegemonic masculinity? Do contemporary popular texts reflect changes that have taken place in American society over the course of the twentieth century due to the civil rights movement, the gay rights movement, and feminism, or do they do more to reflect tensions between traditionally defined masculinity in conflict with a changing world?

Tami Bereska studied thirty popular young adult novels written between 1940 and 1997 and concluded that "a significant portion of the discourse surrounding masculinity has remained unchanged for more than 50 years, despite other social changes having occurred" (Bereska 2003: 162). Ingrid Johnston and Jyoti Mangat surveyed teenaged boys in Canada and the United States and found that "the boys' comments on their own changing roles in society suggest that they feel ambivalent and uncertain about their place in the world. Many boys also believe that traditional notions of masculinity have changed as a result of feminism and not as a result of a reevaluation of male roles per se" (Johnston and Mangat 2002: 144). Susan Faludi, in her best-selling book titled *Stiffed: The Betrayal of the American Man* (1999), argues that many men feel cheated because the traditional gender expectations they have learned do not apply in a changing world. And Kidd argues that much of the discourse underlying discussions about the current boy crisis has its roots in assumptions about masculinity that are a century old: he writes that although some claim that the study of boys is a "hot new field of inquiry," it is instead "a revisitation of early-twentieth-century boyology" (p. 167).

For these reasons, the first chapter of this book—an attempt to understand one of the ways hegemonic masculinity has been and continues to be defined in the United States—is a detailed study of a narrative and a character that have dominated American popular culture for a century. The character of Tarzan is an ideal place to begin a discussion of masculinity in American popular culture, because he is distinctly American, because all of his incarnations have been in decidedly lowbrow genres, and because he has endured as a model of ideal masculinity for generations of boys. In chapter 1, titled "Me Tarzan, You Other: The Evolution of an Icon," I discuss the ways that the various incarnations of Tarzan have embodied and continue to embody ideal (hegemonic) masculinity in the United States and the way this ideal is defined through the abjection of the feminine, the child, the non-Western, the nonwhite, and the colonized. An examination of various characterizations of Tarzan over the century allows us to mark some of the categories of hegemonic masculinity that often go unmarked—whiteness, class privilege, heterosexuality, and American individuality—and to make visible the ways these categories are naturalized through narratives that work to depict any characteristics that are in opposition to these as Other or as abject. The origins, the evolution, and the cultural reproduction of this character, from pulp magazines to films to television shows to toys to Disney films to picture books to video games, can make visible the ways that dominant constructions of masculinity are repeated, reperformed, and reified. For contemporary children, the kinder, gentler version of Tarzan championed in the bowdlerized 1999 Disney film version is only one aspect of a broader cultural narrative because this image competes with repetitions of visual representations of the manly man that dominate the video game, computer game, and television show sequels and product tie-ins. In other words, the image of Tarzan that endures, even in the contemporary context, is not of the sensitive boy holding his ape mother's hand but of a wild, muscled white man in a loincloth gliding smoothly through a jungle over which he is lord.

The chapters that follow explore the ways that dominant masculinity continues to be portrayed, though often in contradictory and complex ways, in popular texts with more contemporary origins. These texts highlight tensions between hegemonic masculinity and nonhegemonic masculinities that often go unresolved. Chapter 2, titled "Reading in the Gaps and Lacks: (De)Constructing Masculinity in Louis Sachar's *Holes*," examines Sachar's novel, which is popular with boy readers partially because it is sanctioned by critics, educators, and award committees. Like Disney's bowdlerized *Tarzan*, *Holes* appears to champion those sorts of masculine behaviors Nodelman points out appeal more to mothers than to boys. On the surface, the two male protagonists of the novel appear to be sensitive, caring, nonthreatening boys able to survive in a harsh world. However, when examined through the lens of abjection, the novel can be seen as working to construct masculinity in opposition to a monstrous feminine that must be silenced, covered over, expelled, or conquered before the boys can come of age. In this way, the novel represents contemporary gendered identity in complex ways that mirror less the ideal versions of masculinity many adults would like to see portrayed in books for boys and more the contradictory, multilayered intersections of culture and dynamic subjectivity that probably more accurately represent the difficult negotiations boys make.

Abjection is an even more overt motif in the books that make up Dav Pilkey's Captain Underpants series, which are mostly enjoyed by younger readers. The overt depictions of the abject—flying food, toilets that eat people, villains who morph into pieces of poop, a boy who becomes a monstrous living booger—repulse many adult readers of the series and seem to appeal to the young boys who are the implied readers of these scatological, carnivalesque texts. In chapter 3, titled "'The Battle of the Bionic Booger Boy,' Bodily Borders, and B.A.D. Boys: Pleasure and Abjection in the Captain Underpants Series," I discuss the ways the grotesque, irreverent illustrations in these early readers work to create pleasurable, playful texts that appeal to even some of the more reluctant younger readers but also work to perpetuate a hegemonic version of masculinity that defines itself, delineates its borders, in opposition to girls, women, and feminized boys. In each of the books in the series, bodily borders are threatened but then reinstated: in this way, the repeated threat of abjection is used to reify a clearly bounded, gendered identity.

A similar use of abjection in a grotesque and violent series of texts for older boys called *Dragon Ball Z* is the main topic of chapter 4, which is titled "And Majin Buu Said, 'I'll Eat You Up!': Consuming Japanese Cultural Imports." Japanese manga (comic books) and anime (animated films and television shows) have a large following in the United States. There is a broad body of cultural exports from Japan representing a range of topics, aesthetic styles, and quality of narrative and artistic representation. I chose to study *Dragon Ball Z* because it is very popular among American boys and young men and has enjoyed relative longevity in the fairly fickle world of children's cartoons and comics. Like the texts I discuss in earlier chapters, it also portrays a deep cultural anxiety about contemporary masculinity. As is the case with the Captain Underpants books, the abject is portrayed overtly and as a literal threat to bodily borders, which works to both trouble and to reify bodily borders between a gendered "I" and a "not I."

The fifth chapter, "Men in Cloaks and High-Heeled Boots, Men Wielding Pink Umbrellas: Witchy Masculinities in the Harry Potter Novels," focuses less on abjection and more on the history of criticism of these popular novels. The Harry Potter novels represent masculinity in complex, varied ways, but many critics, often focusing attention on whether portrayals are stereotypical or nonstereotypical, have chosen to ignore the nuanced portrayals of gender in the novels. When the novels in the series are considered within cultural contexts by accounting for the ways that gendered subjectivity is formed in relation to texts, communities, and larger cultural expectations, they can be used to illuminate the anxieties contemporary boys experience as they work to negotiate their subjectivities within, against, or on the margins of hegemonic masculinity.

1

ME TARZAN, YOU OTHER
The Evolution of an Icon

> Every boy who is good for anything is a natural savage. The scientists who want to study the primitive man, and have so much difficulty finding one anywhere in this sophisticated age, couldn't do better than to devote their attention to the common country-boy. He has the primal, vigorous instincts and impulses of the African savage, without any of the vices inherited from a civilization long ago decayed or developed in an unrestrained barbaric society.
>
> **—Warner (1877: 198)**

Boyhood in the United States is an impossible ideal, viewed as natural and primitive yet also shaped by and contained within civilization and all its prejudices. An object in the process of becoming a subject, it is uncanny—familiar yet disturbingly different, simultaneously the heart and future of the empire and yet a savage in a distant colony always threatening to revolt (and eventually kill the Father). It stakes a claim to universality at the same time as it marks itself as distinctly masculine, heterosexual, white, Western, upper or middle class, Christian, and entitled to a destiny manifest. Kenneth Kidd illustrates in *Making American Boys: Boyology and the Feral Tale* that the myth of the feral boy has been central to the construction of American boyhood in the twentieth century. The lesson we learn from the stories we tell ourselves about feral boys is one "about the white, middle-class male's perilous passage from nature to culture, from bestiality to humanity, from homosocial pack life to individual self-reliance and heterosexual prowess—that is, from boyhood to manhood" (Kidd 2004: 7). The myth of the feral boy, then, does the difficult work of maintaining a paradox, a delicate balance between subject and abject that always threatens to collapse under the weight of its own contradictions and under the uncertainty of all that is tenuously held at bay through abjection. To sustain itself, the myth of American boyhood must continuously be retold, reperformed, and reinvented within public discourse in ways that smooth over its contradictions. It is reified through repetition. One such repetition is the cultural icon of Tarzan: the story of feral boy turned muscle man has been a mainstay of American popular culture for almost a century. Tarzan represents an impossible ideal of American masculinity and its racist, imperialistic, classist underpinnings that sometimes go unmarked: he is aristocratic yet not effete, savage but not barbaric, wild but not native, and civilized but not feminized. Indeed, he represents the fantasy of the primal, vigorous, savage, privileged, white boy ("boys will be boys"), who will naturally and without effort grow into his entitlements as lord of the jungle.

Despite his significance as an influential cultural icon, Tarzan is curiously absent from most children's literature textbooks, anthologies, and critical texts, even though he has been admired by American boys (and girls and adults) for almost a century in a variety of incarnations in novels, comic books, television shows, toys, films, and, most recently, video games.[1] Perhaps Edgar Rice Burroughs's Tarzan has not been extensively discussed by children's literature scholars because the Tarzan stories, originally printed in pulp magazines, are decidedly antiliterary, lowbrow, commercial texts. Or, perhaps, children's literature scholars prefer not to claim the overtly racist, imperialistic, social-Darwinist text of *Tarzan of the Apes* (1912) as part of the children's literature canon because it is an embarrassing reminder of the mainstream racism of American culture. Or, perhaps, Tarzan represents a traditional version of violent, hard-bodied masculinity that many adults would prefer to replace with more feminist depictions of masculinity. Tarzan, however, is an icon of popular children's literature and culture. The original Tarzan stories by Burroughs were read by adults and children; boys and men were major consumers of the Tarzan comic books and films of the early and mid-twentieth century; children made up much of the audience for the Tarzan television programs; and the latest Tarzan films, produced by Disney, are bowdlerized versions of the character and story marketed directly to an audience of young children and their parents.

The latest versions of the Tarzan story produced by Disney (a 1999 film followed by straight-to-DVD sequels, a cartoon television show, and several video and computer games) seem, at first glance, to be far removed from the offensive original text. The gorillas and their habitats seem to be drawn based on research done on primates, though they are anthropomorphized through Disney's animation and dialogue. Jane is spunky, funny, and mildly feminist, and some critics say that her voice-over portrayal by Minnie Driver is the highlight of the first film. The villain of the 1999 film—marked clearly as the bad guy the moment he enters the space of the screen—is a gun-wielding, macho hunter whose name, Clayton, becomes synonymous with the rifle he shoots off numerous times throughout the film. Tarzan, on the other hand, is the ideal sensitive man of the twenty-first century: nonviolent and in tune with nature yet hunky enough to hold Jane with one arm while he swings from a vine he grasps with the other hand, loyal to his mother but willing to follow the woman he loves, and a strong leader who also cares about his family, his community, and the environment.

Disney's *Tarzan* is an attempt to represent a newer version of masculinity that will appeal to modern moms and dads, who will take their young children to the cinema knowing that Disney will not offend, and who will later rent or buy the *Tarzan* video for their child to watch over and over again, committing favorite scenes to memory. In this way Disney's *Tarzan* represents a newer version of dominant masculinity that is most definitely reified through repetition and for a much younger audience than the original novels, films, and comic books. However, Disney's *Tarzan* is filled with contradictions and paradoxically presents hegemonic masculinity as a problem, while simultaneously subtly working to reinforce hegemonic masculinity in ways not very far removed from the original narrative. Robyn McCallum argues that Disney's *Tarzan* is more conservative in its representations of masculinity than some other Disney films of the 1990s such as *Hercules* (1997) and *Mulan* (1998), and may be so because "Tarzan is an iconic figure within popular culture where he is the epitome of hard-bodied muscular masculinity, and hence perhaps does not offer much scope for experimentation with gender representation" (McCallum 2002: 125). Although Disney's version of the Tarzan story works very hard to distance itself from the original narrative's unsavory origins, it is unable to do so and works to perpetuate older versions of hegemonic masculinity. But, as I will discuss later in this chapter, it is precisely these contradictory portrayals of masculinity that are key to the film's commercial success.

Of course, this may be the case with quite a few contemporary, popular children's texts. After studying thirty popular novels written between 1940 and 1997, some of which initially appear to present challenges to hegemonic masculinity, Tami Bereska concluded that within the field of young adult and children's literature, "a significant portion of the discourse surrounding masculinity has remained unchanged for more than 50 years, despite other social changes having occurred" (Bereska 2003: 162). Bereska argues that, on the whole, this body of texts illustrates that the world of boys

> is supposed to be a heterosexual world, comprised of active male bodies, where no sissies are permitted entry. It is characterized by particular types and degrees of emotional expression, naturalized aggression, male hang-out groups, hierarchies within those groups, competition, athleticism, adventure, and sound moral character. (Bereska 2003: 161)

She argues that in fiction written for young readers, depictions of masculinity are changing only in superficial ways and only in reaction to the changing roles of women and girls and that, at their core, representations of masculinity have changed very little over the past fifty years. Tarzan is an ideal starting point for *Boys in Children's Literature and Popular Culture,* because the historical evolution of this popular cultural icon can be used to make visible the ways that portrayals of contemporary hegemonic masculinity are in many ways tied—albeit in subtler and more contradictory ways—to the same constructions of race, social class, sexual orientation, empire, American individuality, and depictions of the abject that have characterized mainstream representations of masculinity for decades.

FROM PULP TO PAP: THE ORIGIN AND EVOLUTION OF AN AMERICAN ICON

Even though most Americans probably have not read Burroughs's original Tarzan books, most Americans have some sense—however far removed from the original text—of the Tarzan legend. Why does the Tarzan story—retold in variation after variation, reinvented so many times that some versions are retellings of retellings—resonate so with Americans? What does our affection for this character and story tell us about our cultural and political values? And how are we in turn affected by it and its repetitions? An analysis of the Tarzan legend can reveal much about the ways masculinity is perceived in the United States.

Despite some critics' attempts to claim literary merit for Burroughs's original Tarzan books, the stories have a decidedly lowbrow origin and history.[2] Of course, the texts that boys most often enjoy and read, and the texts that most alarm the well-meaning adults in their lives, often share this characteristic, something discussed at length in other chapters. The Tarzan story first appeared in 1912 in the pulp magazine *All-Story* and was titled "Tarzan of the Apes—A Romance of the Jungle."[3] The story was later serialized in the *New York Evening World*, where it "reached an enormous readership, including members of the working class, immigrants, and ethnic minorities. Its hero became a cultural icon before the story ever appeared in book form and for readers who would never enter a bookshop" (Kasson 2001: 215, 217). After the success of the first story, Burroughs wrote twenty-three more sequels, which were adapted (often loosely) into movies, television shows, comic books, picture books, toys, underwear, shoes, and computer and video games.

In the first novel of the series, *Tarzan of the Apes*, Burroughs creates a feral white boy with aristocratic origins. British John Clayton, who holds the title Lord Greystoke, and his pregnant wife, Lady Alice, are abandoned on a remote, deserted African shore by a group of cutthroat, mutinous sailors. Lord Greystoke adeptly demonstrates his "genetic superiority" by building a well-crafted cabin and by providing for his weak, dependent wife, who lives long enough to nurse their baby for a year. Shortly after her death, Lord Greystoke is brutally murdered by Kerchak, king of the apes. Kala, an ape who has just lost her baby, adopts the baby British lord who will become Tarzan. The apes depicted in the novel are not any species of gorilla or chimpanzee we might be familiar with today but instead seem to be a strange invention of Burroughs's imagination; half human, half ape, they seem almost to represent for Burroughs African people and are often portrayed as being more human than the caricatures of native Africans Tarzan encounters later in the story. Tarzan, which means "white skin" in the language of the apes, grows up as a feral jungle child who has to fight with apes, the elements, and wild animals to survive. His childhood is a violent one but in adherence with many of our ideals about what boyhood ought to be. Instead of scarring or crippling him, his brutal childhood builds his character so that he becomes a strong young man: a perfect specimen of (white, Western, heterosexual, aristocratic) manly brawn, intellect, and chivalrous morality. As a boy, once he has mastered survival in the jungle, he discovers his father's cabin and collection of books and manages to teach himself to read, write, and use human weapons and tools. As he comes of age, he kills several of the alpha-male apes, murders native Africans, and terrorizes an entire African village by stealing from them, lynching several inhabitants, and making public spectacles of the dead bodies. Tarzan finally meets a group of white explorers, the American middle-class professor Archimedes Porter, his daughter Jane, Tarzan's aristocratic British cousin Clayton, and others in their party in a chapter titled "His Own Kind." He proceeds to rescue them from various jungle threats, and they all admire the body and physical prowess of this mysterious jungle man. Through a series of convoluted, melodramatic events, Tarzan makes his way out of Africa, through Paris, and then finally to Wisconsin, where he saves Jane from a forest fire.

The various adaptations of the Tarzan narrative have mostly only loosely adhered to the original story, some bearing little resemblance to Burroughs's books. For example, with the exception of Hugh Hudson's *Greystoke: The Legend of Tarzan, Lord of the Apes* (which depicts a troubled Tarzan in Africa and then in Britain, unable to reconcile his dual identities), most of the filmic versions of the story depict Tarzan as being vaguely American. Indeed, Walt Morton argues that Johnny Weissmuller's famous 1932 depiction of Tarzan is distinctly American: "classless, ruggedly individual, stoic" (Morton 1993: 118). In some ways, Americanized portrayals of Tarzan can be seen as being more true to the spirit of the original than a British Tarzan, because these more directly portray the ideal American man Burroughs created. For example, in the famous 1932 film *Tarzan, the Ape Man*, Tarzan's origins are ignored and even dismissed. We enter the narrative when Jane comes to Africa and meets an adult Tarzan. When another character says to Jane, "I can't make it out, how did he get here?" she replies, "Oh, what does it matter?" In Burroughs's stories, Tarzan's ancestry is key to his identity, not only in terms of his nobility but also in terms of what Burroughs calls his "superior genetics." On the surface, the Americanized film *Tarzan* can be seen as being more classless or democratic, but he also portrays a myth of assimilation and forgetfulness that allows many Americans to claim that they are "just American" and to ignore the fact that it *would matter* to Jane if Tarzan's skin was a darker shade or if his features were African or if his accent was marked as foreign. Therefore, the Americanized film *Tarzan*—the 1999 version as well as earlier versions—seems democratic but maintains many of the remnants of the original, some of which go unmarked and are taken for granted. However, these remnants do matter, and just like the American Jane of the 1932 film, we sometimes like to pretend they do not.

MODERN MALE FANTASIES: "WE WOULD EACH LIKE TO BE TARZAN"

Burroughs, born in Chicago in 1875, was the youngest son of a successful businessman and Civil War veteran. He felt pressured to follow his father into business but was miserable and ineffectual as a white-collar worker. In his book *Houdini, Tarzan, and the Perfect Man: The White Male Body and the Challenge of Modernity in America*, John Kasson writes that Burroughs wrote the Tarzan stories as "an act of self-liberation," as a fantasy for himself (p. 159). He quotes Burroughs as saying about Tarzan:

> We wish to escape not alone the narrow confines of city streets for the freedom of the wilderness, but the restrictions of man made laws, and the inhibitions that society has placed on us. We like to picture ourselves as roaming free, the lords of ourselves and of our world; in other words, we would each like to be Tarzan. At least I would; I admit it. (quoted in Kasson 2001: 159)

This quote from Burroughs is telling because it draws on several cultural assumptions about hegemonic masculinity. For instance, when Burroughs says "we would each like to be Tarzan," he makes several assumptions about the universal "we," here marked as male, white, and middle class, trapped by the confines of American business and the feminizing influences of modern, industrialized civilization. The assumption, too, is that men and boys should be wild and out in nature, not merely as inhabitants but as lords of it. Finally, these wild white men of privilege are not blue-collar workers in the employ of another man; they are "roaming free" and in control of their own destinies. These fantasies represent not only personal dissatisfactions of the author but also dissatisfactions expressed by many white, middle-class men of the period, and ultimately they contain several of the paradoxes still inherent in hegemonic versions of the ideal American male that are depicted today.

For instance, Kasson points out that fantasies of "natural" masculine wildness are often "explicitly tied to whiteness" (p. 212): the fantasy of being a wild white man represents a complicated negotiation of identity because the wild white man is seen not as a native or a primitive but as an individualistic master of his environment. He also is not a working-class man laboring in the wilderness but instead an aristocratic adventurer. In other words, the illusion of a return to the wilderness is, ironically, steeped in cultural constructions and systems of power. Burroughs's Tarzan novels are set in a make-believe Africa,[4] a colonist's fantasy that represents "geographies of rugged masculinity:

regions within which white men of northern European stock reassert their dominance over physical and moral 'inferiors,' including incompetents, malefactors, weaklings, and cowards" (Kasson 2001: 180). The wild white man is not part of the African jungle and is not native to it—on the contrary, Africa, the jungle, the animals, the African natives, women, and lower-class men all become inferiors against which Tarzan is allowed to test and assert his strength. Burroughs's books work to maintain fantasies of wildness that are inexorably tied to fantasies of superiority and entitlement.

Burroughs's Tarzan, on many levels, is a lengthy, intricate justification of the supposed superiority of the white, upper-class, Western male. Even the structure of the narrative, borrowing heavily from hero mythology, works to achieve this end. *Tarzan of the Apes* is part of a larger tradition and is not alone as a popular hero narrative that works to perpetuate white superiority. In her book *Deconstructing the Hero: Literary Theory and Children's Literature,* Margery Hourihan writes, "The hero is white, and his story inscribes the dominance of white power and white culture. In those versions of the myth which belong to the last four hundred years or so, the period of European expansion and colonialism, white superiority is frequently an explicit theme" (Hourihan 1997: 58). She argues, for example, that in Daniel Defoe's *Robinson Crusoe,* Crusoe is so struck by the inferiority of the natives that he "thanks God he is not like them" (p. 58). Tarzan's identity is similarly established largely by determining all he is *not* like. He is not like an ape, and he is not like the native Africans. When he first meets white explorers, he instinctively and immediately knows he is not like the African American servant accompanying Jane or the lower-class sailors with the party. Finally, although he instinctively knows that the white, Western, upper-class explorers are "his kind," he also knows that Jane is something not like him and is to be desired and protected. Tarzan's identity is established, in part, in comparison to all that he is not.

Tarzan's identity as a cultural icon, however, is more complex than a simple list of negations because the character is also intrinsically tied to the jungle, to the Other that he longs to incorporate at the same time as he is repulsed by it and defined against it. Jacques Derrida writes in *Of Grammatology,* "Man *calls himself* man only by drawing limits excluding his other from the play of supplementarity: the purity of nature, of animality, primitivism, childhood, madness, divinity. The approach to these limits is at once feared as a threat of death, and desired as access to a life without difference" (Derrida 1976: 244). Derrida's list of abjected Others, both feared and desired, places childhood alongside nature, animality, primitivism, madness, and divinity. This dance of negotiation with the Other—always approaching, always repelling—is what Tarzan's growth out of childhood and out of the jungle represents. Childhood is conflated with what is wild, natural, and primitive. Tarzan's manhood is defined in part by leaving the jungle. However, because he represents a fantasy of mastery over the Other, then the Other must always be close by; Tarzan always must return to the jungle, always exists as part of it. He would not be Tarzan if he were not simultaneously both of and not of the jungle. His character, in this sense and in others, is a complex negotiation between abjection and incorporation.

Finally, for the fantasy of the wild–civilized man to work, this complex process must *seem* natural. Whiteness, Westerness, heterosexuality, and masculinity mark themselves as naturally superior in the text precisely because they work very hard to remain unmarked, to seem universally human. It is vital to make visible how the original Tarzan narrative works to naturalize racial, national, and gender identity in ways that construct the ideal American male in precise ways. Burroughs relies on popular narratives of his time about the "science" of race; racist policies of the Jim Crow era; American imperialism, xenophobia, and fears of immigration; the supposed inferiority of the working and lower classes; and the need to chivalrously protect the vulnerable white woman. These are all combined with dominant definitions of masculinity that are represented by a man possessed of a powerful, muscular body, who is able to kill animals and humans with his bare hands, who is the envy of other men who witness his strength, and who is an object of desire for women impressed by his wild virility.

APES, MEN, AND THE SCIENCE OF RACE

For my own part I would as soon be descended from that heroic little monkey, who braved his dreaded enemy in order to save the life of his keeper, or from that old baboon, who descending from the mountains, carried away in triumph his young comrade from a crowd of astonished dogs—as from a savage who delights to torture his enemies, offers up bloody sacrifices, practises infanticide without remorse, treats his wives like slaves, knows no decency, and is haunted by the grossest superstitions.

—Darwin (1871/1981: 404–5)

Although contemporary readers may be shocked by the overt racism in *Tarzan of the Apes*, Burroughs was not a radical. His text reflects many of the mainstream scientific beliefs of his time period, especially those that attempted to prove there were different species of humans, with the white species established at the top of this hierarchy. These scientific beliefs were so infused with racist assumptions that many, like Darwin, argued that white men have more in common with the noble beasts from which they descended than with "savages." These convoluted arguments attempted to account for evolution while still maintaining hierarchies of race. People who believed in white supremacy had much invested in maintaining the "scientific fact" that there were different species of humans, which must have evolved separately. Burroughs's novel reflects these rationalizations in its depictions of different species of apes and different species of men. Although the apes in Burroughs's novel are not always admirable, they are shown in many ways as more human and as morally superior to the native Africans, who are described as having an appearance of "low and bestial brutishness" (p. 72). Indeed, the native Africans in the text, depicted as cannibalistic, cruel, superstitious, and taking great pleasure in ritualistic torture of their captives, bear a striking resemblance to the savages described by Darwin in the above passage. Also, Tarzan's affinity with his community of apes suggests that he has a greater connection to them than to the African humans he encounters. The Africans, although they are given bits of dialogue, are never depicted as more than caricatures, whereas some of the apes are distinct characters.[5]

The science of race is justified in the text by the presence of Jane's father, Professor Archimedes Q. Porter, and his friend, Mr. Philander. These absentminded scholars serve as comic relief in the novel as they get lost in the jungle while they are engaged in philosophical and scientific debates, but they also are learned men, able to provide scientific legitimacy that adds to the verisimilitude of the text. For example, these educated men come across the skeletons of Tarzan's parents, and after examining the skeletons they are able to determine that they "had belonged to a male and female of one of higher white races" (p. 148). Just as physical features are used throughout the novel to construct biological borders between races, they are also used here to separate social classes. The scientists can tell from the skulls that the Lord and Lady Greystoke are one of the "higher white races." Because the reader already knows this to be true within the world created by the text, the text reinforces the science of race as being correct. In these ways, then, *Tarzan of the Apes* performs the fantasy that white, upper-class superiority is natural and tied to biology, not social convention. The titles of chapters—"Heredity," "Man and Man," "His Own Kind"—point to the influence of eugenics and the dubious science of race on Burroughs's worldview.

THE JIM CROW JUNGLE: TARZAN AND THE SPECTACLE AND SPECTER OF LYNCHING

Hand over hand Tarzan drew the struggling black until he had him hanging by his neck in mid-air; then Tarzan climbed to a larger branch drawing the still threshing victim well up into the sheltering verdure of the tree. Here he fastened the rope securely to a stout branch, and then, descending, plunged his hunting knife into Kulonga's heart. Kala was avenged.

> **—Burroughs (1912/1963: 80)**

Because the science of race was used to justify slavery and institutionalized racism for much of America's history, it makes perfect sense that Burroughs's text would function in a similar way. Tarzan is assumed to be superior, whereas the native Africans are depicted not only as inferior but also as deserving of punishment and oppression, as needing to be "put into their places." Tarzan, as a feral child, grows up in an African wilderness devoid of native Africans and first encounters African men and women as a young man. The narrative is structured so that the native Africans move into and invade *his* jungle, which he must then defend against them. Furthermore, the native Africans are depicted using stereotypes of savages, which make them seem dangerous and subhuman. Their first hostile act is to kill his adoptive mother, and he—following the typical path of the hero—must avenge her death.

However, the form his vengeance takes moves beyond archetype and into the specific terrain of the United States in the early twentieth century. While Burroughs was writing *Tarzan of the Apes,* black men and women were regularly being lynched in the United States.[6] Lynchings were effective "as tools of political education and terrorism" (Markovitz 2004: xxv) because they were public spectacles, performances of violence before local and national audiences meant to keep African Americans mindful of their place in the social hierarchy. Jonathan Markovitz, in his book *Legacies of Lynching: Racial Violence and Memory,* writes, "Lynch mobs typically worked to ensure that black audiences were aware of the strength of white supremacy and the costs of violating the boundaries of racial order; at the same time, they wanted to reinforce images of white men as chivalrous protectors of white women" (Markovitz 2004: xvi). White male chivalry (the "knights" of the Klan) was constructed by creating narratives of bestial, sexualized black men seeking to rape and murder vulnerable white women. Therefore, "despite the fact that

48 • Boys in Children's Literature and Popular Culture

rape was only cited as the reason for a minority of lynchings, the need to punish black rapists was the justification most widely cited by the public apologists for lynching" (Markovitz 2004: 8). The stereotype of the black man as sexual predator is linked to the stereotype of the "pure" white woman and to fears of miscegenation. The need to maintain hierarchies of both race and gender are intertwined as the white, male lyncher works to prove his superiority to both the woman in need of protecting and to the black rapist threatening to defile his property.

All of these components of lynching are present in *Tarzan of the Apes,* which transports the terror of the Jim Crow South to the African jungle. One of the most disturbing and offensive justifications of Tarzan's "natural" superiority is the pleasure he takes in lynching native Africans. As a boy, while playing with a rope he has made, Tarzan accidentally throws a noose around the neck of an ape, and he learns a fun new game. Tarzan's ability to make a rope and noose is meant to illustrate his superiority to the animals of the jungle: he is able to use a tool to hunt and gains mastery over them, even though he has no claws or sharp teeth. But the text does not afford the native Africans the same mental superiority, because Tarzan is able to single-handedly terrorize an entire village of Africans. He takes great pleasure in terrorizing the Africans of the village by "picking up solitary hunters with his long, deadly noose, stripping them of weapons and ornaments and dropping their bodies from a high tree into the village street during the still watches of the night" (p. 101). These serial killings are justified within the text because the Africans have been portrayed as cruel cannibals, as less than human, and as being worse, even, than the violent apes. Tarzan (and, presumably, the reader as well) feels no remorse about killing these subhuman Africans.

Tarzan kills the apes and wild animals of the jungle in a variety of ways, but the native Africans are usually killed with a rope. Furthermore, these lynchings are made into public spectacles. For example, Tarzan saves the Frenchman D'Arnot from a tribe of villagers by easily lynching one of them in front of the entire village and, thereby, inspiring terror: "The blacks, their eyes protruding in horror, watched spellbound. Once beneath the trees, the body rose straight into the air, and as it disappeared into the foliage above, the terrified Negroes, screaming with fright, broke into a mad race for the village gate" (p. 199). In this scene, the lone Tarzan has complete control of the village, and the lynching functions in just the same way as public lynching functioned in the American south. In a fantasy of white supremacy, the "Negroes" in the scene witness the lynching, are helpless to stop it, and run away in terror. Tarzan, who then rescues D'Arnot, is constructed as the chivalrous hero saving a white man from a vicious black mob. Tarzan enforces the law of the jungle upon unruly black Africans, and, in this way, the narrative adheres to cultural constructions in which "Blackness is in some sense corporeally constituted in surveillance" and "Whiteness emerges as the bodily schema corresponding to monitoring" (Perkinson 2002: 183). The text of *Tarzan of the Apes* establishes the native Africans as dangerous and in need of control and establishes Tarzan "white skin" as the body able to monitor and police them.

Such cultural narratives of white male paternalism and chivalry are most evident in a scene in which Tarzan saves Jane from a potential ape rapist. Jane is rescued by Tarzan when Terkoz, one of Tarzan's ape rivals, abducts Jane intending to ravage her: "One piercing scream escaped her lips as the brute hand clutched her arm. Then she was dragged toward those awful fangs which yawned at her throat. But ere they touched that fair skin another mood claimed the anthropoid" (p. 171). Kasson writes of this scene, "Burroughs transformed fears of the predatory black rapist and the specter of miscegenation into fears of hybridity between human beings and apes" (Kasson 2001: 208). Because throughout the book the apes have been conflated with native Africans, Terkoz's abduction of Jane represents the greatest fear of white supremacists: miscegenation in the form of the rape of a pure white woman by a black savage. Tarzan's chivalrous nature—he desires Jane but instinctively restrains himself and does not rape her—is constructed in direct opposition to the dark-skinned, savage rapist. Tarzan performs a masculine, white supremacist fantasy when he protects a pure white woman, and her desire to be protected and her admiration of her protector are also part of the fantasy.[7]

LORD OF THE JUNGLE: TARZAN AS COLONIZER

Colonialism is highlighted in *Tarzan of the Apes* in ways that directly connect it to issues of racism and imperialism in the United States. By writing about a British lord in the African jungle, the text can be seen as distancing America from the project of colonialism. Eric Cheyfitz writes that the text creates a space where "Americans could savor, in the act of denying them, their own imperial ventures" (Cheyfitz 1989: 340). Burroughs's text, however, does not deny American imperialism; indeed, the text embraces imperialism in distinctly American ways. By metaphorically transporting early-twentieth-century American policies and prejudices into the jungle of Africa, Burroughs's text works to highlight the connections between colonialism abroad and racism at home and how the ideal American man is constructed in very specific ways in direct relation to these.

Burroughs's Tarzan stories are compared negatively against Joseph Conrad's *Heart of Darkness* because critics argue that Burroughs must have had the same information as Conrad about the atrocities and genocides being perpetuated in Africa at the time but that Burroughs's texts do not condemn the actions of colonizers or work to examine these in the same critical ways Conrad does. Burroughs's romantic texts can even be read as an idealization or celebration of genocide in Africa, especially considering the lynching scenes just discussed.[8] Although the colonizers in *Heart of Darkness* (1902) must face their own corruption, Burroughs's heroes are depicted in unproblematic ways that do little to implicate their own roles in the exploitation of Africa, that do not critique Eurocentric views of the world, and that do not challenge imperialism. Lord Greystoke metaphorically and physically embodies the fantasy of empire because he "was the type of Englishman that one likes best to associate with the noblest of monuments of historic achievement upon a thousand victorious battlefields—a strong, virile man—mentally, morally, and physically" (p. 2). This fantasy of empire shows the colonizer not only as Western but also as distinctly masculine, strong, virile, and morally superior. Neither of these men is distanced from the project of imperialism; they are instead an idealization of it and work to further Eurocentric mythologies about manifest destiny, which are directly tied to depictions of hegemonic masculinity.

The landscape of the novel also works to reinforce the myth of manifest destiny because the jungle where Lord John and Lady Alice are stranded is uninhabited by humans. Africa, in this sense, is depicted as a wilderness that is open for colonizing: a dark, mysterious continent that is foreign, other, and primitive when compared to the civilization of the British colonizers. Shaobo Xie writes, "In Western philosophy, culture or civilization is always opposed to nature or primitivity. Culture refers to norm, canon, modernity; nature designates whatever is unwholesome, irrational, coarse, uncultivated, remote, anthropologically unfamiliar" (Xie 1999: 5). In this sense, then, the wild and dangerous jungle represents the Other, the abject that must simultaneously be held at bay and incorporated. Tarzan, as a British lord raised in the jungle, becomes a physical representation of the relationship between colonizer and colonized: he is both the romance of the feral child and the civilized man separate from and above the wilderness. The myth of the feral child allows him to embody this impossibility, to be both of and not of the jungle, and to be both abject and subject, both of the colony and of the colonizer.

The curious mixture of chivalrous masculinity and feral childhood represented by Tarzan makes visible the ways that dominant American masculinities have been and still are directly connected to race, colonialism, and social class. Mavis Reimer points out that scholars of children's literature have frequently used metaphors of colonization to talk about children and the literature adults write for and about them. In the 1877 quote from Charles Dudley Warner cited at the beginning of this chapter, for example, the boy is colonized, seen as a primitive Other and as an object of curiosity: he is a savage. However, even though the white boy in this passage is seen as a primitive man-in-becoming, he is not as primitive as the African savage he is compared against because the assumption underlying Warner's statement is that the wild white boy will grow into a civilized white man whereas the savage will remain a savage and therefore childlike and in need of a parent, even into adulthood. The metaphor, then, works both to colonize the child and to construct the savage as a child. Reimer writes:

> When we turn to texts specifically produced for children of the colonizers by adult colonizers, the simple analogy between the child and the racialized other begins to break down. For, while as children's literature such texts instantiate the difference between the child and the adult, as imperialist texts they produce, at the same time, the difference between the Oriental and the Occidental in such a way as to include the targeted child audience within the privileged racialized group. (Reimer 1999: 111)

This is indeed what the imperialist texts about Tarzan do. The implied reader of the text is the child of the colonizer, the gaze is that of a Westerner, and the assumptions are those of a privileged group working to hold on to privilege by passing it on to a younger generation. Finally, as is the case with the racism in the text, the hierarchy of colonizer and colonized must appear to be the natural order of things: Tarzan must seem to be naturally superior to the native Africans and must naturally ascend to his position of lord of the jungle.

One way that Tarzan's moral superiority is naturalized shows where the text constructs the native Africans and the space representing Africa as hostile and threatening. Xie argues, "In order to colonize indigenous natives, Western imperialism has to represent otherness as evil" (Xie 1999: 8). The jungle in *Tarzan of the Apes* is a malevolent force and must therefore be tamed and controlled. Lord and Lady Greystoke live in terror for a year, she dies because she is too weak to endure the horrors of the wilderness, and he, weakened by grief, is killed by a vicious ape. The personified apes, in many ways a grotesque distortion of native

Africans, are brutal and violent. Tarzan is depicted as distinct from them through several key aspects: he quickly learns to survive among them, he distinguishes himself as being mentally superior to them, he tames them, and he finally becomes patriarch of the group. But this paternal role soon bores him, and he seeks greater challenges. Cheyfitz argues that the pleasure readers take from the text "may come from never being in doubt about the identity of the hierarchy of race, class, and gender that justifies the imperial system the romance projects" (Cheyfitz 1989: 356). In other words, we know, from the beginning of the narrative, that which Tarzan does not: that he is a nobleman. The text proves the natural superiority of the colonizer who is able to handily master nature and then the natives, and in this way imperialistic assumptions about the superiority of the white, Western man as colonizer are maintained.

Once Tarzan is established as lord of the jungle, he encounters native Africans, who invade "his" jungle. The apes of the jungle are depicted as cruel and dangerous, and the natives are depicted as being worse, as being unnatural, uncanny, and subhuman:

> On their backs were oval shields, in their noses huge rings, while from the kinky wool of their heads protruded tufts of gay feathers. Across their foreheads were tattooed three parallel lines of color, and on each breast three concentric circles. Their yellow teeth were filed to sharp points, and their great protruding lips added still further to the low and bestial brutishness of their appearance. (p. 72)

Burroughs attempts to depict native Africans who are bizarrely different, exotic, and animalistic. Differences in dress and adornment are exaggerated to create a clear distinction between Western self and a monstrous, colonized Other. The word *bestial* is used in several places in the text to describe the native Africans, who are systematically dehumanized. Within the fictional world of the text, they are cannibals, they are cruel, they are superstitious, they are ignorant, and they do not perform gender roles as they are defined in Western cultures. For example, in the fictional African village depicted in the novel, Tarzan notices that the warriors lie about all day while the women work. This depiction mirrors Darwin's description of a savage who "knows no decency" and "treats his wives like slaves."

Gender roles are highlighted as a key difference between civilized and uncivilized men. Tarzan instinctively knows, for example, that he must behave in chivalrous ways toward Jane. The native Africans, though, are depicted as less than human because they are brutal but ultimately ineffectual and emasculated men. Tarzan, for example, is able to prove his physical prowess before the gaze of other white, Western men when a drunken, crazed native African terrorizes a white settlement. The African has "run amok" and charges Tarzan, who joyfully and easily breaks the man's arm with his bare hands (p. 244). The man is left limp after his encounter with Tarzan, who, like his father, shows the other colonizers how it is done. This scene, and others like it, magnifies anxieties about the vulnerability of white, male power that underlie the need to dominate. Jim Perkinson argues, "Black male forms of embodiment represent the deepest moment of challenge to the White middle-class male body" (Perkinson 2002: 177). The black African man who has run amok in this scene represents this fear and challenge to the white, middle-class body, which is soothed by the fantasy of the excessively strong, white, male body of Tarzan that is able to easily gain physical dominance and to emasculate. Furthermore, in the act of proving his manliness, Tarzan also proves himself to be an adept colonizer, able to effectively use violence and terror to keep the native Africans subservient. Once the natives are established as being inhuman, violent, and dangerous, then all forms of violence against them are justified within the worldview established by the text.[9] In these ways and others, the Tarzan story works to neatly delineate and naturalize socially constructed borders. Those borders that are most threatened, that are most at risk of becoming porous or fluid, are those that are most reified as dichotomies by the original text and the repetitions of the Tarzan narrative that have followed: self–other, empire–colony, American–immigrant, white–black, male–female, boy–man, child–adult, and upper class–lower class.

"SWARTHY BULLIES" AND "RAT-FACED" BRUTES: THE LOWER CLASS AS FOREIGN OTHER

Cheyfitz writes of Burroughs's novel, "In this imperial romance the lower class is as much a foreign country to the upper class as Africa is to Europe" (Cheyfitz 1989: 347). His analogy of the lower class as foreign Other is apt here because the text of *Tarzan of the Apes* works to carefully construct Tarzan as upper class and in direct opposition to lower-class characters, who are described with the same dehumanizing terms used to describe the native Africans. The novel makes a direct comparison between the two groups in a scene where Tarzan first sees the lower-class sailors accompanying Jane, Professor Porter, and company. As he observes the sailors, Tarzan notes that they are "evidently no different from the black men—no more civilized than the apes—no less cruel than Sabor" (p. 113). At a glance, Tarzan instinctively knows that the upper- and middle-class members of the group are "his kind" and worthy of his protection. His natural affinity with the upper-class characters and his natural aversion to the lower-class men is so strong that he does not hesitate to kill a "rat-faced" seaman who is fighting with Clayton. Much in the same way the native Africans are constructed, the lower-class characters are portrayed as one-dimensional, subhuman, dangerous, and needing to be controlled by a superior.

For example, the ship that abandons Tarzan's parents on a deserted beach is manned by a crew of mutinous sailors composed of "unhanged murderers and cutthroats of every race and nation" (p. 3), a description that plays on fears of miscegenation by making the diversity of the crew a characteristic that is unseemly. Burroughs explains that even the officers of the ship are "coarse, illiterate fellows, but little above the villainous crew they bullied, and were only too glad to avoid social intercourse with the polished English noble and his lady" (p. 6). In a chilling scene meant to illustrate Lord Greystoke's aloof, British, superior manliness, he leans against a wall, smoking a pipe, while coolly watching the mutinous crew slaughter one another "as though he had been but watching an indifferent cricket match" (p. 13). He is depicted as separate from and above the "swarthy bullies" (p. 3); he is heroic and noble in his distinction from those brutal masses who fall into murderous chaos when not lead and controlled by worthy superiors.

Hourihan argues that the hero is a "symbol of the elite" (Hourihan 1997: 62) and often works to reinforce political and socioeconomic structures. The hero, she writes, often is "an emblem of the patriarchy" (p. 63) in specific ways that mark him as being of a particular race and social class. Tarzan is also such an emblem. *Tarzan of the Apes* does the specific work of maintaining patriarchal and socioeconomic systems by highlighting Tarzan's literal and metaphorical inheritance from his father.[10] Hourihan writes, "Hero tales, especially nineteenth-century adventure stories written for young, potential empire builders, are often overtly concerned with the question of what it means to be a man—a state which is evidently not easily arrived at" (p. 69). In other words, manhood must be earned and proved, and the journey from boy to man is a difficult one marked by trial. The trials must be dramatized in a manner that creates a clear border separating man from boy (and other Others); Tarzan naturally, dramatically, and violently comes into his manhood, and the process he undergoes serves as a model for hegemonic American masculinity.

Kenneth Kidd, by carefully working through a century of narratives discussing what American boys are or ought to be, makes visible a major contradiction that has dominated our twentieth-century perceptions of boyhood and masculinity: boys are naturally masculine and must, at the same time, be taught to become masculine. Tarzan embodies this contradiction because he naturally comes into his manhood but also performs the character-building process needed to make a boy into a manly man. Tarzan's boyhood is brutal: he is abused, beaten, maimed, and almost killed on several occasions, but the text sends the message that this brutality is necessary to produce a man who is physically and mentally strong. Indeed, if Burroughs's book has an intended moral, it is that middle- or upper-class white boys should be reared in the wilderness, not coddled by a feminized society, if they are to grow into the virile men and future patriarchs they already are destined to become.

Tarzan's foil, his cousin Clayton, has the same noble blood but compares poorly against the jungle man: Tarzan is able to easily don the trappings of society, but Clayton is not capable of fending for himself in the jungle. Furthermore, the differences in how these characters perform masculinity also are key to Tarzan's construction as distinctly American. Jean De Silva writes that in much American literature of the late nineteenth and early twentieth centuries, "the ideal American was constructed in direct contrast to the 'feminine' qualities of the Englishman; in others, the modern Englishman's perceived racial purity and command of aristocratic ideals, wealth, and privilege made him the better American—so long as he abandoned England for America and embraced its cultural values" (De Silva 2004: 106). Both Clayton and Tarzan are British nobles, but the wild and independent Tarzan is one step removed from his British ancestry, from the monarchy, and from the feminizing influence of these. In this way, he can embody yet another contradiction: he represents both democracy and aristocracy. The journey Tarzan makes in the first novel from British parents to the African colony and, finally, to the American frontier represented by the woods of Wisconsin "follows a patriotic trajectory, one in keeping with Roosevelt's and later historians' view of American progressive and evolutionary history" (De Silva 2004: 145). Tarzan embodies those qualities that mark him as distinctly, progressively, democratically American, while at the same time maintaining his aristocratic origins. In other words, his "superior genetics" flourish in an environment that allows him freedom of movement and that does not sissify or restrain him.

JANE'S A MUSCLE FAN: GAZING AT THE FEMALE GAZE

The contrast between the two descendents of Lord Greystoke (the effete Brit and the manly American) is most evident when they are viewed through Jane's eyes. Clayton loves Jane, but she is smitten with the strong and manly jungle man who saves her and others in her party, including Clayton, who proves to be ineffectual in the wilderness. Tarzan's strong muscular body, the end result of his rugged boyhood, is described in loving detail by Burroughs. "This man," says a positively gushing Jane, "not only surpasses the average white man in strength and agility, but as far transcends our trained athletes and 'strong men' as they surpass a day-old babe" (p. 224). Burroughs's anatomizing of Tarzan's body literally goes on for pages as Jane talks about things such as "those mighty muscles knotting under the brown skin" (p. 225). However, the intended audience for the novel is not really the sexually desirous woman but instead the heterosexual male reader who is watching her watching Tarzan. For example, the gaze in the following scene is decidedly constructed as that of a heterosexual male: "Jane—her lithe, young form flattened against the trunk of a great tree, her hands tight pressed against her rising and falling bosom, and her eyes wide with mingled horror, fascination, fear, and admiration—watched the primordial ape battle with the primeval man for possession of a woman—for her" (p. 174). If fighting over a woman's body as if she is an object to be possessed can prove traditional masculinity, what better than to have the woman complicit in her own objectification, even turned on by it? Jane, indeed, is so enamored of the virility of the strange jungle man that she quite literally swoons in his arms after he rescues her and carries her off. In a scene that perpetuates the fantasy that women want to be raped, Jane struggles when Tarzan scoops her up and carries her away, but she soon gives in to his manly strength and masculine beauty: "she gave up the futile effort and lay quietly, looking through half-closed lids at the face of the man who strode easily through the tangled undergrowth with her. The face above her was one of extraordinary beauty" (p. 181).[11]

In this scene, Tarzan's body is admired by a woman, but it more often is the case in the text that it is under the scrutiny of the gaze of other men. In scene after scene Tarzan performs feats in front of audiences of other white Western men, who watch in awe. Tarzan's masculinity is proved through public performances of manliness validated by the approving gaze of the other men. Kasson argues, "Tarzan represented Burroughs's conception of the perfect man, a spectacular nude figure of strength, beauty, virility, violence, and command" (Kasson 2001: 159).[12]

It is this fascination with the male nude body as a symbol of American ideals that has made Tarzan such an enduring subject of film.

In the various film versions of the story, we watch Tarzan's body, we watch other men watching Tarzan, and we watch Jane watching Tarzan. In this way, the heterosexual male gaze is preserved by layers of watching. The heterosexual male viewer can gaze at the exposed body of Tarzan without being accused of desiring Tarzan because the gazing characters on screen with Tarzan act as buffers against fears of homoerotic desire. Furthermore, Pat Kirkham and Janet Thumim explain:

> The pleasures to be had in consuming the spectacle of the "perfect" male body are fraught with difficulties, not least because of the contradiction between the vulnerable passivity arguably implicit in the state of being-looked-at, and the dominance and control which patriarchal order expects its male subjects to exhibit. (Kirkham and Thumim 1993: 12)

The Tarzan books and films are about this very pleasure and continuously work to maintain the delicate balance required to construct Tarzan as a manly subject of the heterosexual male gaze. Tarzan cannot represent both the sexualized, passive, silent object of the gaze and heroic manhood. For example, for him to be a heroic subject, his body must be strong and active, rippling with muscles, covered in dirt and sweat, marked by the visual cues that represent physical exertion: "beads of sweat, representative of bodily fluids, may allude to both vulnerability and power. It is the visual mark of the male's power in marshalling and controlling his bodily resources" (Kirkham and Thumin 1993: 13). We watch Tarzan's physical exertions and witness his trials, and Tarzan always ends up able to control his own body, his surroundings, and any antagonist who attempts to threaten these. For Walt Morton, the Tarzan of film represents less an erotic object and more a male protagonist with whom members of a mainstream audience can identify. He writes, "A large part of the male audience enjoys a narcissistic identification with the power-fantasy suggested by Tarzan's strength and command of nature" (Morton 1993: 113).

A further layer of watching is added to this power fantasy when Tarzan is adapted into a film for a child audience, as is the case with Disney's 1999 version. Hamida Bosmajian writes, "The condensations and displacements at work in the author–text–reader relation are problematised in children's literature because of the double reader: adult/child" (Bosmajian 1999: 100). This author–text–reader relation is even more complicated in the dark movie theater where there is the double audience of adult/child, but there is also a physical self-consciousness regarding this double audience. In such a public space as a movie theater there is a community of readers composed of adults and children, who are not only watching the film but also watching one another watch the film. Indeed, part of the pleasure of spectatorship for adults watching a children's film with an audience of children is watching the children watch the film, seeing them laugh or gasp in appropriate (and inappropriate) places. There is also, then, an anxiety for adults watching children watching the film as they worry what may frighten or entice in inappropriate or unexpected ways. The Disney studios have become quite adept at delivering a product that manages this dual audience and that constructs the child viewer through the veiled gaze of the concerned parent or guardian. In Disney's adaptation of the story, Tarzan is reinvented to accommodate the mainstream consumer of Disney—that parent at risk of being offended, that parent working to construct a safe future nostalgia for his or her child. Therefore, whereas Burroughs's Tarzan enjoys hunting, killing, and eating raw meat, Disney's Tarzan eats fruits and the occasional termite. Burroughs's Tarzan finds pleasure in killing his enemies, but Disney's Tarzan accidentally kills Clayton and feels great remorse. Indeed, Disney has bowdlerized Tarzan to such an extent that *Slate* critic Michael Lind calls him a "momma's boy."

DISNEY'S "MOMMA'S BOY": CONFLICTING CONTEMPORARY MASCULINITIES

Me, Tarzan. You, Jane. Nature Good. Civilization Bad. Girls good. Boys bad. ... Disney is evil—not because it's turning children into liberals, but because it's turning them into wimps.

—Lind (1999)

Disney attempts to remove all overt depictions of racism, imperialism, and rigid gender roles from its adaptation of the Tarzan story. The 1999 film manages to avoid the offensive depictions of African natives that are in the original books and earlier films by simply and problematically depicting an Africa that is conveniently free of Africans. The location of the jungle, described in a Phil Collins song as a "paradise, untouched by man," is purposely vague. However, the omissions of specific details do not erase the imperialistic underpinnings of the original narrative but instead work to romanticize these. The generic wilderness without a people, culture, or nation conveniently becomes the exotic jungle (the wilderness, the Other) over which Tarzan can become lord without an overt taint of colonization. Also, in the 1999 Disney

Tarzan, Tarzan's aristocratic origins are smoothed over and romanticized through a pantomimed montage set to a schmaltzy Phil Collins song: Tarzan's parents, white and dressed in Victorian garb, jump from a burning ship (the mutinous crew is also absent) and work together—quite inventively, even effortlessly—to build an elaborate Swiss Family Robinson–style house in the trees. These mimed scenes do not erase Tarzan's noble origins but instead work to romanticize them by showing viewers the fine stock from which he comes.

Furthermore, to simplify the distinction between good and evil (as Disney is often apt to do), both Kala's baby and Tarzan's family are killed by the evil, predatory leopard Sabor, not by fellow gorillas as they are in the original novel. A vegetarian version of the character Tarzan is depicted in the film eating fruits and termites, but he never eats meat in the form of fellow jungle creatures. Apparently he manages to grow to adulthood in the jungle without having to hunt. Tarzan eventually kills the leopard Sabor only when he must do so to defend the gorillas, thereby protecting his community while also, unknowingly, avenging the death of his parents. In keeping with contemporary ideas about the innocence of childhood, Disney's Tarzan kills only once he is an adult. Indeed, the killing of Sabor marks his passage into manhood, which is presented in a ritualized way that includes laying the leopard's carcass at the feet of the gorilla patriarch. Because Disney's Sabor is one-dimensionally evil, has killed Tarzan's parents, and is a threat to Tarzan's gorilla family, Tarzan is allowed to come into his manhood through a ritualized violent act of revenge in which he is not fully implicated.

Later in the film Tarzan "accidentally" kills his rival Clayton when Clayton—like all good Disney villains—is done in by his own one-dimensional, excessive evilness. This is another way in which Disney's Tarzan can be manly and violent but not blood thirsty or macho; it is another way that Disney can rely heavily on traditional hero narratives and tropes of masculinity while appearing critical of these. Clayton, with his over-the-top Hemingwayesque machismo, represents a brutal version of masculinity and serves as a foil for the more sensitive Tarzan. This is especially fascinating because Tarzan's cousin Clayton in the original text is also a character foil—he represents the effeminate man who has been softened by modern civilization and, as a man, he pales in comparison (especially under Jane's gaze) next to the wild, strong jungle man. In the Disney version, however, Jane clearly disapproves of the gun-wielding British Clayton and falls for the sensitive, Americanized Tarzan. Curiously, Disney's British Jane teaches Tarzan to speak English, but he "naturally" speaks back in an American accent. Disney's version of the character is also quintessentially American in his movements: instead of simply swinging from vines, this Tarzan surfs along the limbs of trees like a cool skateboarder or surfer. Indeed, the young American wild man depicted in this film is a handsome, tanned, muscular California dude who treats both nature and women with respect and resorts to violence only when he must protect those he loves.

Disney rewrote the Tarzan narrative significantly, in part so that it neatly fits the Disney film formula. Disney's version fits the mold of a watered-down hero narrative and also fits into a formula that "imitates the standard Hollywood musical of the 1930s" (Zipes 1995: 110). Jack Zipes writes about film adaptations of folktales that, because the plot of Disney films is formulaic, "the incidental characters and their antics play a larger role in the film version of the story. They are always funny, adorable, infantile, and mischievous" (p. 111), and these work to entertain audiences when the predictable plots become tedious and boring. The plot of Disney's *Tarzan*, although based loosely on the original novel, is also interchangeable, in spots, with the plots of such films as *The Lion King* (1994), *Hercules* (1997), *Dinosaur* (2000), and *Finding Nemo* (2003) because we see a male hero who is orphaned and threatened at birth and who faces a series of trials that eventually lead him into heroism. Furthermore, in Disney's *Tarzan*, cute anthropomorphized animals sing and dance to catchy tunes, schmaltzy Phil Collins songs accompany montage scenes and reveal character and relationships, and Tarzan is accompanied by the wisecracking gorilla Terk and the self-effacing elephant Tantor, who together provide many of the film's jokes and one-liners. Lind writes that Disney's *Tarzan* is the "politically correct heir of several generations of Hollywood Tarzans—a facsimile of a facsimile" (Lind 1999). The film is, more accurately, a bricolage recombining Disney conventions with portions of the original novel with bits and pieces from earlier Tarzan films. For example, a scene in which Tarzan takes off Jane's shoe to playfully examine her foot is taken almost verbatim, not from the original novel but from the 1932 film. In these ways, the Disney film is less about the character from Burroughs's novel and more about the cultural icon that Tarzan has become. The Disney film manages to reproduce, for better or for worse, a new version of the Tarzan myth for a new generation of children.

It is important to note, though, as Ian Wojcik-Andrews points out in his book about children's films, that "the world of franchises, stock options, cash and short-term investments, mergers and acquisitions, operating budgets, territories, commodities, products and so forth can no longer be inhabited only by corporate leaders" (Wojcik-Andrews 2000: 47). Scholars of children's literature, film, and culture have a responsibility to acknowledge that Disney films (television shows, games, and books) are products "designed to secure the dominant economic position of the media giant" (p. 47). The main goals of the Disney franchise and its *Tarzan* films and television shows are to make money, to sell more products, and to perpetuate belief systems favorable to a free market system. Disney's *Tarzan* achieves these commercial goals in two ways: it is specifically an advertisement for other products, and it is generally an endorsement of dominant social structures. The movie, like many children's films currently produced, is a product designed to sell other related products for a multinational, multifaceted corporation, and it uses narrative conventions to achieve this.

When viewed within this context, Disney's *Tarzan* products, it can be argued, follow generic narrative formulas because they work in the marketplace. Disney's *Tarzan* works to sell the DVD or video version of the film, book adaptations of the film, toys based on the film, other Disney films and straight-to-DVD sequels, and video and computer games, all of which must appeal to children and to the parents who do most of the buying of wholesome family entertainment. The film uses the myth of the white feral boy grown into a hard-bodied and powerful young man to tap into fantasies of power that are linked inextricably to constructions of whiteness, imperialism, middle-class status, American individuality, and consumer culture. For example, Ellen Seiter argues that commercials directed at child audiences often offer "an appealing vision of a world where 'kids rule,'" but that, when examined more closely, "access to this child-centered utopia is restricted; full citizenship is denied to girls of all races and to boys of color" (Seiter 1993: 116).

This child-centered utopia is evident in the 1999 film but becomes a major focus of the video game versions of the narrative. Indeed, within the larger cultural narrative created by a matrix of consumer products all based on Disney's *Tarzan,* the kinder, gentler version of Tarzan championed in the film version competes with the visual representations of the mostly mute manly man that dominate the video game, computer game, television show sequels, and other product tie-ins. In other words, the contemporary image of Tarzan that endures through repetition is not so much the sensitive boy holding his ape mother's hand but a wild, muscled white man in a loincloth gliding effortlessly (often with the help of video game controls) through a jungle over which he is lord. According to Henry Jenkins, video games allow children a freedom of movement, an access to wide open imagined spaces that are no longer afforded most of them in contemporary urban and suburban America. However, it is significant that these depictions of space are based on assumptions about gender that allow boys to have greater access to this imagined space than many girls and female characters, who are often restricted in movement (Jenkins 1998a). Both the film and video game versions of *Tarzan* produced by Disney depict a freedom of movement that, when examined more closely, is marked as distinctly masculine. Fantasies of power and freedom are embodied in the physical representation of the white, male, American cartoon Tarzan and in the ways he moves through the utopian space created by the mise-en-scène. Empowered with a physical prowess bestowed by animation, Disney's Tarzan is able to physically claim the space of the jungle as his own without having to resort to the obvious domination and violence used by the original Tarzan. It is a claiming of space that seems innocent and free of markers of race, class, and empire but that embodies all of these.

On the surface, then, Disney's Tarzan is a version of a new sensitive man: an emotionally aware environmentalist, vegan, feminist, and passivist. But Disney's *Tarzan* would not be popular with children or with their parents if he were truly the momma's boy that Lind accuses him of being. The discourse surrounding the current boy crisis reveals that American adults are conflicted about boys because we want them to be sensitive and critical of hegemonic masculinity but not *too* sensitive and certainly not feminine or gay. Disney's Tarzan fulfills these contradictory adult expectations of boyhood because he is sensitive but is still also manly in very conventional ways. His rugged masculinity, sense of entitlement, and mastery over nature are depicted often through a freedom of movement; as a boy, he playfully wrestles with gorillas and other jungle animals, he takes a dare and jumps off a cliff, he snags the hair from an elephant's tail, and he mischievously causes an elephant stampede in which other animals are almost injured. Disney's adult Tarzan does not awkwardly swing from vines; he surfs through the trees flying impossibly from limb to limb like a cool skateboarder, surfer, or snowboarder. Cartoon animation creates an impossibly fit and agile body shown flying through the trees and sliding along branches: he is the young, white, male, middle-class, extreme-sport athlete with six-pack abs, broad shoulders, handsome face, and a tan. His "natural" American accent marks him as not British, not Southern, not Black, not lower class, not effeminate but "just" generic (i.e., middle-class, heterosexual, and white) American.

The tan and muscles visually signify the leisure time and freedom of movement afforded to young white men of the American middle class who have the time and disposable income to pursue surfing or skateboarding and the education to be environmentally conscious. Jim Perkinson writes, "The white male body is not innocent of social history or ethical content. Whiteness and maleness and middle-classness intersect in a form of embodiment that populates certain social spaces with a living norm of ontological power" (Perkinson 2002: 175). Disney's *Tarzan* subtly works to perpetuate America's myth of classlessness, while simultaneously marking Tarzan as a member of the middle or upper class. And it highlights the popular American truism that race, class, and gender "don't matter," at the same time as it celebrates the whiteness, Americaness, class privilege, and rugged masculinity of its hero.

The film, in this sense, reenforces the contradictory statement Jane makes in the 1932 film version of the story when she claims that Tarzan's origins do not matter, when indeed they matter a great deal to her and to the audience watching the film. For example, in Disney's *Tarzan*, Kerchak, the stern alpha-male gorilla, complains when the baby Tarzan is brought into the tribe that "It's not our kind" and later says, "Kala, look at him. He will never be one of us." Kerchak is the blackest of the gorillas, whereas Kala, Tarzan's adoptive mother, is brown and lighter skinned than many of the others. Disney has, in this way, subtly adopted the physical characteristics described in the original text. Disney also includes, but changes, the scene from the original novel in which Tarzan looks into a pond and sees himself as ugly compared to the gorillas. Disney uses this scene not to overtly highlight Tarzan's superiority to the gorillas but to include didactic messages about acceptance of difference and the importance of family and motherly love. When Tarzan covers his face with mud to look like a gorilla, Kala shows him that they each have two eyes, two hands, two feet, and one heart. "Forget what you see," she says. "Now, what do you feel?" she asks him. The surface message of the film that we hear again and again in dialogue and in Phil Collins songs is that we are all the same underneath and should learn to see past difference. But the film belies this message because we know that Tarzan and Jane are superior to the animals (especially the comic sidekicks); to the native Africans we never see; to the goofy, old, and frail Professor Porter; to the brutish, clumsy Clayton; and to the swarthy working-class seamen who work for Clayton.

Disney's *Tarzan* is an attempt to rewrite an offensive text in ways that make it appealing to contemporary audiences of children and their parents. To do this, the film also must negotiate new versions of masculinity that are rife with contradictions and unresolved tensions. In some ways, it is almost as though the original character of Tarzan has been symbolically split in two to account for these current tensions. For example, Clayton is Tarzan's foil in the original novel because he represents an effete aristocracy, but in the 1999 film he is a foil because he represents an excessive version of older, hegemonic masculinity. This new Clayton represents the brutal colonial invader: we hear his gun before we meet him, he takes joy in capturing animals, and the first time we see him, he is slicing through the jungle with a machete and firing his gun at anything in the jungle that moves. It is ironic that Disney's villainous Clayton is closer to Burroughs's Tarzan than any other character in the film. In this way, this film represents two versions of masculinity—a supposedly older version and a contemporary version—at odds with one another. Tarzan is depicted as an environmentalist who lives in harmony with nature, and Clayton is a macho brute who has come to the jungle to capture gorillas to sell to zoos. Like the Clayton in the original text, he is still British, but his Britishness is performed as imperialistic arrogance: "If I can teach a parrot to sing 'God Save the Queen,' I can certainly teach this savage a thing or two," he says of Tarzan. But Clayton fails miserably at teaching, and Jane becomes Tarzan's English teacher. Clayton, like Tarzan, is large and excessively muscled, but he is meant to represent a hyperbole of machismo and the dangers of patriarchy: he patronizes and bullies Jane and her father, he exploits the environment, and he is a violent, greedy, and dangerous imperialist.

One contemporary mainstream children's film formula championed by Disney and other major studios seems to be increasingly that of the sensitive man versus the excessively macho man. Movies such as *Beauty and the Beast* (1991), *The Iron Giant* (1999), and *Toy Story* (1995) feature "good" versions of masculinity (sensitive men and boys) that are pitted against male antagonists who embody "bad" versions of masculinity. These "bad" men and boys are represented in excessive ways: they are power hungry and violent, they destroy the environment, they are rough with women, and they are excessively muscular, but, ultimately, they also fail at being manly because they cheat, or lie, or bully, or manipulate. These battles between good masculinity and bad masculinity not only contain conflicting messages about what our culture believes men and boys ought to be but also embody the internal battles many boys experience as they work to negotiate their identities within the context of such mixed messages.

For example, Disney's Tarzan, to come into manhood in ways that symbolically follow the generic heroic narrative, must participate in the oedipal struggle without appearing, on the surface, to be violent or even overly aggressive. The film achieves this difficult task by depicting the alpha-male father figures he must destroy (Kerchak and Clayton) as brutish, dangerous, and excessively masculine. In other words, to come of age as a contemporary man, Tarzan must destroy men who are traditionally masculine, who then will be replaced by him as a kinder and gentler patriarch. These convoluted machinations work to create far-fetched scenarios in which Tarzan both is and is not traditionally masculine. As discussed earlier, because the sensitive Disney Tarzan does not endorse violence, he must accidentally kill his foils. Kerchak is killed taking a bullet for Tarzan, which neatly does away with the alpha-male father figure standing in the way of Tarzan becoming lord of the jungle. Also, in a climactic scene where Tarzan and Clayton are battling, Clayton drops his gun and Tarzan picks it up. Clayton smiles, and says, "Go ahead. Shoot me. Be a man." To which Tarzan replies, "Not a man like you," as he throws the gun away and prepares to fight Clayton without a weapon. This gesture simultaneously marks Tarzan as a passivist while also marking him as a brawny man of extraordinary strength who does not need a weapon. Eventually, Clayton, a victim of his own excessive evilness, manages to hang himself with vines that entangle him while he swings at Tarzan with a knife. This neatly disposes of Tarzan's nemesis, without making Tarzan into a murderer. Indeed, Tarzan looks on helplessly and tries to warn Clayton of the danger he is in.

On the surface, drastically conflicting constructions of contemporary manhood are pivotal to this scene and are highlighted in the terse exchange about manhood that serves as a climax for the film: "Not a man like you." Thick-necked, square-jawed, British Clayton is depicted in the film as a construction of masculinity that supposedly was dominant in some remote past, whereas tanned, agile, long-haired Tarzan is depicted as a new, feminist version of masculinity that supposedly has replaced it. However, Clayton is such a hyperbole of brutish übermasculinity that Arnold Schwarzenegger seems like a "girly man" in comparison. McCallum points out that although the Tarzan and Clayton of the 1999 Disney film seem to be opposites, "the contrast between Tarzan and Clayton, however, is really only one of degree; the film is playing off of what are really two versions of muscular, hard-bodied masculinity" (McCallum 2002: 129). The new sensitive Tarzan seems gentle compared to Clayton but actually maintains many of the traits of his literary ancestor in subtler forms. Like the original Tarzan, he is, for example, naturally superior to the sinister, swarthy, working-class crew of the ship, who obey Clayton's orders to capture Tarzan, his friends, and the gorillas. He is still the feral jungle boy who grows into a strong man because he has survived a difficult and wild childhood. He is still the subject of adoring female and male gazes as Disney's Jane looks longingly at him, draws pictures of him, and talks obsessively and excitedly about the man in the loincloth who saves her from a wild pack of baboons. He still gains a, albeit benign, mastery over the inhabitants of the jungle and becomes their lord. His broad-shouldered body is as physically impossible for a man as a Barbie doll's body is for a woman, and his strength and agility are possible only through animation. He represents a kinder and gentler version of masculinity but ultimately still becomes a patriarch (who just happens to be white, American, heterosexual, and upper class). The narrative structure of the film, much like that of the original text, works to justify an existing social hierarchy as "natural." There is much pleasure, in the form of plaisir, at the film's end, when Tarzan beats his chest, bellows his familiar yell, and takes his rightful place as ruler: it feels comfortable, familiar, and like the way things ought to be.

The contemporary ideal American manhood portrayed in Disney's *Tarzan* is a direct descendent of the dominant masculinity portrayed in the original text, even while it attempts to distance itself from some of the more obviously troubling aspects of this construction that have come under scrutiny in the past few decades. The result of this negotiation is a complex and contradictory masculinity, an impossibility that real boys may measure themselves against but cannot possibly embody. An examination of other texts, such as *Tarzan,* popular with contemporary American boys shows that there is still a hegemonic masculinity (white, heterosexual, Western, upper- or middle-class, manly, athletic, etc.) we have inherited from the past and that still influences and is influenced by cultural consensus about what boys and men ought to be. It is significant, however, that a major difference between the original Tarzan narrative and contemporary Disney adaptations is the portrayal of a struggle on the part of the protagonist against a narrowly defined, traditional, hegemonic masculinity that seems to have been overtly embraced by the original text. This struggle, embodied by confrontations between Tarzan and Clayton, represents complicated battles over contemporary masculinity that many boys and the adults in their lives are working to negotiate, especially within the context of the boy crisis discussed in the prologue. A similar pattern emerges in quite a few popular children's texts, many of which reveal an ambivalence about contemporary masculinity and about what we, as a culture, expect our boys to be and to become.

2
READING IN THE GAPS AND LACKS
(De)Constructing Masculinity in Louis Sachar's Holes

> You will have to fill in the holes yourself.
> —Louis Sachar (1998: 231)

Louis Sachar's novel *Holes* has received much praise from both critics and child readers who love the complex tall tale he has woven about two boys whose lives are connected by fate and an almost magical legacy of ancestral curses and obligations. Sachar creates characters and situations that seem realistic but always teeter over to the side of the magical because they are wonderfully excessive and draw on common motifs from legends, folktales, and popular culture. Pat Pinsent describes the novel as a modern fairy tale, "partly because it possesses so many elements of the genre, but also since, like many fairy tales, it conveys a sense that Fate and Fortune are at work in ensuring the happy ending" (Pinsent 2002: 207). The novel does not easily fit into any one genre: although it is often classified as contemporary realism, it could also fit into the categories of fantasy or magical realism. Stephanie Yearwood argues that it is this "transgressing its own boundaries" that marks *Holes* as a postmodern text. Such postmodern texts, she writes, create "dialogues with other texts, either other previously-written literary texts or other stories, creating new stories in the interstices and frictions and contradictions of various other stories" (Yearwood 2002: 50). This rich and complex novel—also on the border between children's and young adult literature—has been awarded the Newbery Medal, the

National Book Award, the American Library Association Best Book for Young Adults award, the *School Library Journal* Best Book of the Year award, and several other major awards.

Furthermore, at a time when educators, parents, and U.S. policy makers are becoming increasingly concerned about reports of boys' declining levels of literacy, *Holes* can be seen as a useful book that can interest boys in reading: it is easy to read, the plot moves quickly, it is adventurous, and it features likeable boy protagonists. Mark Bauerlein and Sandra Stotsky wrote a controversial column in January 2005 for the *Washington Post* titled "Why Johnny Won't Read?" They claim that "few strong and active male role models can be found as lead characters" in the books boys are required to read in school and that "publishers seem to be more interested in avoiding 'masculine' perspectives or 'stereotypes' than in getting boys to like what they are assigned to read." *Holes* can certainly be characterized as a book with "strong and active male role models" and as a book with many young male fans. Indeed, in a surface reading of the text, the two protagonists, Stanley and Zero, can even be seen as the best possible male role models because they are masculine yet also kind and sensitive, because they break the rules but only when treated unjustly by corrupt adults, and because they seem to be bad boys but ultimately are revealed to be good kids who love their moms.

However, because the novel is not (on many levels) realistic and relies heavily on folktale motifs, fantastically exaggerated characters and situations, and surreal imagery, the boys, and the fictional world surrounding them, are constructed in less politically correct ways than fans of the book might initially recognize, or even want to admit. Yearwood argues that *Holes* "bypassed fantasy altogether and edged out into the surreal" (p. 51). This is a compelling point because there is much in Stanley's and Zero's situations—in the landscape of the camp, in the structure of the narrative, in the series of outlandish coincidences, and in the over-the-top villains—that gives the novel the quality of a dream. Read within this context, the psychosexual imagery that is present in the novel can have several implications: *Holes* may be so popular because the author, through his use of surrealism, is tapping into the unconscious in ways that resonate with readers. The coming-of-age story in *Holes* may be another version of coming into subjectivity that is characterized by what Karen Coats describes as a "separation from the mother and the taking up of a position with respect to the Law of the Father" (Coats 2004: 7). In her book *Looking Glasses and Neverlands: Lacan, Desire, and Subjectivity in Children's Literature,* Coats argues that taking up a modernist subject position also requires internalizing certain societal norms: "Closure means heterosexual marriage, secure gender roles, and father-led families" (p. 7). Furthermore, as these behaviors are established as the norm in the stories we tell our children, other behaviors and people who represent these other behaviors are distanced and constructed as abject or abnormal. Literature written for children can function as a cultural artifact, working as part of a larger cultural narrative to construct readers' identities in normative ways. Therefore, although *Holes* may, on the surface, appear to champion a kinder and gentler version of masculinity, on the level of the subconscious, it champions a more visceral, more oedipal version of boyhood attempting to distance itself from its mother (or (m)Other) and all things feminine.

Holes is set at a juvenile correctional facility for boys, ironically named Camp Green Lake. The camp is a harsh and intimidating place because of the physical labor the boys must endure, the geography, and the surly inmates and counselors. "You're not in the Girl Scouts anymore" (p. 13), Mr. Sir, a camp counselor, says to Stanley on his first day at camp.[1] Mr. Sir is an excessive character, whose over-the-top machismo is evident in his doubly masculine name. This cruel adult character can be interpreted as an indictment of the stereotypical gender expectations placed on boys and of the misogyny inherent in these expectations. Mr. Sir's repeated references to the Girl Scouts make clear the difference he sees between boys and girls. The Girl Scouts, at least according to Mr. Sir, do not "build character," and girls do not (cannot) do difficult physical labor. The repeated comments about the Girl Scouts are also insults meant to demoralize the boys who are inmates at the camp. These comments are similar to the way a military sergeant insults new recruits at boot camp by calling them "ladies." Both examples imply that the worst insult one can say to a man or a boy is to call him a woman or a girl. Every day each boy at the camp must dig a hole in the dry lakebed that is five feet deep and five feet in circumference. The desert is crawling with rattlesnakes, scorpions, and poisonous lizards and is described as a "dry, flat wasteland." No wires, fences, or guard towers are needed to keep the boys there because the camp has the only water for one hundred miles. "You want to run away?" asks Mr. Sir. "You'll be buzzard food in three days" (p. 15).

Like many texts written for children, *Holes* is a Bildungsroman. Specifically, it is a story of its main character coming into manhood. When we are introduced to Stanley Yelnats, the palindromic protagonist of the novel, he is a fat kid who gets picked on by school bullies. Stanley is a good boy who has been sent to Camp Green Lake for a crime he did not commit. Although most of the counselors and inmates at the camp are tough characters, Stanley befriends a quiet African American boy named Zero. He teaches Zero to read and eventually saves Zero from dying in the desert. Stanley and Zero come out of the desert at the end of the novel as friends who have earned one another's trust and respect. They also vanquish the evil female warden of the camp and her counselor minions by finding and claiming ownership of a buried treasure she has been seeking. By the end of this novel, filled with near-magical coincidences, Stanley finds the buried treasure, teaches Zero to read, loses weight, gains strength and confidence, and removes a curse that has been plaguing his family for four generations.

Kimberley Reynolds argues that *Holes* can be seen as being a "fictional homage" to Robert Bly's *Iron John,* in which "traditional masculinity is personified and enacted by the strong male body in combination with the restoration of all-male communities and connection with the natural world must be restored. In this reading of *Holes,* the Warden, the only female, takes the role of the ultimate bad mother who is blamed so relentlessly by Bly and his followers" (Reynolds 2002: 106). However, Reynolds backs away from this reading, claiming that Stanley's coming-of-age is "gender neutral" because it highlights a "lack of focus on self and increased alertness to the needs of those around him" (p. 107). Stanley's coming-of-age is not, however, gender neutral, and, moreover, the ways in which it is distinctly masculine should be marked, especially because the construction of his identity relentlessly relies on the motif of overcoming "the ultimate bad mother," who is represented throughout the text in a variety of ways, both literal and metaphorical.

Stanley's dramatic coming-of-age does indeed force him to acquire many positive traits. For example, he discovers both mental and physical strength in himself, and he nurtures his friend Zero. However, far too much of Stanley's coming-of-age story also involves conforming to stereotypical constructs of masculinity, which require the boy both to endure grueling physical trials and to negate the feminine to become masculine. Michael Kimmel argues that even though many people think of masculinity as innate, it is socially constructed:

> Manhood is neither static nor timeless; it is historical. Manhood is not the manifestation of an inner essence; it is socially constructed. Manhood does not bubble up to consciousness from our biological makeup; it is created in culture. ... We come to know what it means to be a man in our culture by setting our definitions in opposition to a set of "others"—racial minorities, sexual minorities, and above all, women. (Kimmel 2003: 119)

Conforming to dominant constructions of manhood in the course of this novel, Stanley (and the reader) learns to define his manhood as "not feminine" and "not gay." Within the world of the novel, he can become a man only by disowning the feminine within himself and, therefore, on a metaphorical level, also by negating the feminine that surrounds him as well. In the process of its narrative, *Holes* often treats feminine traits, symbols, and characters as frightening, disgusting, or excessive aspects—like the gaping holes in the landscape—that need to be filled in, covered over, silenced, or expelled. Furthermore, the novel also depicts masculinity in a stereotypical way that reinforces hegemonic ideas about the way "real" boys ought to behave to become "real" men. Although some researchers argue that many contemporary boys do not face the same expectations boys faced twenty or thirty years ago[2] and that boys from different socioeconomic, religious, ethnic, or racial groups have varied expectations that are specific to their group, others also argue that there are still culturally dominant versions of masculinity within which many boys feel pressure to conform.

In his book *Messages Men Hear: Constructing Masculinities,* Ian Harris compiles a list of traits that define stereotypical masculinity in the contemporary United States. Men should take risks and be tough guys, they should be stoic and learn to ignore pain in their bodies, they should "achieve even though it hurts," they should protect and provide for family members, they should be in control and be self-reliant, they should defy authority, they should be knowledgeable, and they should be able to pass a series of tests (Harris 1995: 12–13). Through the course of the novel, Stanley passes from childhood into manhood by meeting most of these requirements: he pushes past physical pain by digging holes, he defies authority by stealing a water truck, he stoically endures several physical and mental trials, he finds a buried treasure that makes him financially successful and helps him to pull his family out of financial difficulty, and he heroically saves Zero by carrying him up the side of a mountain. Stanley neatly conforms to many of our society's expectations of masculinity. Although masculinity or becoming a man is, of course, not inherently sinister, the stereotypical version of hypermasculinity espoused by dominant culture and reflected in this novel may be. In his book *Proving Manhood,* Timothy Beneke argues, "Brutal manhood rituals set in relief what is too common for men in many western cultures: boys are brutalized into their identities as men" (Beneke 1997: 64). Stanley, Zero, and the other boys at Camp Green Lake are brutalized, and the message of the novel, ultimately, is not that this brutalization is psychically damaging for boys but, on the contrary, that Stanley and Zero are much better off at the end of the novel because they have endured this series of trials. As Don Sabo argues, "Boys are taught that to endure pain is courageous, to survive pain is manly" (Sabo 1992: 159).

The camp's warden wants the boys to dig holes and wants to know if they find anything "interesting" (a buried treasure) in their excavations, but the camp has authorities convinced that by digging holes the boys are building character. Although the novel's narrator seems to mock the idea of hard labor as "building character," Stanley does indeed become stronger, less feminine, and more of a "man" as he sheds weight and builds muscle. Stanley's feminized childhood is a common trope in the boy story, where coming-of-age means moving through and past the feminine. In the male coming-of-age story, childhood, with its vulnerabilities, is viewed as tied to the mother, as feminine, and it is "imagined as a stage to be suffered through and then surpassed" (Kidd 2004: 59). This is precisely the pattern the narrative of *Holes* follows. As Stanley begins to dig his first hole at Camp Green Lake, he is ineffectual, weak, and feminized: "The shovel felt heavy in Stanley's soft, fleshy hands. He tried to jam it into the earth, but the blade banged against the ground and bounced off without making a dent" (p. 26). However, by the end of the first day he has already begun to "build character." After he finishes digging his first hole, he turns down a ride to camp from a counselor and walks back to camp feeling proud of his accomplishment. The digging of the hole is described as grueling, miserable work he and the other boys must endure: "Stanley's blisters ripped open, and new blisters formed. He kept changing his grip on the shovel to try to avoid the pain. Finally, he removed his cap and held it between the shaft of his shovel and his raw hands. This helped, but digging was harder because the cap would slip and slide. The sun beat down on his unprotected head and neck" (p. 33). Beneke argues that many men often must submit themselves to tests of physical endurance to prove their manhood. "Why is it that successfully enduring distress is so central to proving manhood and proving superiority to women, not just only in the United States, but in most other cultures of the world? And why is it that manhood is something to be proved?" (p. 35), he asks. Beneke argues that for men to prove their manhood, they must endure pain in almost ritualistic and public ways.

Digging holes at Camp Green Lake is a sort of ritual for the boys there. They tell each other stories about digging their holes to reinforce the commonality of their shared experiences. Stanley is quickly accepted by the boys because he understands the need to mimic their ritualistic behavior. On his first full day at the camp, Stanley partakes in a ritual, for example, when he follows the other boys' lead and spits into his completed hole before he heads back to camp. The spitting can be read as an act of defiance: the boys are made to dig the holes, but they spit in them to show their displeasure. It can also represent a primitive way of marking territory. The spitting into the hole also can be read as a sexual metaphor, especially considering some of the other images from the novel, which I discuss later. Finally, the spitting can be a sign of strength and endurance because Stanley (and the other boys too, we assume) is so thirsty he has little saliva to spare. When Stanley gets back to camp after digging his hole, his fellow inmates give him his camp nickname, "Caveman," after Stanley grumbles at another boy. "You don't want to mess with the Caveman," X-Ray warns. Armpit replies, "The Caveman's cool" (p. 44). This is quite a change in image for an overweight boy used to being picked on by other school children. Stanley, or Caveman, continues to win approval from the other boys by following the rules of their hierarchy: he takes the blame for stealing a bag of sunflower seeds from a counselor, for instance, even though another boy stole them. It is significant that this proving of masculinity happens within the gaze of his peers, another key component in the compulsory construction of hegemonic masculinity. Kimmel says, "We are under the constant careful scrutiny of other men. Other men watch us, rank us, grant our acceptance into the realm of manhood" (p. 125).

By performing prescribed masculine behaviors before an audience of his fellow inmates, Stanley is able to move up in the camp hierarchy above Zero, an African American boy. Depictions of race in *Holes* are complex and contradictory because the text simultaneously wants to claim that race is not an issue and that the race of several characters in the novel is key to their relationships with others, their situations, and their identities. "Stanley was thankful that there were no racial problems. X-Ray, Armpit, and Zero were black. He, Squid, and ZigZag were white. Magnet was Hispanic. On the lake they were all the same reddish brown color—the color of dirt" (p. 84). In this passage, Stanley is portrayed as a naive white boy who is oblivious to racism and the "racial problems" that exist, whether he is aware of them or not. In her insightful analysis of issues of race in *Holes,* Coats argues that Stanley is "in denial": "Specifically, Stanley is part of a larger conspiracy of white denial of the privilege that comes with being a white male" (2004: 133). She argues that Stanley may not initially seem privileged because he has been wrongly accused of committing a crime and imprisoned but that his privilege becomes visible through the ancestral legacy that links him to "an entire history of both privilege and the denial of that privilege" (p. 133). His Latvian ancestor, Elya Yelnats, literally owed a debt to Zero's Egyptian ancestor, Madame Zeroni, that he never repaid. Coats argues that Stanley and his ancestors have failed in their "responsibility to the Other." "It is this failure, this erasure or even mere forgetfulness of the debt to the Other for one's position as subject, that haunts Whiteness" (pp. 133–4). Later in the novel Stanley's naïveté is once again visible when he is taken aback by other campers' reactions to the relationship he has developed with Zero. Zero offers to dig some of Stanley's daily hole in exchange for reading lessons. When the other boys spot Stanley resting while Zero digs for him, they taunt the pair for being an overseer and a slave. Coats argues that, at this point in the story, "Stanley begins to assume his position of white privilege before he takes responsibility for it" (p. 134). Stanley can come into subjectivity only by taking responsibility for his white privilege—not earned but conferred upon him in part by racist actions in the past by characters such as Trout Walker and Elya Yelnats—when he makes reparations of a sort by carrying Zero up the mountain, nursing Zero when he is ill, and then sharing the treasure with him at the novel's end.

The fact that Zero and Stanley are linked through several generations and that they, in many ways, rely on one another for their successful journey out of Camp Green Lake makes visible the ways blackness and whiteness are dependent on one another and on history for definition. Perhaps the most important and positive aspect of *Holes* is that it can potentially illuminate the ways that contemporary racism is part of the continuum of history. Read in one way, the text can make visible the inheritance of white privilege and its continued effect on both whites and blacks. Henry Giroux argues in his essay "White Noise: Toward a Pedagogy of Whiteness," "Defining 'whiteness' largely as a form of domination, [much] scholarship, while rightly unmasking whiteness as a mark of ideology and racial privilege, fails to provide a nuanced, dialectical, and layered account of whiteness that would allow white youth and others to appropriate selective elements of white identity and culture as oppositional" (Giroux 1998: 43). In other words, if white children see only negative portrayals of racist white characters, they have no role models to read about who illustrate ways to behave as allies against racism; they may feel helpless to change their current situation, as if there is nothing they can do to work to alter a racist culture. Therefore, when Stanley takes responsibility for his inherited privilege by working together with Zero, he offers up a model of whiteness for young people to follow that is not merely oppressive or merely crippled into inaction by "white guilt" but positive and proactive. Despite Stanley's earlier perception that the campers are all the "color of dirt" and that race is not an issue at the camp, his race, the race of other characters, and their relationships are vital to his coming-of-age and becoming a subject.

Furthermore, although Stanley and Zero are both protagonists and must both make a difficult journey toward manhood, that journey is different for each boy because of his racial identity. Stanley must move from a feminized position to manhood, but his access to the subject position is not as difficult or as far removed as Zero's. This is most fully illustrated through each character's initial access to language, through ancestry, and by the quality of attention they receive from adults and the larger systems of power these adults represent. The lack of access Zero is given to the Symbolic Order is most characterized by his silence and his inability to read and write. He is often quite literally spoken for by other characters in the novel because he is silent: "Zero's one weird dude," says ZigZag (p. 37). Also, whereas Stanley has an ancestral background that he can easily trace all the way back to his European heritage, Zero is an orphan because he cannot find his mother and does not know his ancestry. Zero explains to Stanley that before he came to the camp he rarely went to homeless shelters because "if they'd found out I didn't have a mom, they would have made me a ward of the state" (p. 183). Outside of the juvenile correction facility, Zero existed on the margins of society. As the novel progresses, Zero's identity is even erased in the correctional system's computers. Pinsent points out that Zero's identity is yet another repetition of the hole motif in the story: "Many people think of Zero's mind being as empty as his name, and his apparent nothingness is emphasized by the hole in cyberspace into which Zero's records have fallen, together with the fact that 'no one cares for Hector Zeroni'" (Pinsent 2002: 208). Therefore, whereas Stanley must work to move from boy to man (which, as Coats points out, includes claiming an inheritance of white privilege), Zero's journey as a homeless African American boy is more treacherous and difficult to navigate because he is judged by how he measures up to dominant versions of masculinity yet always already is denied access to these because they are most often defined by white privilege. Like Stanley, Zero grows up and comes into manhood by moving from a feminized position to a masculine one by the end of the novel. Like Stanley, he must stoically endure physical pain and pass several trials to prove his manhood. Unlike Stanley, Zero gains his manhood by the end of the novel by gaining access to language and gaining enough of a mastery over language to read the key clue that secures ownership of the buried treasure for himself and Stanley. Also, unlike Stanley, he has had to create his own inheritance, which Stanley must share by acknowledging an ancestral debt and a current affinity. He and Stanley must, ultimately, work together to break the ancestral curse that has been plaguing both of their families.

Although some aspects of Zero's and Stanley's coming-of-age are positive, others are not, partially because they entail some of the more damaging trials boys in our culture often are expected to endure. The depictions of Stanley's and Zero's brutal transformations into manhood not only reinforce our culture's need to put boys through physical trials but also work to reinforce stigmas against boys who have feminine traits. Eve Kosofsky Sedgwick argues that our cultural obsession with making "men out of boys" is partially based in homophobia. Sedgwick claims in her essay "How to Bring Your Kids Up Gay" that for boys, human identity or a healthy sense of self is equated with masculinity: "[A researcher] uses the phrases 'sense of masculine self-regard,' 'masculine competency,' and 'self-evaluation as appropriately masculine' as synonyms for any self-esteem and, ultimately, for any self" (Sedgwick 1998: 234). As many earlier feminists have argued, if "masculine" is equal to "human," then "feminine," the opposite of "masculine," is equal to "nonhuman." Therefore, according to this equation, men (and women, as well) who have feminine traits are not human but inhuman, subhuman, and other. Sedgwick goes on to argue that even though we live in a culture that seems to be (at some level, at least) accepting of adult gay men, we have little tolerance for gay boys or boys who have feminine traits. No parenting book, she argues, gives parents tips on how to raise a son to be gay. "Fag" is still one of the more popular insults thrown around on school playgrounds in the United States, and mandatory heterosexual (masculine) behavior is still the enforced norm for many boys.

The insistence in *Holes* on the development of a specific brand of heterosexual masculinity works to negate the feminine both outside of and within boys and works to construct this masculinity through the exclusion of the other. Judith Butler claims:

> The construction of gender operates through exclusionary means, such that the human is not only produced over and against the inhuman, but through a set of foreclosures, radical erasures, that are strictly speaking, refused the possibility of cultural articulation. Hence, it is not enough to claim that human subjects are constructed, for the construction of the human is a differential operation that produces the more and the less "human," the inhuman, the humanly unthinkable. (Butler 1993: 8)

Therefore, the portrayal of masculinity in *Holes* as something that is in opposition to femininity works to delineate an other—the girl, the woman, the feminine boy—that must be distanced or expelled to construct masculinity. Furthermore, Beneke argues, "compulsory masculinity is inexorably tied to sexism—in proving manhood a man is proving his superiority to women by enduring distress that women supposedly cannot endure" (p. 47). In other words, the physical trials Stanley and Zero must undergo to prove their manhood also require them to prove they are definitely not feminine. The novel devalues the feminine as something other that boys must overcome to mature and to become human.

Barbara Creed argues that this fear of the feminine other is personified in horror films, which often depict the monstrous in ways that are feminine. Creed reexamines Freudian and Lacanian theories about gender identity within the context of Julia Kristeva's work on the abject to argue that "human" or "masculine" is often defined in opposition to the abject or to the monstrous. Although depictions of the monstrous vary, she argues, the outcome of these various depictions of the monstrous feminine is "to bring about an encounter between the symbolic order and that which threatens its stability" (Creed 1993: 11). Creed argues that Freud might interpret these representations of the monstrous as symbolic of the "Phallic Mother," who represents a fear of castration because, to a young boy, she appears castrated. Creed, however, argues that the monstrous feminine creature "is primarily a terrifying figure not because she is castrated but because she castrates" (p. 22). She goes on to analyze the recurring motif of Vagina Dentata (vaginas with teeth) as an embodiment of the male fear of castration.

Although Creed uses horror films as examples of these recurring motifs, I think her ideas can also be applied to a reading of *Holes*, a book that often depicts the monstrous as feminine. According to Creed's definition of the monstrous, both major female characters in *Holes*—Kissin' Kate Barlow and the Warden—are monstrous. Creed writes,

> In some horror films the monstrous is produced at the border between human and inhuman, man and beast …; in others the border is between the normal and the supernatural, good and evil …; or the monstrous is produced at the border which separates those who take up their proper gender roles from those who do not …; or the border is between normal and abnormal sexual desire. (Creed 1993: 11)

The mythical Kissin' Kate Barlow is monstrous in the ways her character is a conflation of feminine sexuality with criminality and death. She begins as a tragic character whose African American lover is murdered by ignorant townspeople, but she evolves into an outlaw who gives men red lipstick kisses before she murders them. She is what Creed might call a representation of "the archaic mother" because she signifies both life and death and she is both castrated and castrating. "She is either the tamed, domesticated, passive woman"—the sweet schoolteacher who makes the best canned peaches in Green Lake—"or else the savage, destructive, aggressive woman" (p. 116)—the nice girl gone bad who is out to avenge her lover's death by robbing and killing as many men as she can. The canned peaches are a safe, nurturing, motherly form of female sexuality, and the red lipstick she applies to give her kisses of death is an excessive and grotesque form of feminine sexuality that is destructive and deadly. Kate Barlow embodies both aspects of the "archaic mother."

It is interesting that Kissin' Kate Barlow's actions set into motion many of the events in the novel. She robbed Stanley's ancestor, Stanley Yelnats I, and buried his treasure under the dry lakebed. Although she didn't kill Stanley Yelnats I, she symbolically emasculated him and four generations of Yelnats men by denying them their ancestral inheritance, by taking away their entitlement. The mythical Kissin' Kate Barlow is also present in the present time of the novel in the form of "Sploosh," the one-hundred-year-old jars of peaches that keep Zero alive in the desert. He finds the jars of sticky sweet brown "Sploosh" under an overturned and half-buried boat in the desert and makes this new hole in the ground (a motherly womb) his home for a few days. In keeping with the contradictory images of the archaic mother, the "Sploosh" is both life sustaining and deadly because, although it keeps Zero alive for a few days, it also gives him a case of food poisoning that threatens to take his life.

Another poisonous and monstrous female in the novel is the Warden. Because the Warden is referred to in genderless terms in the first part of the novel, the reader assumes this Warden, who frightens even the threatening Mr. Sir, is a man. We are just as surprised as Stanley is to discover the Warden is actually a woman. She is the only woman at Camp Green Lake and is a cartoonishly evil witch of a woman, who terrifies all the children and counselors. When we first meet her, we see her from Stanley's point of view: "A tall woman with red hair stepped out of the passenger side. She looked even taller than she was, since Stanley was down in his hole. She wore black cowboy boots which were studded with turquoise stones" (p. 66). Stanley, "down in his hole," looking up at the Warden, is overcome by the feminine at this point in the novel. And the feminine is poisonous and debilitating. The holes, which the boys dig and which are not filled in, make up the grim landscape of Camp Green Lake. They become treacherous places to avoid because, like mythical images of vaginas with teeth, the vacant holes become homes for poisonous yellow-spotted lizards, scorpions, and rattlesnakes.

Reading in the Gaps and Lacks • 79

The Warden, who dominates the males at the camp, also is poisonous in a strikingly feminine way. In one of the more disturbing scenes in the book, we come to understand why the counselors all fear her:

> The Warden held up a small jar of dark-red nail polish. "You see this, Stanley?"
>
> He nodded.
>
> "This is my special nail polish. Do you see the dark rich color? You can't buy that in a store. I have to make it myself."
>
> Stanley had no idea why she was showing it to him. He wondered why the Warden would ever have the need to wear nail polish or makeup.
>
> "Do you want to know my secret ingredient?"
>
> He raised and lowered one shoulder.
>
> The Warden opened the bottle. "Rattlesnake venom." With a small paintbrush she began applying it to the nails on her left hand. "It's perfectly harmless … when it's dry."
>
> She finished her left hand. She waved it in the air for a few seconds, then began painting the nails on her right hand. "It's only toxic while it's wet." (p. 90)

Then the Warden lightly brushes her hand against Stanley's face in a moment that seems almost sexual, especially considering the last bit of dialogue. Right after she finishes painting her nails, she "[runs] her sharp wet nails very gently down his cheek. He [feels] his skin tingle. The nail on her pinky just barely [touches] the [two-day-old] wound behind his ear. A sharp sting of pain cause[s] him to jump back" (p. 90). When she finishes with Stanley, she turns on Mr. Sir like a wildcat. She strikes him across the face, he falls to the floor writhing in pain, and he is left with three envenomed scars that leave his face swollen and purple for several days afterward. The Warden is literally poisonous. In this scene, Mr. Sir is violently emasculated by her.

The Warden's makeup case, which is covered with pink roses and which reminds Stanley of his own mother's makeup case at home, becomes associated with pain and with the emasculation of a grown man. This connection to Stanley's mother, though small, can be explained using psychoanalytic theories that assert that men must, symbolically, separate themselves from their mothers or from an identification with their mothers. This is a complex switch of identity, because to conform to hegemonic versions of masculinity, boys must learn to identify with men, without becoming sexually attracted to men. Beneke writes, "The little boy realizes that he will grow up to be a man and so must shift his identification to his father—a difficult and wrenching trial. His mother pushes him to identify with his father" (p. 50). For Stanley to reach manhood and to gain access to the Phallus, he must first distance himself from his mother. In *Holes* this distancing is aided by the painful associations between Stanley's mother and the Warden. The scene just described gives physical representation to Stanley's oedipal struggle: his mother, the Warden, and a feminine sexuality represented by painted fingernails gently brushing his neck and making his skin tingle are all conflated in a surreal scene that combines sexual arousal for a mother figure with violence and fear. The Warden is fascinatingly feminine with her flowered white-and-pink makeup case filled with lipstick tubes and nail polish and then monstrous and poisonous in the way she symbolically castrates the most macho counselor at the camp. Kimmel argues, "The flight from femininity is angry and frightened, because the mother can so easily emasculate the young boy by her power to render him dependent, or at least remind him of his dependency" (p. 124). Moreover, Creed argues that this fear and anger associated with the flight from the pre-Phallic mother is often embodied in depictions of the monstrous feminine.

Therefore, in addition to working to distance Stanley from (desire for and identification with) his mother on a symbolic level, the scene with the Warden also works to mark the feminine as something monstrous, frightening, and abject. The feminine act of painting nails becomes something dangerous: the message to boy and girl readers is that feminine beauty is used to hide something monstrous underneath. The rich red of the polish, also feminine in its association with menstruation, is indistinguishable from the blood on Mr. Sir's face: "[Mr. Sir] had three long red marks slanting across the left side of his face. Stanley didn't know if the redness was caused by her nail polish or his blood" (p. 90).[3] Once again, in the novel, the feminine becomes something treacherous to avoid. Furthermore, Mr. Sir, powerless to take out his revenge on the Warden, takes his anger out on Stanley later by refusing to fill his water bottle in the desert. If masculinity is proved when it is performed before an audience of other men, Stanley has become an unwitting spectator in Mr. Sir's emasculation at the hands of the Warden. Mr. Sir must work to reestablish himself as a man in Stanley's eyes. The man and boy are pitted against one another by a powerful and dangerous woman, who knows how to use her feminine wiles to gain power over men. Therefore, the Warden, praised by critics for being a fascinating and original villain—"Shades of Freddy Krueger and Hannibal Lecter"

(Hipple and Maupin 2001: 40)—is actually a stereotypical domineering female. Pinsent unambiguously states that the Warden "is certainly a witch" (2002: 208).

The Warden is part of a long tradition of emasculating fictional female characters whom heroes must overcome to prove their manhood. Joseph Pleck argues that such portrayals of female characters support the myth that domineering women, and not men, are responsible for the oppression of women. He cites as an example the film *One Flew Over the Cuckoo's Nest:* "This film portrays the archetypal struggle between a female figure depicted as domineering and castrating and a rebellious male hero (played by Jack Nicholson) who refuses to be dominated by her" (Pleck 1992: 20). The message of this film, he argues, is that violence against women is justified because domineering, emasculating women deserve to be put in their place. He also ties such characterizations to a "mother domination theory": men, as boys, feel controlled by their mothers and powerless. Therefore, they feel the need to dominate women when they become adults. This adult behavior is something Stanley learns at the end of the novel in a scene I discuss later.

The trope of men's need to gain dominance over women because they are dangerous is further emphasized in the novel by the repeated juxtaposition of the Warden with the poisonous reptiles.[4] On the first page of the first chapter, this connection is made immediately by these three paragraphs describing the camp:

> The only trees are two old oaks on the eastern edge of the "lake." A hammock is stretched between the two trees, and a log cabin stands behind that.
>
> The campers are forbidden to lie in the hammock. It belongs to the Warden. The Warden owns the shade.
>
> Out on the lake, rattlesnakes and scorpions find shade under rocks and in the holes dug by campers. (p. 1)

The poisonous animals, with which the Warden is linked, own the shade just as she does. This association between a female and a familiar animal is also a common motif. "In classical art the figure of a beautiful woman was often accompanied by an animal companion with open jaws and snapping teeth; the creature represented her deadly genital trap and evil intent" (Creed 1993: 108). Another parallel between the Warden and the reptiles is made when the narrator explains that, like the grumpy counselors, the rattlesnakes and the scorpions are not the greatest threat to the campers at Camp Green Lake. "You can't be bitten by a yellow-spotted lizard. That's the worst thing that can happen

82 • Boys in Children's Literature and Popular Culture

to you. ... If you get bitten by a yellow-spotted lizard, you might as well go into the shade of the oak trees and lie in the hammock" (p. 4). The Warden is as threatening as these mythical deadly lizards and is set up, through the book's opening, as being kin to a deadly reptile: crossing the Warden by lying in her hammock is as dangerous as being bitten by a poisonous reptile.

As is often the case in plots treating the common motif of the poisonous woman, the boys must overcome her and put her in her place to negate the threat she represents and thereby prove their masculinity. Before Stanley and Zero are able to vanquish the domineering woman (and mother figure) that is the Warden, they must first gain access to the power of the Phallus, at least on a symbolic level. Zero, tired of being mistreated at camp, hits a counselor in the face with a shovel and runs away into the desert. The counselors and Warden use Zero's marginal status as an excuse not to look for him, because if he dies in the desert, they believe no one will miss him: Mr. Pendanski says of Zero, "He had nobody. He was nobody" (p. 144). After Zero has been missing for three days, Stanley flees the camp to go out into the desert to look for him.

At this point in the novel, the depiction of the geography becomes key to its subconscious significance. The boys move out of the dry lake, filled with holes, to search for a mythical mountain peak called "God's Thumb" or "Big Thumb." "The peak looked to him exactly like a giant fist, with the thumb sticking straight up" (p. 128). About eighty years earlier, Stanley's great-grandfather, also named Stanley Yelnats, was robbed by the outlaw Kissin' Kate Barlow. Instead of killing Stanley's great grandfather, she robbed him and left him to die in the very desert that later became Camp Green Lake. He saved himself by finding God's Thumb, and he passed the story down to his family. The two boys head for God's Thumb because they hope to find water and refuge there. The story of God's Thumb is part of Stanley's patriarchal inheritance. The imagery of the different landscapes is significant: the boys leave the feminine wasteland (the holes and dried-up lake, ruled over by the castrating Warden), and they find refuge at a phallus atop a mythic mountain, where the water runs uphill. God's Thumb, a giant precipice sticking straight out of the mountain, is a masculine and magical site of fertility and wetness when compared to the dry, barren desert. God's Thumb is surrounded by a surprisingly fertile field of wild onions that the boys eat to restore their strength. When Stanley reaches the top of the mountain, he realizes he is "in a field of greenish white flowers that seemed to extend all the way around Big Thumb" (p. 174), almost like pubic hair or sperm adorning the base of the Phallus. Later, Zero can only surmise that "[God's Thumb] must have a hole in it ... filled with water." He says to Stanley, "Where else could the water be coming from? ... Water doesn't run uphill" (p. 185).

This journey to God's Thumb marks the turning point in this coming-of-age novel. When Stanley carries Zero, the great-great-grandson of the very Madame Zeroni who cursed Stanley's family, up the side of the mountain, Stanley breaks the curse that was put on his family. Stanley and Zero are healed at God's Thumb, and they build up their strength by eating wild onions and drinking muddy water. The boys are then ready to head back to camp to face and defeat the Warden: the onions have made them smelly and distasteful to the poisonous lizards that inhabit the holes, Stanley's patriarchal inheritance gives him a claim to the treasure the Warden has been seeking, and Zero's newly acquired literacy gives him the access to language that allows him to read the meaning of the treasure they have found. A suitcase Stanley and Zero find buried in the lakebed, which once belonged to Stanley's great-grandfather, has the name Stanley Yelnats on it. When Zero reveals this information to the Warden and witnesses, the vanquished Warden is left at the end, as all threatening women should be, speechless: "The Warden stared in disbelief. 'That's im ... imposs ... It's imposs ...' She couldn't even say it" (p. 216). The silencing of the Warden is directly connected to a symbolic triumph over the monstrous feminine. To claim their treasure the boys must spend the night in a hole filled with yellow-spotted lizards, which climb onto their bodies but do not bite them because the boys smell of onion. Metaphorically, their recent entry into the Phallic Order protects them from the Vagina Dentata and from the Warden. From this point on in the novel, the holes begin to be filled in and the female characters, like the nurturing lawyer and the obedient wife of Clyde Livingston, fall into their prescribed roles within the Phallic Order.

The epilogue of the book, aptly titled "Filling in the Holes," shows the two boys, a year and a half later, living happier, wealthier lives. We learn that, in a few years, Camp Green Lake will become a Girl Scout camp. The threatening, poisonous holes at Camp Green Lake have been filled in to create and to foster a more docile, nonthreatening femininity. Zero finds his mother, who is represented as a quiet, beaten woman. Other holes in the narrative also are filled in, creating closure and putting gender roles into their proper places. In a short, final scene, which is meant to be funny, the two boys watch television with family and friends. A woman in this scene teases her husband, Clyde, who then covers his wife's mouth with his hand:

"You've made your point," said Clyde, covering her mouth with his hand. He looked back at Stanley. "Will you do me a favor, Stanley?"

Stanley raised and lowered his left shoulder.

"I'm going to get more caviar," said Clyde. "Keep your hand over my wife's mouth." He patted Stanley on the shoulder as he rose from the couch.

Stanley looked uncertainly at his hand, then at Clyde Livingston's wife.

She winked at him. (p. 232)

In this scene another hole, a woman's mouth, is symbolically filled in by her husband's silencing her. Stanley feels uncomfortable: "he felt himself blush." Is this because he is embarrassed by seeing a grown woman silenced or because she is older than he and not yet someone he can silence? She certainly makes him feel more comfortable by winking and making light of the matter, by being complicit in her own silencing.[5]

This final scene is a reversal of the structure of Camp Green Lake, a place where the female Warden did much of the talking and the men cowered. In its apparent normalcy and its attempts at closure, the final scene shows the way things "ought to be" and the proper roles men and women should take within a patriarchal society. Stanley and Zero have proved their manhood not only by conforming to the expectations of hegemonic masculinity but also by overcoming the feminine. However, the holes in the narrative can never entirely be filled in, and the final scene also shows that manhood can never be finally and completely proved; one must continuously work to prove oneself a man. Butler claims that performing one's gender is "not a singular 'act,' for it is always a reiteration of a norm or set of norms, and to the extent that it acquires an act-like status in the present, it conceals or dissimulates the conventions of which it is a repetition" (p. 12). The gaps and lacks made visible in this narrative work to construct the boys' masculinity, yet at the same time they call the boys' masculinity into question as a construction. Therefore, whether or not they are fully conscious of their behavior, Stanley and Zero must continually prove their masculinity in the future to be considered men: more trials await them.[6]

3

"THE BATTLE OF THE BIONIC BOOGER BOY," BODILY BORDERS, AND B.A.D. BOYS

Pleasure and Abjection in the Captain Underpants Series

"Abject" is always negative. You can't experience "abject joy" unless you're being deliberately paradoxical.

—Brians (2004)

KA-BLOOOOOSH!

—Pilkey (1999a: 33)

People, perhaps, do not experience abject joy, but many do experience joy in reading about the abject. Dav Pilkey's wildly popular, gross, and irreverent Captain Underpants books are partially about taking pleasure in reading about abjection. The books are also pleasurable for child readers because they present reading, writing, and literacy as activities that work to subvert adult authority. Although these books have been challenged and censored by some parents and educators who are worried they will harm children, they also can be seen as excellent texts that appeal to early or reluctant readers (often boys). Even though the books have a few didactic moments, through their use of parody and metafiction they often function as intertextual, interactive texts that construct children as intelligent subjects who have agency. In this sense, the books also may be pleasurable for child readers partially because the self-conscious structure of the narratives works to undermine the parent–child, author–reader relationship by creating active roles for readers and thereby constructing child readers, both within and outside of the text, as authorities able to make meaning. For these and other reasons, these books are very popular with younger children, especially boys, and examining the reasons for this popularity—as well as the reasons that some adults challenge and censor these books whereas other adults successfully sell them as mass-marketed consumer products—can make visible the ways that a cultural text may contribute to the construction of younger children as readers, thinkers, and gendered subjects.

As cultural artifacts or as literary texts, these books are ultimately both positive and negative for child readers. On one hand, the books use parody and word play in sophisticated ways that are delightful for child readers, who are included in on humor that mocks adult authority. These books often satisfy children's needs for power fantasy by ridiculing adults and playfully inverting hierarchies that most often place children at the bottom. On the other hand, much of the ridicule in the books is directed toward women and feminized boys and men. Therefore, although the books allow readers to question some hierarchies, they also work to maintain others, specifically a dominant version of masculinity that places heterosexual males above females and feminized males. Although these books may help young boys to enjoy reading, they often do so by working to construct the two male protagonists, and, therefore, the young male imagined readers who might identify with them, as whole, gendered subjects defined in opposition to a female or feminized abject.

In other words, the pleasure of reading in these books comes partially from identifying with boy protagonists whose gender identities are clearly, sometimes rigidly, drawn and not identifying with the porous, fragmented, fluid, feminized "others" depicted in the texts. This dichotomy is not one that Pilkey invented; he is tapping into deeply held cultural ideas about gender. Indeed, his texts may be so popular with boy readers because they simultaneously perform anxieties about gender identity that young boys may have and then resolve or smooth over those anxieties in conventional ways that reinforce our perceptions of gender identity as something always already fixed and stable. Furthermore, such portrayals of gender in books for young readers may help to set up patterns that shape a young person's later reading habits: various studies have found that although many girl readers are perfectly willing to identify with both female and male protagonists, boys often say they do not identify with female protagonists and do not want to read books about girls. For example, when Michael Smith and Jeffrey Wilhelm examined the body of research published over the past twenty years that studied the reading habits of boys and girls, one of the main conclusions that they reached was that "boys tend to resist reading stories about girls, whereas girls do not tend to resist reading stories about boys" (Smith and Wilhelm 2002: 9). Examining the Captain Underpants books as cultural artifacts for early readers can highlight one way in which both boys and girls are taught to identify with male protagonists and distance themselves from the feminine.

Furthermore, some researchers mark the age when most children begin school (about age six years) as being a moment when gender roles begin to become reified. Up until then, some claim, children view gender in more performative ways. For example, one study found that children ages four to six years often see gender as alterable:

> Emmerich et al. (1997), for example, reported that when children in this age group were asked questions such as, "If Janine cut her hair short and played with trucks, could she be a boy?", a majority of respondents indicated that gender was indeed variable as a function of such features. By the age of about seven, however, children are reported to have acquired a strong concept of gender constancy, coming to see maleness and femaleness as basic and immutable biological categories. (de Castell and Bryson 1998: 241)

It is significant that some researchers also describe a period between these two phases that is "suffused with anxiety about the unalterable fact of sex versus the mutable appearance of gender" (p. 241). Many children are first introduced to the books in the Captain Underpants series at these ages, and they may be so fond of these books because they both raise and work to resolve anxieties about gender identity; they threaten to dissolve bodily borders but then reinscribe and solidify them.

"YOU'D BETTER STRAIGHTEN UP, YOUNG MAN": *CAPTAIN UNDERPANTS* AS SUBVERSIVE PLEASURE

The humor of kids in school is primarily oral and physical, whereas schooling tends to focus on reading and writing. It is primarily subversive, mocking adult authority so that any humor we propose to "teach" may be too domesticated and sanctioned to appeal to kids. And male humor in particular deals with the body in ways that are designed to make adults uncomfortable.

—Newkirk (2002: 145)

Despite, or perhaps even because of, their status as mass-marketed, lowbrow cultural texts, the books in the Captain Underpants series illustrate the complex relationship children have with the media as readers, consumers, and subjects, who are continuously negotiating their identities, and who simultaneously resist and submit to authority. These often censored and grotesque books for young readers feature George Beard and Harold Hutchins, two little boys who are stereotypically masculine in almost every way, except that they like to write and illustrate their own comic books. At a time when there is much alarm and debate about American boys' slipping levels of literacy, George and Harold can even be seen as role models because they make writing and language play seem fun, subversive of adult authority, and boyish. George and Harold are often in trouble at school for pulling pranks, being silly, changing the lettering on school signs, and, mostly, making rustic comic books that ridicule adults at their school. In the first book, they hypnotize their cruel principal, who then believes he is a comic book superhero the boys have invented named Captain Underpants. Because the boys think that most superheroes look like they are wearing underpants, they decide to literally dress their parody of a hero in tighty-whities. When their principal transforms into Captain Underpants, he strips off all his clothes and toupee and is left bald and wearing tighty-whities and a red cape as he has various adventures fighting for truth, justice, and "all that is pre-shrunk and cottony." The books in the series are all propelled by scatological humor and feature talking toilets that eat people, mad scientists who shrink people, space aliens who disguise themselves as lunch ladies in an effort to turn all the students into "zombie nerds," and one nemesis who turns into a giant piece of poop and another who turns into a giant booger. The silliness and comic book format make the books easy for younger children to read and enjoy, and the books are especially popular as early readers for kindergartners through third graders.

According to critics of the series and to even the author, the books are not meant to be high art or moralistic. The major didactic messages in the books are that boys are often unfairly labeled and targeted for criticism, that literacy is fun, and that censorship interferes with the pleasure of reading and writing. Indeed, reading and writing are depicted in the books as subversive activities that clever children can do to annoy unimaginative adults. Each book, for example, depicts George and Harold removing letters from or changing around the lettering on school signs to subvert official announcements by turning them into jokes: "See our big football game today" becomes "boy our feet smell bad," "Please wash your hands after using the toilet" becomes "Please wash your hands in the toilet," and the lunch menu changes from "New tasty cheese and lentil pot-pies" to "Nasty toilet pee-pee sandwiches."

Such verbal playfulness presented in opposition to adult prohibitions against imaginative play is a common motif in many early readers. Karen Coats argues that there are simultaneous feelings of loss and pleasure that accompany learning to read: children miss the comfort of being physically close to an adult reading to them but take great pleasure in finally having a more direct access to language. They are torn between wanting to read themselves and still wanting to be read to. "Hence the Symbolic has to run a sort of PR campaign to convince the reluctant child that the space he is entering has as much if not more to offer than the space he is leaving behind" (Coats 2004: 60). As part of this "PR campaign" children must be seduced by playful language that gives them feelings of pleasure and power.

Another pleasure for child readers of the Captain Underpants books can come from identifying with boys who are unfairly labeled and criticized by teachers and other adults and who then are able to gain (at least temporarily) some power over those adults. For example, in the fourth book in the series, *Captain Underpants and the Perilous Plot of Professor Poopypants,* the boys are described in the first few pages as being labeled by various adult authorities in their school:

> All of the "experts" at Jerome Horwitz Elementary School had their opinions about George and Harold. Their guidance counselor, Mr. Rected, thought the boys suffered from A.D.D. The school psychologist, Miss Labler, diagnosed them with A.D.H.D. And the mean old principal, Mr. Krupp, thought they were just plain old B.A.D. But if you ask me, George and Harold simply suffered from I.B.S.S. (Incredibly Boring School Syndrome). (pp. 14–15)

Children diagnosed with attention deficit disorder or attention deficit/hyperactivity disorder may identify with the protagonists because they may also feel that they have been simply labeled as B.A.D. by educators.[1] The author here, who often writes in second person, is working to seduce his child readers, to convince them that he is one of them and not an adult author(ity) like the teachers, parents, and administrators he ridicules in his books. Dav Pilkey is clearly modeling the protagonists on himself and his experiences as a boy, something he shares in several different short biographical statements. According to his online biography, "After setting the school's all-time record for the amount of time spent in the principal's office, Dav was diagnosed with Attention Deficit Disorder and severe hyperactivity" (Pilkey 2003c). His teacher sent him out into the hallway so frequently that she ended up moving a desk out into the hallway for him. Pilkey filled the hallway desk with paper, pencils, and crayons. "I used to staple sheets of paper together and make my own books," he writes. "I remember one teacher who used to rip up my books and tell me I'd better start taking life more seriously" (Pilkey 2003c). The "about the author" blurb included on the last page of some of the Captain Underpants books highlights this specific episode from his life: "Dav's teacher told him, 'You'd better straighten up, young man, because you can't spend the rest of your life making silly books.' Dav was not a very good listener!" (Pilkey 1997: 123). Teachers who mislabel and discourage bright, creative children are targets for Pilkey in all of the books in the series, and this blurb is clearly included to encourage those child readers who may be in circumstances similar to his.[2]

Many schools have recently started to ban violent writing in student essays, and some schools have even punished students for writing considered to be threatening.[3] In this climate, there are probably quite a few children who have experienced the same feelings of frustration that Pilkey did as a child. Pilkey gives children an outlet for such frustration by mocking adults who censor children's imaginative play by giving them silly names such as Mr. Rected, Miss Labler, and Miss Singerbrains and also by depicting George and Harold as being quite clever. Despite being labeled as having learning and behavior problems, the boys are clever enough to be able to gain power over the adults who have labeled them. It is interesting that the comic books—and the imaginative play they represent—are what often give the boys power over authority figures: Principal Krupp turns into a superhero the boys created; the talking toilets who eat teachers are the boys' invention; and Super Diaper Baby, who vanquishes several adults, exists entirely in a rustic, error-filled comic book within a comic book, supposedly written by the boys.

Although the Captain Underpants books have been credited by many educators and parents for getting reluctant readers, especially young boys, to be excited about reading, they have also been challenged and censored by some adults concerned that the texts will exert a negative influence over impressionable children who might imitate the naughty behavior of the protagonists, learn to ridicule adult authority, or pick up poor spelling habits. According to the American Library Association Web site, the Captain Underpants books were the fourth-most censored and challenged texts in 2004, and they were most often challenged for having "offensive language and modeling bad behavior" (American Library Association 2005). It is interesting to note that the adults challenging these books seem to be mostly concerned about those aspects of the books that might be a threat to adult authority over children. For example, a "PTA Mom" from Mission Viego, California, wrote, "Our principal will not allow Dav Pilkey's 'Captain Underpants' series to be sold at the book fair. Her impression is that the characters portray bad behaviors and thus encourage bad behavior by the readers (the students)" (Trelease 2003). George and Harold do indeed receive poor grades, are always in trouble with their teachers, cannot sit still at a desk, pull lots of pranks, destroy school property, and ride skateboards over ketchup packets in the gym. But to assume that child readers will imitate their behavior is to assume that children are easily duped. Furthermore, Jim Trelease points out, "The students with the worst behavior problems are—right—the poorest readers. So if they do the least reading, they can't be modeling on the bad behavior of book characters" (Trelease 2003).

Another school district in California, the Bakersfield City School District, "banned this series completely from its 42 libraries because it shows 'a lack of respect toward authority'—the principal in his BVDs, I'm guessing" (Trelease 2003). The series blatantly ridicules adult authority figures in every book: they have names such as Miss Anthrope, Ms. Ribble, and Professor Pippy Poopypants; the gym teacher, Mr. Meaner, is routinely eaten or killed; Mr. Fyde, the science teacher, is inept; and parents are often depicted ignoring their children while reading tabloids. However, children, who often feel powerless in their interactions with many adults, need texts that feature power fantasies. In other words, the mockery of authority and adults in the books is psychically necessary. Thomas Newkirk argues that although some adults believe that children should always be respectful and obedient, "to be completely compliant is psychologically dangerous, for in over-identification we lose a sense of self; we become the institution" (Newkirk 2002: 166).

The books that children love, and that many of us loved as children—from *Alice's Adventures in Wonderland* to *Matilda*—often are loved precisely because they ridicule arbitrary adult authority, which children sometimes fall victim to. They allow children to fantasize about having the power they frequently lack in their lives. In contrast to the silly adults in the Captain Underpants books, George and Harold—like folktale tricksters—usually come off as being the cleverest characters in each comic book in the series, and they often are able to exert power over cruel adults. Both fans and censors of the series acknowledge that some children's literature may even be subversive, working to undermine established systems of power and hegemony—in other words, if children read enough of this sort of literature, they may start to question authority. Bill Osgerby argues that censors have historically cited challenges to adult authority, that these challenges are often linked to issues of taste, and that lowbrow texts are subversive simply because they are lowbrow and a challenge to adult standards and aesthetics. The "media panics" and the acts of censorship that accompany them—for example, the comic books scares in the 1950s—are "an attempt to re-establish the generational status quo" and represent broader "struggles over taste and cultural autonomy" (Osgerby 2004: 70).

Therefore, the status of these books as lowbrow literary junk, of which many adults seem to disapprove, further increases their capital as subversive texts for children to enjoy. In the later books in the series, the author openly mocks adults who censor his books, thereby including child readers in on the joke and making them his coconspirators and active participants in an adult debate, which affects children but in which they often do not have much of a voice. In book seven of the series, *Captain Underpants and the Big, Bad Battle of the Bionic Booger Boy, Part 2: The Revenge of the Ridiculous Robo-Boogers,* the school librarian is named Miss Singerbrains and she presides over a library devoid of books. The library, the text explains, had once been a lively site of learning, but "now the library was filled only with rows of empty bookshelves and posters that warned of the potential subversive dangers of reading" (Pilkey 2003b: 50). Posters hanging in the library state "Only Schnooks Read Books," "Reading Might Offend You—Why Take a Chance?" and "Challenge Books, Not Minds." By including these textual references to the censorship of his books, Pilkey avoids talking down to children and constructs them as intelligent readers who are able to make intertextual connections, who are aware of the world they inhabit, who are able to understand word play and jokes, and who might even be able to engage in adult debates about censorship. Furthermore, he uses the adult disapproval of his books to his advantage: if some adults want to keep books from children, then those books become a subversive pleasure precisely because they are forbidden.

Another compelling point is that among the reasons given to censor the Captain Underpants books, the author's excessive use of grotesque bodily functions is not cited nearly as frequently as the other reasons cited previously. As the series progresses, the books become increasingly disgusting and increasingly focused on the disruption of bodily borders; the blurring of the distinction between inside and out. Perhaps those wanting to censor these books focus on the books' supposed challenges to adult authority because that is precisely what the bodily disruptions depicted in the books represent. Deborah Thacker argues that in children's literature, "the carnivalesque and its roots in 'low' culture, bodily functions, and notions of the 'Other,' continually [challenge] notions of bourgeois social conformity, resemble and include those child-like uses of language that repeatedly test the authority of imposed structures of meaning" (Thacker 2000: 10). She convincingly argues that such challenges to hierarchies may be one reason why much children's literature is ignored and marginalized. Therefore, the frequent objections to the Captain Underpants books may represent censors' reactions to these books' assaults on middle-class social mores.

In this context, Mikhail Bakhtin's work on carnival is a useful tool to discuss the possible subversive pleasure of the Captain Underpants books, texts characterized by scatological folk humor, inversions of hierarchies, parody, laughter, food, grotesque bodies, and mild curses. Although Bakhtin focuses much of his discussion in *Rabelais and His World* on the specific practices of the Renaissance carnival, he also argues that there are vestiges of carnival in modern texts and practices—especially in humor. Carnival challenges the status quo by turning hierarchies inside out, by contesting the borders between high and low, king and peasant, adult and child, and author and reader. "This carnival spirit offers the chance to have a new outlook on the world, to realize the relative nature of all that exists, and to enter a completely new order of things" (Bakhtin 1984: 34). Carnival can, ideally, work to undermine hegemony, but, conversely, it can also lead the masses to experience a temporary release of tension so that systems of power ultimately remain unchallenged and intact. This dichotomy is especially useful to consider when discussing children's literature. Would any adult truly write or teach or share with children a text he or she believes to be wholly subversive of adult authority? Do we sanction—through schools and through the mass-marketed consumer goods we purchase—only those books that offer children an illusion of power but that ultimately work to release tension so that hierarchies can be maintained?

The childish, lowbrow, folk humor featured in the Captain Underpants books has many of the characteristics Bakhtin discusses and may function in the same ways, and with similar mixed results, as carnival. The childish, scatological humor in the books specifically works to illuminate the "ever unfinished nature of the body" (p. 29). Each book employs mild curses—*poop, pee, butt, booger*—that refer to bodily excretions and that mark the body as open and leaky, with shifting borders. Adults are called "Deputy Doo-Doo" and "Professor Poopypants." These mild curses are amusing to children partially because they call up sexual pleasure or the pleasures of the body. Also they involve an inversion of social rules on a very literal level because many children are not allowed to say "poop" in front of their teachers or their parents. Therefore, an adult character named "poop" creates a double pleasure— pleasure of the body and the pleasure of subverting adult authority.

Mark West offers a slightly different reading of the use of the grotesque in children's literature in *Psychoanalytic Responses to Children's Literature*. He writes, "Adults often deplore as tasteless many of the stories, situations, and jokes that children find humorous. This conflict, however, involves more than taste; it also involves differences in the psychology of children and adults" (Rollin and West 1999: 92). West defends the work of Roald Dahl against adults who are appalled at Dahl's depictions of the grotesque, explaining that Dahl's books tap into children's anxieties about toilet training and other forms of parental control over their bodies. Younger children, who can no longer empty their bladders or bowels whenever and wherever they like, find a release for their anxieties by saying words like "poop." Older children find more complex ways to express "the pressures of measuring up to adult standards of cleanliness and neatness" (p. 93), which often take the form of scatological humor. Furthermore, texts that depict adults as the butt of such jokes are even more pleasurable for children who "enjoy jokes and stories that poke fun at the moral authority of adults" (p. 93). Therefore, the depictions of Deputy Doo-Doo and Professor Pippy Poopypants delight children, who often must submit to adult control over their bodies.

The books also are filled with illustrations of grotesque bodies—characters that literally morph into poop or boogers. The images in the books blur the borders between inside and out: food is thrown and splattered on people, not eaten; teachers are eaten by talking toilets and then regurgitated like vomit; and Melvin Sneedly's runny nose takes over his entire body, covering him and everyone around him in snot. Melvin's excessive, leaking, inside-out body is also accompanied by an excessive narrative:

> Melvin squished and sloshed as he jiggled over to his chair. Each gooey footstep coated the floor with a foamy trail of slime, and everything he touched became wet and encrusted with warm, bubbling, syrupy phlegm. When Melvin sat down, generous helpings of yellowish, pudding-like goo slowly dribbled down the chair collecting into creamy, gelatinous puddles beneath him. The puddles themselves were slightly transparent and speckled with thick, shimmering nose hairs and dark red chunks of coagulated blood, which—"ALRIGHT ALREADY!" yelled George to the narrator. "Enough with the descriptions—you're making us all sick!" (pp. 92–93)

The pleasure in this portion of the text is performative and interactive: child readers or children being read the book by an adult squirm, giggle, and yell "ew!"; they show the book to adults hoping for an appropriate reaction of disgust; and they laugh even more when George tells the narrator that he has gone too far. The author is self-consciously mocking his own writing, or, perhaps, he really has gone too far in this interesting example of self-censorship.

On one level, then, the books can be seen as fulfilling the joyous, celebratory goals of carnival: "The unfinished and open body (dying, bringing forth and being born) is not separated from the world by clearly defined boundaries; it is blended with the world, with animals, with objects" (Bakhtin 1984: 26–27). This Bakhtinian concept of the open body is a celebratory inverse of the concept of the open body as abject. Although abjection relies on the fear of that which threatens perceptions of the self as whole and impermeable, the grotesque Bakhtinian body revels in the disruption of borders. In a positive sense, then, the uses of the grotesque in these books can, ideally, make visible and open up the constructed borders that delineate gendered identity. Unfortunately, however, I believe they have the opposite effect and instead work to reify normative gender identity by continuously challenging and then continuously reestablishing bodily borders.

"YOU'D BETTER STRAIGHTEN UP, YOUNG MAN": ABJECTION, GENDER PERFORMANCE, AND NORMATIVE MASCULINITY

Performativity is thus not a singular "act," for it is always a reiteration of a norm or set of norms, and to the extent that it acquires an act-like status in the present, it conceals and dissimulates the conventions of which it is a repetition.

—Butler (1993: 12)

"Oh, no!" cried Harold.

"Here we go *again!*" said George.

—Pilkey (1997: 120)

As the books in the Captain Underpants series progress, they become more excessive and more grotesque. As the series progresses, the borders that establish the identity of a gendered subject, those borders between outside and in, between self and other, are increasingly disrupted. But these eruptions of the abject in the Captain Underpants books are always brought under control at the end of each book by the heroic actions of the boy protagonists or by Captain Underpants. Furthermore, and most significant, with each new book, the abject always threatens to erupt again, which means that characters must be ever vigilant about clearly defining their bodily borders. Indeed, this threat is reinforced because almost all the books end with the phrase "here we go again," implying that the adventures—and the threats to subjectivity they enact—are bound to be repeated.

Judith Butler discusses abjection when she uses the idea of gender performance to complicate the biological–constructivist dichotomy often used to explain gender identity and to instead discuss gender identity in ways that simultaneously acknowledge the influence both of culture and of personal agency; one's gender is continuously being formed and reformed as part of a complex, shifting web that includes the body or the self negotiating with culture and with others through public discourse. Gender, she argues, not only is performed but also must continuously be reperformed to maintain its tenuous, fluid boundaries. This performance of gender identity often necessarily relies on abjection—on creating a border between self and other, between outside and inside, between subject and object, and between the normal represented by the social body and the abnormal represented by those relegated to its margins. It is paradoxical that gender identity that is established in opposition to an abject is never stable and is always tenuous because the very existence of an abject threatens borders, threatens to engulf, enter, seep into, or leak out of both social and individual bodies. Although the abject is crucial to the maintenance of a gendered identity, then, it also works to open up gaps that make the performance of gender visible. In other words, if the identity borders we erect were indeed "natural" and fixed, then they would not always and continuously need to be reestablished.

The Captain Underpants books are examples of texts for children that illustrate this tenuous relationship between abjection and gender identity: specifically, masculine identity portrayed in opposition to a feminine abject. The abjection portrayed both through language and through illustrations in the books can be seen, as I discussed in the first half of this chapter, in the positive light of carnival. However, it is significant that Bakhtin defines carnival as all-encompassing parody and festive laughter. No one is above ridicule or set apart; even the reader or spectator is laughed at:

> The people do not exclude themselves from the wholeness of the world. They, too, are incomplete, they also die and are revived and renewed. This is one of the central differences of the people's

festive laughter from the pure satire of modern times. The satirist whose laughter is negative places himself above the object of his mockery, he is opposed to it. (Bakhtin 1984: 12)

Although Bakhtin may be overly romanticizing the idea of festive laughter as democratizing, this distinction between laughter that includes the self and laughter that requires an other to ridicule can be used to better understand the function of the grotesque humor in Pilkey's books. The humor in the Captain Underpants books sometimes verges on the festive laughter of carnival but most often takes a distant and satiric point of view. This distant humor—humor that distances the subject from the object of ridicule—is closely tied to the ways that abjection is repeatedly used in these books as something that the masculine identity of the protagonists is defined against.

In the second book in the series, *Captain Underpants and the Attack of the Talking Toilets,* George and Harold are banned from the annual "Invention Convention" because at the previous year's convention they had glued the teachers and other students to their chairs—literally. The boys get revenge for being banned from the convention by sabotaging other children's inventions: they fill an automatic dog washer with ink and reverse all the spray nozzles, they put butterscotch pudding in a student's volcano project, and they put eggs into an electric ping-pong ball server. Subsequently, everyone—except George and Harold (who have been banned from attending)—is covered in a spray of ink, pelted with eggs, and splattered with butterscotch pudding. In the third book, everyone—except George and Harold—is turned into an "evil zombie nerd." "They're all wearing broken eyeglasses held together with masking tape ... and they've all got vinyl pocket protectors!!!" says George (Pilkey 1999a: 60). In the fourth book, the boys get back at teachers who have mocked them by sabotaging the teacher's lounge. The teachers are sprayed with water, covered in powdered paste, and then sprinkled with worm-shaped bits of Styrofoam; essentially the faculty is benignly tarred and feathered by George and Harold. George and Harold—the protagonists one assumes most boys identify with—repeatedly stand back watching and laughing while other characters in the books are covered in goo or splattered with food. The illustrations reinforce this distance between the objects of ridicule and the subjects gazing at those being ridiculed.

Some illustrations in the fourth book in the series highlight the way this distance is created. After seeing their science teacher make a bubbly volcano using baking soda and vinegar, the boys decide to trick the lunch ladies into making a recipe containing these ingredients. The lunch ladies multiply the ingredients by one hundred so they can make enough for the entire student body, and when they pour in the two hundred bottles of vinegar, the mixture explodes: "KA-BLOOOOOSH!" (Pilkey 1999a: 33). The lunch ladies are propelled through the air by a "giant wave of green goop" that covers three pages of text as it

> crashed through the cafeteria doors and splashed down the halls, swallowing everything in its path. Book bags, bulletin boards, lunch boxes, coat racks, trophy cases … nothing could stand in the way of the gigantic green glob o' goo. It traveled down to the north, east, and west wings of the school, covering everything from the drinking fountains to the text on this page. (pp. 34–35)

The glob o' goo ends on page 36, where it engulfs several students and stops short just at the feet of George and Harold, who are left intact and unscathed. The fifth book in the series features similar illustrations where the boys hide behind a column while everyone else is covered in food that was meant to cater an ill-fated wedding: "The creamy candied carrots clobbered the kindergarteners. The fatty fried fish fritters flipped onto the first graders. The sweet-n-sour spaghetti squash splattered the second graders," and so on, until fruit punch "rained down upon the wedding guests like a torrential downpour" (Pilkey 2001: 62–67). At the end, George and Harold run away, once again untouched after the wedding cake lands—"Splat!"—on the angry bride's head (p. 70). The splattering food depicted in several of the books is often associated with women: the lunch ladies who prepared the goop and the angry bride, who later will become "Wedgie Woman." It is interesting that Kristeva writes, "Food loathing is perhaps the most elementary and most archaic form of abjection" (1982: 2). Splattering food—an inversion of inside and out because food is meant to be eaten, not worn—challenges bodily borders but, in this case, only of the feminized others who are being splattered and not of George and Harold, who remain clean with their bodily borders still well defined.

Bodily borders also are challenged in the books through transformations: characters—usually villains—physically morph into monsters. In the fifth book, the jilted Ms. Ribble morphs into Wedgie Woman, who uses her superpowered hair to terrify the boys and others. In *The Adventures of Super Diaper Baby*, a comic book supposedly authored by the two boys, the villain, Deputy Dangerous, morphs into a piece of poop. Much of the humor in this book comes from poop jokes: Deputy Dangerous's dog starts to call him "Deputy Doo-Doo," asks him if he is "pooped," and calls him a "party pooper." After Deputy Doo-Doo is turned into a giant piece of walking poop, he terrorizes the city: "You know," says a person running away from the monster, "I've seen people step on poo before, but I've never seen poo step on people" (Pilkey 2002: 88). Super Diaper Baby and his sidekick Diaper Dog wrap Deputy Doo-Doo in giant toilet paper and fly him to, of course, Uranus.

As excessive and gross as this plot seems, the most disgusting story line by far is in the two-part story of *Captain Underpants and the Big, Bad Battle of the Bionic Booger Boy*. It is in these books—the sixth and seventh in the series—where bodily borders are most challenged and, therefore, where the masculine identity of the protagonists must be most clearly defined. The boys' antagonist in these books is Melvin Sneedly, who is a tattletale and class nerd. Melvin wears a bow tie and glasses, slavishly follows school rules, and gets George and Harold into trouble by reporting them to the principal. In the seventh book, to distance Melvin from themselves as masculine subjects, the boys create a comic book about Melvin that feminizes him further. They depict him lying in his bed hugging a doll and surrounded by dolls, a dollhouse, and posters that read "Dollys are cool" and "I ♥ unicorns" (Pilkey 2003a: 64). When Captain Underpants calls Melvin a "nerd," he says, "I'm not a nerd. I'm cool!!! My mommy said so!" (p. 67). Melvin is depicted by George and Harold as a momma's boy who likes to play with dolls: he becomes a feminized other who can be safely ridiculed because he has been emasculated.

It is significant, too, that the emasculated Melvin is characterized as a momma's boy in a book written for children in the process (a lengthy process, of course) of gaining independence from their mothers. If learning to read on one's own involves a movement away from mom's lap, then do texts for young children also necessarily highlight the idea that the mother (or (m)Other) must be expelled before the child (the boy) can enter into the Symbolic Order? Although such psychoanalytic readings are useful to understand the proliferation of and the appeal of such literary motifs, they do not fully account for the everyday ramifications of an accretion of words and images that repeatedly depict a feminized other. In other words, momma's boys or feminine boys are often ridiculed and ostracized. For boy readers, girls, women, and sometimes anything that can remotely be considered feminine become that "thing" one must vigilantly avoid being or seeming to be. For girl readers, the negotiation with the text becomes even more complex and treacherous because they must simultaneously identify with the masculine protagonist and with the feminized other. This becomes increasingly difficult when the feminine is continuously portrayed as the inhuman or the abject.[4]

Melvin's feminization is conflated with his abjection as his body is literally turned inside out. Melvin creates a machine that he hopes will turn him into a bionic boy by combining him with a robot, and he fantasizes about making George and Harold his slaves who will "carry his books, sharpen his pencils, and be his personal footstools during each class" (p. 79). But Melvin's plan backfires when he sneezes as the machine is combining his body with the robot, and instead of becoming a bionic boy, he becomes a bionic booger boy. "At once the children recognized the terrifying creature that stood before them. 'Melvin?!!?' they cried. 'Yes, it's me,' gurgled the wet, jiggling monster angrily" (p. 90). As Melvin enters the classroom, part of his hand comes off on the doorknob, he oozes and leaks as he walks, and parts of his body stick to his chair. As Bionic Booger Boy, "Melvin now won every football game he played … because no one wanted to tackle him. And when he served a volleyball, nobody on the other team would dare to hit the ball back" (pp. 96–97).

Melvin clearly does not represent the festive laugher of carnival and instead has become abject. What might be seen as a depiction of the invisible cooties of the unpopular kid on the playground has become excessively visible through Pilkey's language and illustrations. George and Harold, and those boys and girls identifying with them, are able to define themselves against the porous, leaking, monster (i.e., feminine, queer, momma's boy, nerd) represented by Melvin. "The construction of gender operates through *exclusionary* means," argues Butler. "The construction of the human is a differential operation that produces the more and the less 'human,' the inhuman, the humanly unthinkable" (p. 8). For example, Melvin is not afforded human qualities when his desires for power over those who oppress him—George, Harold, and the author, who ostracize him for being feminine—are characterized negatively. In other words, children who perform their genders appropriately are allowed to fulfill their power fantasies through the text, but children who do not do so have no outlet. Melvin is not portrayed sympathetically, because to do so would mean that he could then no longer be an object of ridicule against which the normative-sexed identity of the boy protagonists is defined.

It is a paradox, however, that the act of constructing the gendered self against an abject, inhuman other simultaneously calls the self and the borders that delineate self into question. When the gendered self is articulated against an abject other, that abject other, in turn, by its very existence, threatens the stability and the borders of the self, which then must be reperformed, reestablished, and reified. In other words, the more grotesque the Captain Underpants books become, the more the boy protagonists must reassert and prove their masculine identity. And what Butler argues about several works of literature for adults—"the instability produced by the effort to fix the site of the sexed body challenges the boundaries of discursive intelligibility" (1993: 16)—also can be applied to some texts written for children. Cultural anxieties about the instability of gender make their way into texts such as the Captain Underpants books. Indeed, I argue that the excessive and grotesque portrayal of these cultural anxieties about gender identity is what makes the books in this series so popular among boys, who are in early elementary school and at a moment when they are increasingly called on to perform their gender in normative ways.

4

AND MAJIN BUU SAID, "I'LL EAT YOU UP!"
Consuming Japanese Cultural Imports

> Japan's future in influencing, even leading, global culture, will come through three industries—video games, *anime* (animation), and *manga* (comic books). The market for these three industries has surpassed that of the car industry in the last ten years, leading some economists to hope this will pull Japan's economy out of the red.
>
> **—Allison (2004: 36)**

> First it was Pokémon, then it was Digimon and now it's Dragon Ball Z. When you see your kids enjoying that sort of high quality television, you have to ask yourself as a parent, "Where did I go wrong?"
>
> **—Bloomberg (2003: 144)**

Scholars of children's literature have long observed a disconnect between those texts that children enjoy and those texts that adults value, but this disconnect is further complicated by the recent popularity of Japanese cultural imports that feel foreign to many Westerners (at least those of us born before the 1980s) because of the unfamiliar media, technologies, aesthetics, narrative techniques, and ways of seeing and knowing these texts reflect. Many children in the United States currently are fans of Japanese texts (comics, television shows, films, games), about which many adults seem to know very little. This lack of familiarity has not kept some adults, though, from voicing their disapproval about texts they see as violent or morally corrupt or as lowbrow junk. Despite (or perhaps because of) adult ignorance and disapproval, younger children in the United States enjoy Japanese animation (anime) in the form of television shows and trading card games, and older children and teenagers enjoy these shows as well as anime films, video games, and comic books (manga) that are cultural exports from Japan and that are quickly increasing in popularity:

> According to a recent survey by the Marubeni Research Institute, exports of Japanese comics, films, art and video games leapt by 300 percent between 1992 and 2002, where other sectors showed only 15 percent growth. American culture may have dominated the world for most of the 20th century, but the 21st century is seeing a phenomenal boom in Japanese cultural exports, to the point where they are now nearly neck-and-neck with American ones. In recent years manga have become the fastest-growing category in American publishing. (Gravett 2004: 152)

For example, just a few years ago manga occupied one shelf in the "graphic novels" section of my local Borders; now there is an entire section of six *bookcases* filled with a variety of manga, which are purchased mostly by teenagers and young adults in their twenties. Several comic book stores in town cater specifically to the growing number of fans who are purists and insist on renting original films and shows that have not been edited to appeal to Western sensibilities and on buying manga that have not been altered for Western audiences to read from left to right. It is clear that this is a publishing trend to which children's literature scholars should pay attention if we want to work to understand those texts that young people currently read and enjoy. Furthermore, these and other Japanese cultural imports in the forms of television shows, films, and video and computer games are influencing the aesthetic sensibilities of this generation to such a degree that scholars of children's literature would be remiss not to pay critical attention to these popular texts.

For this chapter, I have chosen to closely read the Japanese anime television show *Dragon Ball Z* because it has had longevity in American markets (relative to several other short-lived series) and because it is a narrative that is especially popular among American boys, teens, and young men. I also chose it because the *Dragon Ball Z* franchise expands beyond the television show to include films, manga, toys, video games, and Internet discussion groups and fan sites. Also, as is the case with other texts discussed in this book, *Dragon Ball Z* is a text that focuses on issues of masculinity, specifically the masculine body in relation to the abject. Finally, like many other Japanese cultural exports, *Dragon Ball Z* has come under fire by Western adults concerned about possible negative effects on children and teenagers and therefore further illustrates the gap that often exists between the tastes of adult and child readers.

The television series *Dragon Ball Z*, not to be confused with the other television shows in the popular franchise such as *Dragon Ball* or *Dragon Ball GT*, is—at first glance through Western, middle-aged eyes—a loud, obnoxious, violent, offensive Japanese anime with little redeeming cultural value. Episodes, backed with speed metal soundtracks, often resemble professional wrestling matches where opponents spend half their time talking trash to one another and the other half engaged in brutal hand-to-hand combat. Indeed, the video game versions of these narratives dispense almost entirely with plot or character development and require players to participate in one battle after another in which they throw punches and kicks until they have knocked out their opponent. In the games, manga, and television show, both the villains and the heroes are exaggerated versions of masculinity (females seldom fight)—the superevil villains are almost always sadistically intent on destruction, simply for destruction's sake, whereas the stoic heroes sacrifice themselves to save their friends or city or world. The good guys are excessively muscled martial arts warriors who are able to fly and to channel their energy into powerful blasts they hurl at their opponents. According to one Web site, "Their leader, Goku, [is a] Saiyan Warrior born to battle and destruction, now sworn defender of his adopted world. Pure of heart, with super-honed battle skills and mental powers of extraordinary magnitude, he is a walking one-man nuclear war" (Talsorian Games 2004). Sagas—or story lines that are typically structured around drawn-out, melodramatic battles against a particular villain or group of villains—can last for dozens of episodes and can be more convoluted than a soap opera. To make matters more confusing, some characters are ambiguous in their affiliations and switch sides, and their bodies morph, transform, divide, join together into one combined body, and sometimes characters can die and be reborn. These bodily distortions and various disruptions of the boundaries between self and other can seem grotesque and disturbing to adult viewers unused to the program.

Many Western adults have been suspicious and critical of Japanese cultural imports such as *Dragon Ball Z* since they started to capture the attention of children, who seem disturbingly mesmerized by television shows such as *Pokémon* and *Yu-Gi-Oh!* and the trading cards, games, toys, stuffed animals, movies, and action figures that often accompany the shows. In an essay analyzing critiques of Pokémon from around the world, Christine Yano explains, "Moral panic pervades much of this critique. Pokémon is variously seen as the devil, evil incarnate, a manipulator of vulnerable minds, and/or an instigator of violence and crime. Schools ban it, religious organizations prohibit it, parents gnash their teeth over it" (Yano 2004: 108). It is significant that she says that critiques against Pokémon come from "both the left and the right sides of the political spectrum":

> On the left, critics attack Pokémon for its excessive consumerism, preying upon young children with multiple marketing strategies epitomized by the slogan, "Gotta catch [acquire] 'em all!" On the right, Christian religious groups attack Pokémon as a promoter of dangerous occultism, evolution, reincarnation, and idolatry. Islamic groups attack Pokémon for its encouragement of gambling, espousal of evolutionism, and use of a hexagon star (interpreted as the international Zionist symbol). (p. 132)

Yano argues that these critiques of Pokémon reflect adult ambivalence about global capitalism: we actively participate in and promote it but want to shield our children from it. We are then disturbed when we see our children so overtly mirroring our own consumer desires when they in turn desire products specifically designed for and marketed toward children—trading cards and video games—that they do not need and for which a desire has been blatantly manufactured. We work to censor those children's texts that reflect those aspects of adult culture that make us most uncomfortable with ourselves.

Other critics argue that these moral panics about Pokémon and other Japanese cultural imports are more about fears of an Other culture, which feels too unfamiliar or exotic and too at-odds with Western ways of seeing and knowing. Many of these texts, after all, were originally produced for Japanese audiences who share similar religious beliefs and cultural values "without regard to possible foreign responses to their treatment of sex, Christianity, and other sensitive subjects" (Gravett 2004: 152). Cultural differences also appear in these exports in the ways childhood and the imagined child reader is portrayed. Yano argues that there is "less separation of childhood practices from adult ones" in Japan than in many Western countries and that many texts are viewed or read by both children and adults (2004: 111). Furthermore, she argues, "far from shielding children from consumerism, marketers and many parents in Japan actively work to socialize a child for consummate consumership" (p. 112), an attitude that differs sharply from the attitudes of many liberal Westerners, who actively work to shield children from (at least, overt) consumerism and commercialism.

Although some misunderstandings of Japanese cultural texts are the result of different cultural mores, others reflect Western prejudices against the Japanese. In his book *Manga: Sixty Years of Japanese Comics,* Paul Gravett argues that American reactions to manga have often reflected either a xenophobic fear of the "yellow menace" or a patronizing attitude toward Japan as being a childlike or immature culture:

> Westerners often have a number of preconceptions about [manga]: "All the characters have big, Bambi-like eyes"; "The magazines are as thick as phone directories"; "Businessmen devour them in public on trains"; "They are full of sex and violence." Often misrepresented as little more than "tits and tentacles," manga were, and still are, open to being doubly damned in the West for being Japanese, and for being comics. (Gravett 2004: 8)

Gravett argues that prejudices against manga are twofold: whereas part of the adult critique of manga and other Japanese imports may be the result of xenophobic misconceptions or cultural misunderstandings, other critiques are based on the same perceptions about genre and aesthetics that often present challenges to those of us studying children's literature: manga are comic books, in other words, children's books, and therefore not worthy of serious critical attention.

Furthermore, although some of the disdain for manga and anime may be the result of not understanding that these genres are rich and complex forms of art or literature, these misunderstandings about genre are doubled by cultural misunderstandings that result not only from differences in subject matter but also from different ways of seeing and knowing and different aesthetic sensibilities. Scott McCloud, in *Understanding Comics: The Invisible Art,* explains the different illustrative and narrative techniques used by Japanese manga artists. There are fundamental aesthetic differences between European and American comics and Japanese comics, which not only differ in subject matter but also differ in narrative pace and sequence and in visual depictions of perspective, movement, layout, and narrative structure. In other words, the storytelling and the illustration of Japanese comics are different enough to be unsettling to those of us used to Western-style narrative techniques. For example, McCloud writes, "Traditional western art and literature don't wander much. On the whole, we're a pretty goal-oriented culture. But, in the East, there's a rich tradition of cyclical and labyrinthine works of art" (McCloud 1994: 81). Many manga, such as *Dragon Ball Z,* are series of books that are thousands of pages long and tell winding stories with characters that shift and plots that move in circular ways or sometimes do not move at all. Because these texts are much longer than the traditional American thirty-two-page comic book, they are "not under the same pressure to move quickly" (p. 80). Indeed, even movement is depicted differently within the illustrations: whereas most Western comics (at least traditionally—this is beginning to change because of Japanese influences) depict movement from the perspective of an observer who is standing still, many Japanese artists use "subjective motion," which McCloud explains, "operates on the assumption that if observing a moving object can be involving, being that object should be more so" (p. 114). It is. But for my untrained, middle-aged eye it is also headache inducing and disorienting, which may be another reason that many Western adults are critical of these Japanese imports: they seem foreign and unfamiliar and therefore unsettle our aesthetic expectations. Of course, that which discomfits many adults may be pleasurable for younger readers, precisely for this reason.

In the early 2000s *Dragon Ball Z* was consistently one of the most-watched cable television shows among American boys, teenage males, and men in their early twenties. Furthermore, the June 2003 *Business Wire* reported:

> Dragon Ball is celebrating its 200th consecutive week of ranking in the Top 10 most-searched terms on The Lycos 50 (http://50.lycos.com), a weekly list of the most popular people, places, and things Lycos users are searching for online. Because of its popularity, the term "Dragon Ball" has been at the top of the weekly report since August 1999. It is the only topic that has been in the Top 10 for 200 consecutive weeks. (*Business Wire* 2003)

As is the case with several other Japanese anime television shows, *Dragon Ball* is not just several cartoon series; it is an international franchise of television shows, videos, games, action figures, and other products that have become major exports from Japan to the United States and other nations, and the staggering popularity of the term on the Internet reflects the global commercial success of the *Dragon Ball* franchise. Why are so many boys and young men so drawn to these narratives about which adults seem to know so little? Do the television shows and other texts that make up the franchise work to reinscribe hegemonic versions of masculinity or to perpetuate misogynistic or homophobic views? Do they work to construct masculinity in ways that negatively affect our children? Should adults be concerned, or are adults who are critical of the shows simply misunderstanding these texts because of cultural and generational differences?

Quite a few adults in the United States and other Western nations (at least those who are aware of the show) are offended by the grotesque violence of the program. Because many adults in Western countries are offended by Japanese anime in general, perhaps because it is unfamiliar in its aesthetics, in its ambiguous, convoluted characters and situations, and in its depictions of violence and adult themes, Japanese publishers have responded by editing much of their work that is exported. Hirofumi Katsuno and Jeffrey Maret report that many Japanese cartoons are edited to be less violent for American audiences, but even after editing, shows such as *Dragon Ball Z* still come under fire because many American adults worry that violent television shows will cause kids to behave aggressively or affect them in other negative ways (Katsuno and Maret 2004: 80–84).

As I have discussed earlier, underlying these concerns are assumptions about contemporary childhood, children's culture, and children's texts. Henry Jenkins states that currently in the United States, "our modern conception of the innocent child presumes its universality across historical periods and across widely divergent cultures" (Jenkins 1998b: 15). He challenges this notion by pointing out that constructions of childhood—like constructions of gender and race—have evolved over time and vary across different cultures. The changes that must be made to Japanese cultural imports reflect some of these differing assumptions about childhood and children's texts. Furthermore, Jenkins argues that the myth of the innocent child in the contemporary United States is currently evolving in the midst of conflicting cultural messages that work to posit an "ahistorical conception of the innocent child as eternal, even as our political rhetoric poses childhood as constantly under threat and on the verge of 'disappearing' altogether" (p. 15). It is a paradox that in our contemporary culture, children seem to be both innocents in need of protection and violent savages who need to be controlled lest they gun us all down—we project onto children both our nostalgia and our fear. These projections matter because "our beliefs about childhood have some impact on our treatment of children" (p. 21). All one has to do is witness teenagers being sentenced to the death penalty or watch talk show hosts send "rotten kids" to "boot camp" to understand that "contemporary America may be a far less 'child-centered' nation than it imagines" (p. 22). According to these current paradoxical views, then, children are innocent, unless, of course, they are the monsters we all already know they are.

In actuality, child subjectivity is far more nuanced than these dichotomous adult perceptions will allow but is in turn influenced by these perceptions. Children are psychologically complex beings and must work to negotiate their subjectivity within the context of these current conflicting constructions of childhood and within postmodern, global capitalism but without the same agency that adults are allowed. Keeping all of this in mind, we must consider the texts that children enjoy as cultural artifacts that are both shaped by and work to shape a children's culture that we, as adults, often misread and misunderstand. If we think of children as complex subjects and as active readers who possess at least some agency, then we need to look at violent children's programming such as *Dragon Ball Z* in more nuanced ways than we have in the past, in ways that give children some credit for the choices they make, however limited those choices may be within popular consumer media culture.

In his book *Misreading Masculinity: Boys, Literacy, and Popular Culture*, Thomas Newkirk critiques past studies that link violent behavior and television viewing. He says that researchers in some of these studies create artificial situations in which they show violent programming to children and then put the children into a room with a Bobo punching bag to see what they will do. When the children punch the Bobo doll, perhaps reenacting a scene they viewed on the show, researchers interpret this role-play as violent behavior. (Who wouldn't be tempted to punch a Bobo doll?!) "It is assumed that the children have nothing interesting to say about the visual stimulus—so they aren't asked," argues Newkirk. "The film is treated not as a text that is interpreted by the child, not as something processed in any way. The child is presumed to have virtually no capacity to interpret, to resist or to mediate" (Newkirk 2002: 98). Newkirk and other scholars argue that middle-class anxieties about the television-viewing habits of children are often based in class bias that assumes that well-brought-up, middle-class children should not watch television. Newkirk, who observed more than one hundred school-age children, argues that children use television creatively in play and writing, though not in ways that are always sanctioned by adults, who often seem to prefer quiet, passive play. Ellen Seiter, another researcher of children's media, argues that children are more savvy viewers of television than many adults know and that recent studies show that children are far more active viewers and readers of television shows than once was thought. "Children spend a lot of time discussing television, arguing about it, and criticizing it, both on the playground with friends and at home with parents and siblings" (Seiter 1998: 313). By looking at children's viewing habits—what they do and say while they are watching television—and not just at the amount of time the television is on in a household, researchers are learning that children are not as passive before the television as was once assumed.

Web-based discussions about *Dragon Ball Z* support this argument because creative role-play is evident even in online *Dragon Ball* discussion forums that are not role-playing games. Judging by the enormous *Dragon Ball Z* Web presence, many fans spend as much time writing about the show (and related programs and products) as they do watching, playing, or reading *Dragon Ball Z*. As is the case with many Web forums, the discussions often involve fast-paced one-liners that frequently devolve into flame wars, but a number of the discussions also involve clever examples of parody and playful social interactions that are quite creative. Newkirk argues that teachers often misread violent banter in writing by boys as destructive or semiliterate. But he convincingly argues that boys often use writing to recreate their favorite action stories and characters and to establish or reinforce friendships. Although teachers want boys in their classrooms to write about acceptable topics such as an adult role model or their favorite tree, many boys model their writing after their favorite games or cartoons. "The students I interviewed treated fiction writing as a free utopian space where they could act out, claiming power or skill that they didn't possess in 'real life'" (Newkirk 2002: 88).

For example, a participant on the "Unrivaled Dragon Ball Discussion Board" was quickly grilled by other participants for daring to even broach the topic of television violence and its effect on viewers. He asked, perhaps sarcastically, "Does *Dragon Ball Z* contribute to violent behavior?" The discussion quickly turned into a series of flames and playful verbal sparring. One participant wrote, "I watched *Dragon Ball Z* for the first time, and as soon as it was finished I went and found someone with blond spiky hair and fought them." "And you were handed your ass in a basket," replied another member of the group, to which the first participant responded, "No, he was only a SSJ, I had the mystic power up." Another member joined in with, "You also had the 'crack cocaine' power up," and so on. Although some researchers, educators, or parents might interpret this exchange as violent, rude, or even silly, it seems more like evidence of active viewing and imaginative play that involves parody and creativity and an awareness and ridiculing of adult objections to their viewing practices. Newkirk argues that when children or teenagers engage in this type of banter, they are "doing something far more complex than mimicking stories drawn from video culture" (2002: 124–5). He argues that when boys write, they do so within a system of acceptable boy discourse (bantering, parodying, mocking, one-upping, etc.) that works to limit and to restrict nonmasculine behavior but that also "offers abundant opportunities for shared adventure, for ingenuity and humor" (p. 126). In other words, these exchanges on the Web illustrate that, for this group of viewers at least, watching *Dragon Ball* shows on television is not passive and solitary but instead creative and social, albeit within the confines of a space that favors certain sorts of masculine discourse.

Through Web-based fanzines, discussion groups, and self-publishing on the Web, fans of *Dragon Ball Z* seem to gain a sort of mastery over these complex texts by compiling elaborate lists of characters and genealogies or by entirely rewriting plots. Differing levels of expertise create hierarchies among fans. For example, those who boast of seeing the original and unedited Japanese versions of the shows are better, more committed fans than those who merely watch the versions of the shows shown on the Cartoon Network. Some of the material on the Web seems time-consuming to produce and obsessive in its attention to detail, but Newkirk argues in a section of his book titled "Make Room for Obsession" that "some degree of obsessiveness, even narrowness, is essential for literacy development" and that many avid readers probably fondly remember "phases," times when they focused narrowly on the work of one author or one subgenre, as times that helped them to develop as readers (p. 183). In this sense, then, and in others, these fans are improving their levels of literacy, by both writing about and carefully reading texts—even if these are texts and responses that might not initially appeal to literary scholars.

Keeping these more complex understandings of children's reading, viewing, writing, and agency in mind, we can look at *Dragon Ball Z* not as a show that works to one-sidedly construct the identity of its boy viewers but as a show that boy viewers use to negotiate their subjectivity. Although many of the Japanese anime cartoon shows such as *Sailor Moon, Yu-Gi-Oh!,* and *Pokémon,* which are currently popular in the United States, have audiences of both boys and girls and although many manga are specifically marketed to audiences of girls and young women, the shows that make up the *Dragon Ball* series are watched mostly by boys and young men. Although it is apparent the show has some girl viewers, there are many girls who share the opinion of this *Sailor Moon* fan, who started a petition to replace the *Dragon Ball* shows being shown on the Cartoon Network with *Sailor Moon.* She writes, that the Cartoon Network "dumped a wonderfully entertaining magical girls show which was filled with warmth, charm, and underlined with values of love, friendship, loyalty, and family in exchange for mindless violent testosterone-driven male-leaning programs like *Dragon Ball Z*" ("*Sailor Moon* Petition" 2004).

One can easily agree with this fan and argue that *Dragon Ball Z* is so popular among boys because of its stereotypical "testosterone-driven" portrayals of gender: episodes often resemble highly choreographed professional wrestling matches where hard-bodied heroes battle campy, exaggerated villains who threaten to destroy the heroes' friends and family and even the entire world. The convoluted, drawn-out sagas—many spanning dozens of episodes—often are centered on the traditionally masculine narrative of seeking revenge. The official Web site for Talsorian Games, which produces the *Dragon Ball* role-playing games, explains that "rage is also a powerful force in Saiyan physiology; anger kicks their hyper evolutionary abilities into overdrive." Male characters in the show, both men and very young boys, fight in brutal, bare-knuckled combat, while motherly female characters worry about them and admonish them to be careful. Although *Dragon Ball Z* can indeed be viewed as perpetuating hegemonic versions of masculinity, the show is more nuanced and complex than this. By examining the most popular *Dragon Ball Z* saga and villain, the "Majin Buu Saga" and the monster Majin Buu, I will look at one of the ways in which *Dragon Ball Z* performs anxieties about contemporary masculinity or boyhood and the conflicting messages that boys and young men hear and must work to negotiate.

Although the Saiyan hero Goku is the main protagonist of all the *Dragon Ball* shows, the most fascinating character is featured in the *Dragon Ball Z* "Majin Buu Saga": the monster Majin Buu. Buu, like the twisting plot of the series, is difficult to describe. He is a creature made of a flexible, mutating pink material and has a body covered with many orifices that occasionally spew steam or fluid. Buu, who sometimes is childlike, often kills people by turning them into candy and eating them. In many ways, Buu is the epitome of the Bakhtinian grotesque "body in becoming." He constantly changes shape and size, and there is no one Buu: although he is always pink and rubbery, he sometimes is fat and squishy and other times he is muscular and fierce looking. Sometimes he is childlike with a round body and baby face. Other times he has no body at all because he transforms himself into a liquid with no shape or into gobs of goo that can float in the air and separate from his body so as to sneak up on his opponents from behind. Buu uses his abilities either to ingest other bodies or to invade the bodies of others. For example, in an early episode of the saga, he kills a man by turning himself into liquid, pouring himself into the man's mouth, thereby invading the man's body, and exploding the man from inside out. In a later scene, Majin Buu attempts to enter a Saiyan warrior's body in the same way—but he is unable to control the warrior's body and is spit out like vomit.

As I discussed in chapter 2 on the novel *Holes*, the abject has been typically portrayed in film (especially horror films) in ways associated with women, the feminine, or homosexuality. Even though Buu is male, one can easily argue that his association with the abject and grotesque, his pinkness, his ever-changing body, and his excessive number of orifices mark him as feminine. In the scenes described earlier, the monster Buu can easily be seen as the threat of the homosexual—the abject monster sneaks up from behind and threatens to violate male orifices. He is able to invade a weak man, but the solid, heterosexual, erect Saiyan warrior is able to fight off the monstrous threat by maintaining his bodily and identity borders. Buu's femininity is further accentuated by being juxtaposed against the exaggerated masculinity of the Saiyan heroes who fight him. As is the case in the books in the Captain Underpants series, abjection functions in the narrative to reify gendered identity because the tenuous construction of the borders that delineate gendered identity are briefly made visible, exposed to be vulnerable and porous, but then recontained when the abject monster is defeated. However, this narrative formula is complicated in *Dragon Ball Z* on several levels.

For example, the portrayal of the Saiyans as superpowerful, excessively muscled men fighting an abject monster can have implications in terms of racial or ethnic borders, not just borders delineating gender. Even though *Dragon Ball Z* is a Japanese anime, the Saiyans look Western. Koichi Iwabuchi, in an essay titled "How 'Japanese' is Pokémon?" argues that in an effort to make products that will have mass global appeal, the exporters of anime create characters that are "culturally odorless" (2004: 57). He writes:

> The cultural odor of a product is closely associated with racial and bodily images of the country of origin. [Technologies, comics, cartoons, and video games exported by Japan] are cultural artifacts in which bodily, racial, and ethnic characteristics have been erased or softened. This is particularly evident in Japanese animation where the characters, for the most part, do not look "Japanese." Such non-Japaneseness is referred to in Japan as *mukokuseki,* which literally means something or someone lacking any nationality, but which is also used to refer to the erasure of racial or ethnic characteristics and contexts from a cultural product. ... Consumers of Japanese animation and games may be aware of the Japanese origin of these commodities, but they perceive little "Japanese bodily odor." (p. 58)

The Saiyans have light skin and facial features that appear more European than Asian. The most powerful of the Saiyans are able to transform themselves into "Super Saiyans," at which time their hair changes from black to blond and their eyes from brown to green. At this point they turn from beings of neutral ethnic or racial identity to beings who are decidedly Nordic in character. Now, to point out that Saiyan sounds a bit like Aryan and that Super Saiyan can be abbreviated as SS is a bit of a stretch. However, examining some literature about Saiyans on the Web reveals some disturbing imagery. For example, the official Web site for Talsorian Games explains the "rules" for being a Super Saiyan: "It is written that only a Saiyan who has a purity of heart can achieve the powers of Super Saiyan," and "To become a Super Saiyan, you must be: of at least partial Saiyan birth, and have a pure heart or pure purpose" (Talsorian Games 2004). Words such as *Saiyan birth, purity,* and *pure* combined with the image of the Super Saiyan with his solid muscular body, blond hair, and green eyes work to form an image of masculinity that is quite possibly fascistic, especially when it is presented in opposition to the threat of the abject monstrous body that is Buu.

In *Male Fantasies,* Klaus Theweleit uses the diaries, novels, and other writing of SS soldiers and officers to show fascistic masculinity as an exaggerated version of manliness that must be exaggerated because it is under a constant threat of the abject (the feminine, the queer, and the nonhuman that threatens carefully constructed bodily, racial, and national borders). In his examinations of the writing by these soldiers, Theweleit discovered an obsession with the abject, which was often associated with women and feminine or feminized bodies. To maintain an exaggerated masculinity, the abject must be controlled or expelled—eliminated from both the social body and the individual body. Theweleit argues that a common conclusion in the writing he studied is that the greatest defense against a perceived invasion of the abject is not weapons but the "erect, soldierly body" (Theweleit 1987: 409). He writes that, from the fascists' point of view, "weapons aren't much use against the threat of sinking into a confused heterogeneity. The man within, with his 'fire of enthusiasm,' is to be called upon here to fight the 'miserable morass of the present'" (p. 402). The hard-bodied and erect warrior protects himself, and the social body, from the leaking, uncertain borders that threaten individual and nationalistic identity.

On one level, then, the "Majin Buu Saga" of *Dragon Ball Z* can be read as presenting our boys and young men with a dangerous view of what it means to be a man. Although it is unlikely that young viewers of *Dragon Ball Z* will be enticed to join their local white supremacist group after watching the show, the hardened version of masculinity portrayed fighting the feminine abject does work to perpetuate damaging ideals of masculinity on both a symbolic level and a literal level. For example, Goku's wife and Gohan's mother, Chi Chi, is turned into an egg and crushed by Buu. Her young son, Gohan, who appears to be six or seven years old, is allowed to cry a single tear before he is admonished to use his anger to train so that he can fight Buu and avenge his mother's death. As the male heroes fight the abject and monstrous Buu, they also must fight the feminine (leaking, emotional, soft, abject) within themselves. In other words, boys are allowed to feel and use anger to fight but must stuff down all other emotions such as affection or fear or sadness if they are going to be warriors. Scholars in the field of men's studies, such as Michael Kimmel and Timothy Beneke, have long argued that boys are damaged by societies' expectations that boys must learn to stifle emotions to be considered appropriately masculine. Dan Kindlon and Michael Thompson argue, "Stereotypical notions of masculine toughness deny a boy his emotions and rob him of the chance to develop the full range of emotional resources," which boys need to deal with emotional stress and conflict in productive ways (1999: 4). In other words, if boys are allowed to feel only happiness or anger, they never learn to manage the wide range of complicated, often contradictory, emotions we all have and often learn to repress emotions that are perceived as being not masculine.

Saiyan warriors, then, clearly are not positive role models for boys and young men working to negotiate their masculinity in the early twenty-first century. And they certainly are not the sensitive male protagonists discussed in my introduction of which most mothers would approve. However, to simply write off *Dragon Ball Z* as a negative influence on our boys is to discount children as active spectators, consumers, and readers of culture. As Jenkins and other theorists who study children's culture have pointed out, children often do not read or consume texts in ways we expect them to, and children are far more savvy and complex than many adults give them credit for. If we work to reimagine children as complex psychological beings who possess agency, we can begin to look at a child's spectatorship and reading and consuming of texts in more nuanced ways that involve a negotiation of identity rather than an imposition of identity, ways that assume children are active and not merely passive consumers of culture.

For instance, a quick search of the Web yields Majin Buu sites that affectionately speak of Buu as being many viewers' favorite villain on the program. My son once said, "I wish Majin Buu fought for the good guys," and some of my adult male college students tell me that Buu is "cool." It is clear that the Saiyan warriors are not the only ones with whom viewers choose to identify. It is no surprise that some boys and young men identify with or are fascinated by the abject Buu, especially because our culture often works to construct them as such through increasingly contradictory public discourse about the boy crisis and the troubles boys pose, discourse about which many boys are aware.

And Majin Buu Said, "I'll Eat You Up!" • 117

Also characters such as Buu are not so uncommon in children's literature, a world populated by monsters who eat people and characterized by bodily transformations that often blur the lines between self and other, human and animal, and human and machine. In *Psychoanalytic Responses to Children's Literature*, Lucy Rollin and Mark West argue that children often identify with what Rollin calls the "Freudian Child": the wild children of Maurice Sendak's books who are associated with cannibalism, the uncanny and primitive Mickey Mouse of the 1920s, and the grotesque bodies in Roald Dahl's fantasies. As most anyone who grew up loving the books of Sendak and Dahl can attest, the texts that children love often feature the grotesque, abject, wild, and uncanny. Rollin argues that the original Mickey Mouse "represented a different kind of child: sadistic, aggressive, mischievous—a remarkable icon of the primitive, id-driven child which civilization aims to repress" (1999: 31). Majin Buu, who often is a trickster and who sometimes takes the form of a pink, pudgy, candy-eating baby unable to control his impulses, perfectly fits this description. Baby Buu is naive and greedy and acknowledges no boundaries between self and other. He is able to turn people into candy, and by doing so he literally consumes a city's entire population to satisfy his voracious hunger and desire. He embodies the threat of the abject that not only invades other bodies, or blurs bodily borders, but also incorporates others by consuming them, pulling them into himself. And he does all of this with great glee and playfulness, which makes him more childlike than any of the serious Saiyan warriors, even the child warriors. Even the more frightening incarnations of Buu are closer than the emotionally repressed and serious Saiyans to a representation of the id or the Freudian child. Furthermore, thinking of Buu as an example of the uncanny Freudian child that is present in much children's literature also helps to explain adults' revulsion to him. Rollin argues, as discussed in the introduction, that adults often work to censor images of the uncanny child: "almost never do we see the raging, craving inner child in the books we give our children—so deep is our need to protect ourselves from that image" (p. 79).

Many children, even some teens and young adults perhaps, may not feel the need to protect themselves from such images and in fact may enjoy the very portrayals that most deeply disgust their parents. If many boys either identify with or are fascinated by Majin Buu, it may be because he represents what is repulsive to many adults and, therefore, what is subversive for children. Majin Buu also may conversely represent some of the deeper frustrations and threats that accompany coming-of-age within contemporary global capitalism: the young people who enjoy consuming the text also risk being consumed by it. Or perhaps boy viewers find both Majin Buu and the Saiyan warriors, and the battles between them, equally intriguing because they represent battles that boys and young men must wage within themselves as they work to conform to, to resist, or to negotiate conflicting versions of contemporary masculinity and childhood. In *Ways of Being Male,* John Stephens writes that the fact that "many boys themselves find the contemporary world bewildering is often attributed to a lack of correspondence between their experiences of living in the world and a perceived demand to conform to the hegemonic masculinity in their society" (Stephens 2002: ix). As children, boys are often denied agency while at the same time being told that to be masculine is all about having agency. Furthermore, boys who do not very easily conform to hegemonic versions of masculinity (most boys, some would argue) face an even more dramatic separation between their lived experiences and culturally imposed ideals of masculinity. Even traditionally masculine boys are under fire in a post-Columbine culture suspicious of play or talk that seems aggressive. It is no wonder then that the abject, monstrous Majin Buu is a site of fascination or even identification for many boys, who may have ambivalent feelings about the masculinity performed by the hard-bodied, tough, and angry Saiyan warriors. Buu's grotesque battles against the Saiyans may indeed represent the boys' battles against or within hegemonic masculinity.

This is not to say that *Dragon Ball Z* is a work of art that will stand the test of time. Indeed, as I write this in early 2007, the franchise's popularity seems to be ebbing. I also do not see the franchise as a particularly enlightening or liberatory text that can help to make dominant ideology visible or help to challenge current constructions of masculinity—it is, after all, a collection of products that children and young people are induced to consume. Jack Zipes points out:

> Paradoxically the freedom taken by young people and adults to question or to articulate their opposition to homogenization is often used and co-opted by a hegemonic culture industry to represent and rationalize a false freedom of choice, for all choices are prescribed and dictated by market systems. (Zipes 2002: 4)

In other words, the producers of children's popular texts know that children enjoy power fantasies and that boys like to gross out their parents. *Dragon Ball Z* is such a popular television show because it delivers both of these criteria. In fact, one can cynically argue that the show is simply a brilliant piece of marketing with tie-ins to other consumer products such as action figures and computer games. However, it is simplistic to say either that *Dragon Ball Z* is a site of resistance for teenage boys or that it is an Althusarian machine intent on programming our boys for hegemonic masculinity and slavish consumerism. Instead, examining the show and its varied, conflicting portrayals of masculinity is one way to look at some of the ways that boys living in America work to negotiate complex subjectivities within the context of contemporary global capitalism. In *Dragon Ball Z* this is portrayed as being a difficult negotiation fraught with threats and fears: the text combines the traditional image of the macho warrior, both with and against the feminine abject, both as and against the monstrous, both consumed and consuming, in ways that cannot be simplistically interpreted because of the texts' status as Japanese cultural imports, as lowbrow mass media, and as texts for younger readers and consumers. This is because what it means to be masculine and a child and a participant in global capitalism—specifically, to be a teenage boy in post-Columbine America—is elusive.

5

MEN IN CLOAKS AND HIGH-HEELED BOOTS, MEN WIELDING PINK UMBRELLAS
Witchy Masculinities in the Harry Potter Novels

> Children's culture is not the result of purely top-down forces of ideological and institutional control, nor is it a free space of individual expression. Children's culture is a site of conflicting values, goals, and expectations.
>
> —Jenkins (1998b: 4)

J.K. Rowling has been accused of perpetuating patriarchal social structures by relying on traditional male-centered heroic narratives, and she has been lauded for creating feminist fairy tales. She has been vilified for championing feminist-inspired witchcraft while being praised for getting reluctant boys to read, and the characters who populate the fictional world of her novels have been described as sexist and stereotypical or, conversely, as feminist role models. Although not always directly stated, what is at stake in these debates is not so much the meaning of literary texts but the effect that meaning may have on the children who read the texts and, in this case, on the gendered beings they will eventually become. The assumption often underlying these debates is one of an innocent childhood, a conception of the child as a blank slate onto which culture is written, which "'empties' the child of its own political agency, so that it may more perfectly fulfill the symbolic demands we make upon it" (Jenkins 1998b: 1). Instead of assuming a "top-down" relationship between Rowling's texts and her readers, I want to instead read the space between reader and text (identity and culture) as one of continuous negotiation marked by contradictions and conflicting values, goals, and expectations. In other words, the contradictory readings by critics of portrayals of gender in the Harry Potter series coexist because, as is the case with many of the better children's texts, these complex novels function in a space between, where dominant ideology is simultaneously reinforced, challenged, and negotiated. These books are ultimately popular with so many child and adult readers not because they didactically advocate *either* feminist or patriarchal ideals but because, through their complex portrayals of characters, gender, and relationships, they depict the anxieties, tensions, and uncertainties about contemporary gender roles that readers of all ages are continuously working to define and to negotiate.

Several critics have already focused much attention on Hermione and other female characters in the series such as Professor McGonagall, Mrs. Weasley, and, increasingly, Tonks and Ginny, but the following discussion will focus primarily on the male characters in the novels and the ways they perform a variety of masculine identities. Much attention has been paid, in feminist children's literature scholarship, to depictions of female characters. Although this is necessary and important work, a continued focus on women and girls as the primary subjects of the study of gender in children's literature could run the risk of further naturalizing masculinity and of perpetuating the assumption that girls are gendered whereas boys are just naturally boys. Furthermore, the scholarship that has discussed at length the male characters in the Harry Potter novels has tended to focus on the extent to which male characters are or are not stereotypical. Although calling attention to stereotypes is important, it also can assume that there is a direct, unproblematic correlation between the behavior of characters portrayed in texts for children and children's behavior. Identifying and listing stereotypes does not take into consideration the multifaceted and interactive relationship readers have with a text within a culture and the complexities of shifting, layered, gendered identities that exist within, on the margins of, or in opposition to cultural norms.

Through her novels, Rowling shows us that—although there is a dominant version of masculinity that is favored in Western culture and that often is imposed through mainstream society—many boys and men do not easily conform to this hegemonic masculinity. In the previous chapter, I cited John Stephens's argument that many boys' anxieties about gender roles can be "attributed to a lack of correspondence between their experiences of living in the world and a perceived demand to conform to the hegemonic masculinity of their society"

(Stephens 2002: ix). The Harry Potter novels depict this tension that exists between societal expectations and the experiences of boys who don't always conform. Furthermore, by highlighting this tension, Rowling not only creates complex male characters whom boys can relate to but also opens up possibilities for redefining masculinity in broader, more inclusive, less confining ways that ultimately can benefit both boys and men, and the girls and women in their lives.

As discussed in the prologue, boys have been the subjects of much scrutiny over the past few years as parents, educators, and psychologists work to understand what has been called the "boy crisis." This so-called crisis has created an entire body of pop psychology and parental advice books aimed at helping us to cope with boys who are—depending on the expert—too masculine, too gay, too illiterate, too tied to biology, too much under the influence of feminism, too angry, too unemotional, and so on. Some say that feminism has emasculated our boys and claim that boys will be just fine if we acknowledge their biology and just let boys be boys. Others claim that patriarchy, not feminism, puts too much pressure on boys to be unemotional and tough at the expense of their emotional well-being. Shifting definitions of masculinity and conflicting views about the boy crisis play themselves out in children's real, lived experiences in school, at home, on television, in interactions with parents and other adults, and in the texts that make up children's culture and literature. In fact, these conflicting messages play themselves out in much of the criticism written about the Harry Potter novels, where boy characters are criticized for a range of behaviors and attitudes, including being interested in sports, being insensitive jerks, and, conversely, being feminized wimps. Indeed, much of our ambivalence about contemporary masculinity—especially our anxieties about boys and what boys ought or ought not to be—is visible both in the body of criticism written about gender in the Harry Potter novels and in the books themselves. In her essay "Accepting Mudbloods: The Ambivalent Social Vision of J.K. Rowling's Fairy Tales," Elaine Ostry writes, "The popular response to *Harry Potter* seems to reflect a truth that we adults do not want to own up to: when it comes right down to it, we do not really know what we want from children's literature, comfort or change" (Ostry 2003: 90). Ostry is discussing Rowling's ambivalent portrayals of race and social class in the Harry Potter series, but her observation can also apply to responses about depictions of gender in the books: the body of criticism discussing portrayals of gender in the books shows that we do not really know what we want.

HARRY POTTER AND THE GREAT GENDER DIVIDE: THE CURRENT DEBATES

The Harry Potter novels have received a vast amount of critical attention in both the popular press and the academic press, especially considering their recent publication and the fact that the series is not yet complete. Within this body of criticism, the novels have been both praised and vilified for their depictions of gender. Much of this criticism has focused on female characters in the novels and has argued that girls and women are not portrayed as often or as richly as the boys and men in the books. Some critics also complain that the female characters are boring when compared to their fun and adventurous male counterparts and that the girls and women are often portrayed in ways that are one-dimensional and stereotypically feminine. These criticisms are valid because the portrayals of gender roles in the Harry Potter novels often are not ideal and sometimes do border on the stereotypical: Professor McGonagall often is stern whereas Professor Dumbledore is delightfully eccentric and wise, and groups of girls whisper and giggle whereas the major boy characters concern themselves with serious and life-threatening situations. For example, in the most recent book in the series, *Harry Potter and the Half-Blood Prince,* except for female Death Eaters watching Dumbledore's murder, the most dramatic and important moments are played out among the male leads: Dumbledore is killed by Snape when Draco is unable to complete his task, and, earlier, Harry and Dumbledore travel to a treacherous cave to search for a Horcrux that contains part of Voldemort's soul. The women are engaged in battle, but clearly on the sidelines and in less important supporting roles. Furthermore, as some critics have pointed out, the focus on the male protagonist and his struggles with the various father figures in his life is a common motif that assumes and works to perpetuate an inheritance of patriarchal systems of power and that plays out an ancient oedipal struggle that distances women and constructs them as Other. In response to these critiques of gender portrayals in the novels, other critics and fans have rushed to the defense of Hermione, McGonagall, and Rowling. Some claim that Hermione is a role model for girls because she is strong and clever, that girls in the novel play equally with boys on the Quidditch field, that Ginny and Tonks are smart and capable, that Mrs. Weasley's nurturing should be valued, and that McGonagall is a respected adult character, who is a role model and mentor for boys and girls alike. Yet others argue that the characters in the novels are indeed imperfect and, therefore, believable and likeable.

These varied, sometimes opposing, interpretations of the series are all valid because the Harry Potter novels are complex, character-driven works that often depict gender in nuanced, layered, and contradictory ways. Some critics have come to the conclusion that these books are so popular with fans because they reinforce hegemonic notions of gender (and social class, imperialism, race, etc.) and that readers prefer books that make them feel comfortable with conventional beliefs and do not challenge the status quo. Others conversely claim that readers are drawn by the books' feminism and that the books work to subvert dominant ideology. These novels, however, would not be as popular as they have been if either of these generalizations was true.

In 2000 Christine Schoefer started a furor among Harry Potter fans when she published an essay in *Salon* critical of Rowling's depictions of gender in the first three Harry Potter novels. In the essay "Harry Potter's Girl Trouble," she wrote, "Girls, when they are not downright silly or unlikable, are helpers, enablers and instruments. No girl is brilliantly heroic in the way Harry is, no woman is experienced and wise like Professor Dumbledore." Her short essay drew harsh criticism from Harry Potter fans, who "protested Potter's innocence on e-mail discussion lists, barraged *Salon* with negative letters, and even sent hundreds to Schoefer herself" (Elliott 2001). Many fans saw accusations of sexism as a wholesale dismissal of the books and characters they held so dear. They jumped to the defense of Rowling by saying that Schoefer was overreacting, and they pointed out aspects of the books that are not sexist. In an article titled "Stepping on the Harry Potter Buzz," Jane Elliott criticizes the fans' defense of the books. In her analysis of Schoefer's article and the backlash that followed it, Elliott claims that the women readers who disagree with Schoefer, even those who consider themselves feminists, do not want to be critical of Rowling: "For Schoefer, the reluctance of readers to discuss sexism in the Potter series indicates that we take comfort from the conventional roles reproduced in the books" (Elliott 2001). Elliott, here, seems to dismiss defenses of portrayals of gender in the novel as coming from naive readers who simply do not understand the ways we all are being constructed by our culture.

Elizabeth Heilman makes similar assumptions about Harry Potter fans when she adds to this argument in her essay titled "Blue Wizards and Pink Witches: Representations of Gender, Identity and Power," where she points out, "Ordinary people do not realize the extent to which their ideas of gender are culturally created" (Heilman 2003: 231). Heilman thoroughly works through the first four books in the series, creating an exhaustive list of examples to support her argument. There are more male characters than female characters, and the male characters receive more attention, are portrayed in more positive ways, and are more important. Hermione, she argues, is relatively powerless and is Ron and Harry's helper rather than an equal partner in their adventures. According to Heilman, in addition to perpetuating negative stereotypes of girls and women, the novels also portray men and boys in stereotypical ways: "In the *Harry Potter* books, boys are stereotypically portrayed, with the strong, adventurous, independent type of male serving as a heroic masculinity, whereas the weak, unsuccessful male is mocked and sometimes despised" (p. 231). According to Heilman, Harry succeeds at being masculine not only because he is good at sports and accomplishes heroic deeds but also because he is being compared to men and boys who fail at masculinity: for example, she claims that Cedric Diggory is from a lower class and Neville Longbottom is feminized. I disagree with Heilman on these points because it is never clear what social class the popular and handsome Cedric belongs to and because Neville's character is quite complex. In fact, by the end of the fifth book, Neville is parallel to Harry on many levels, and his difficult childhood, painful family history, and quirky behavior make him one of the more interesting and admirable secondary characters in the novels. Neville is neither popular nor handsome, and he is neither good at sports nor is he an outstanding student, except in the study of herbology. However, Harry and the reader learn, with each additional book in the series, that Neville has a strength of character that many lack: he bravely battles Death Eaters in the fifth and sixth books in the series, and, like Harry, he wants to avenge the hurt that Voldemort has done to his family. Neville is an important character because he is always portrayed sympathetically by Rowling even though he is rarely stereotypically masculine. He is part of a large cast of characters depicting a wide range of gendered behaviors. The complexity of his character—a stammering lack of self-confidence contrasted to bravery in the face of real danger, secrecy about his family, loyalty to his male and female friends, and evidence of a deep pain and loss that parallels Harry's—makes him far more than a mere character foil for Harry or a stereotypical or conventional character.

In another recent article, Terri Doughty also argues that the Harry Potter books appeal to readers because of conventional portrayals of boys and men. In her essay "Locating Harry Potter in the 'Boys' Books' Market," an essay that considers the books' mass appeal to boy readers, she writes, "The *Harry Potter* books do not problematize masculinity; this is, perhaps, one reason for their appeal for boy readers. Rowling follows an older narrative tradition, in which the boy-hero comes to maturity supported by a cast of 'fathers' who are there when he needs them, but who also let him make his own way when he needs to do that" (Doughty 2002: 253). Harry must "fight a man's battles" and does so with the help of male mentors and against a powerful male antagonist. Doughty does not see this traditional male-centered hero narrative as negative, though. On the contrary, she believes that boy readers—who often must read about flawed male characters in much fiction written for young adolescents—need positive role models. "Rowling has tapped into a kind of collective unconscious need to be reminded that boys have a path toward maturity to follow, and they can indeed make it, both with help and on their own" (p. 257). Although I agree with many of Doughty's points, especially the idea that boys (and girls) can benefit from positive male role models, I question whether boys need traditional models of masculinity to follow. Perhaps more unconventional, more nuanced portrayals of masculinity might be more useful, especially in a world where constructions of masculinity are evolving and researchers are questioning the effects of the expectations of traditional masculinity on boys. "Paradoxically," write Nodelman and Reimer, "traditional assumptions about maleness are repressive mostly because they claim not to be" (Nodelman and Reimer 2003: 165). Many boys who do not conform to hegemonic masculinity are, at times, ridiculed or bullied, and those boys who do conform are often brutalized into manhood through physical and mental trials. Therefore, simply demanding that boys behave in ways that are nontraditional is unrealistic considering the complexities of identity within culture and could even be potentially dangerous in a playground culture that sometimes violently polices a "boy code" of traditionally gendered behavior.

To say that gender is socially constructed is not the same as saying we can easily adopt gendered behaviors that are unconventional without facing social consequences. On the other hand, individuals with agency are not entirely helpless before cultural forces. In other words, to say that gender is entirely imposed by culture onto individuals who are blank slates is just as deterministic as claiming that gender is shaped solely by biology. In *Bodies That Matter*, Judith Butler uses the idea of gender performance to complicate the biological–constructivist dichotomy and to address questions of agency. We should be wary of positing the natural as something that can simply be written over by discourse, just as we should be wary of claiming that the body is something outside discourse. She argues instead that gender performance involves a "matrix of gender relations" that is both imposed and performed in ways that are tenuous. The gendered foundation of the subject is always tenuous because identity must be established in opposition to an abject, and that abject always threatens the subject at the same time as it works to construct it. If masculinity were natural, boys would not need to police gendered behaviors of themselves and their peers on the playground, and boys and men would not need to continuously prove that they are not feminine. Therefore, the continuous performance of a masculine identity working to establish itself in opposition to anything feminine paradoxically works to mark those aspects of gendered identity that are performed, that need to be proved. In other words, the abject is an "enabling disruption critical to the matrix of gender performance" (Butler 1993: 23). Although the abject—that which disrupts bodily borders or a conception of a whole and fixed self—is crucial to gender identity and performance, its presence also opens up gaps that can make performance visible and create moments of "productive crisis." The Harry Potter novels open up spaces of this productive crisis through their depictions of nonhegemonic masculinities existing in opposition to cultural expectations and through depictions of nontraditional heterosocial relationships. These contradictions and tensions may be what draw in savvy child readers, who would not be as attracted by didactic texts that advocate rigidly defined gender roles. The construction of gender is fluid and ongoing (for both children and adults); it requires subjects who are thinking, acting, conforming, and resisting and who are influenced by but are not always blind to or helpless in the face of a monolithic "Culture."

This is not to say that children's negotiations of identity within culture(s) are the same as adults'. Children have less experience of the world than adults and are afforded less agency because of unequal power structures. As Jenkins writes, "Children *are* subject to powerful institutions that ascribe meanings onto their minds and bodies in order to maintain social control," and "Children's culture *is* shaped by adult agendas and expectations, at least on the site of production and often at the moment of reception, and these materials leave lasting imprints on children's social and cultural development" (Jenkins 1998b: 26). On the other hand, children also are not entirely helpless before culture. Children often "resist, transform, or redefine adult prerogatives, making their own uses of cultural materials and enacting their own fantasies through play" (p. 27). The fan culture surrounding the Harry Potter books is a perfect example of such agency on the part of readers because some fans of the books rewrite story lines and reinvent characters, situations, and relationships in fan fiction, on fan Web sites, and in e-mail discussion lists.

Several Harry Potter fan Web discussion lists, for example, treat the topic of gender in the novels in intelligent ways that we, as academic critics, should not be so quick to dismiss. The fans of these books are not oblivious to the sexism in them, but they also see gender in the novels in more nuanced, less dichotomous ways that show that many fans are able to think critically about what they read. For example, in a lengthy discussion about gender issues in *Harry Potter and the Order of the Phoenix*, fans posting on the Internet said such things as, "Why should we expect a world more or less perfect than our own if the Wizarding world is supposed to exist next to our own?"; "If the characters, both female and male, behaved in such a way as to create [a 'feminist haven'], the books would be very dull indeed"; and "I think most readers of all ages would rather engage with the complexities of flawed but real characters rather than [a vision] of a perfect feminist world." One fan is particularly on the mark in pointing out that the critics who want the Harry Potter books to portray an ideal feminist world "seem to be operating on the basis that somehow, books written for or read by children should have a 'message'—they should reinforce whatever is Politically Correct or Socially Desirable at the time, never mind whether or not it is realistic" (*Sugar Quill* 2003). These fans—whose age or gender we can't tell from the pseudonyms they use on the Web—are clever enough to see that debates about issues such as gender focus mainly on what we believe is at stake culturally and politically in children's identity development.

One critical article that looks at gender in the Harry Potter books in a more complex, less polarized way is Eliza Dresang's "Hermione Granger and the Heritage of Gender." Dresang argues in defense of Hermione and McGonagall but does so by looking at the books and the characters through various feminist lenses that offer a multiplicity of readings. Some critics, for example, are critical of Hermione's plastic surgery in *Harry Potter and the Goblet of Fire*—Hermione's big front teeth are straightened and made smaller and her hair is no longer bushy when she attends the Yule Ball with Viktor Krum. But Dresang acknowledges that feminist criticism is not monolithic and discusses the different ways Hermione's actions can be viewed using different feminist approaches: "Radical-libertarian feminists maintain that females have the right to do whatever they want to with their bodies, while radical-cultural feminists would more likely disapprove of using the body in this manner to attract male attention" (Dresang 2002: 233). Dresang acknowledges that the portrayal of gender in Rowling's novels creates a "mixed and inconclusive picture" (p. 236) and that the books do not represent utopian possibilities but instead depict "the far less than ideal reality of the late twentieth and early twenty-first centuries" (p. 238).

This brief summary of the body of criticism about gender in the Harry Potter novels shows that Rowling has been able to tap into some of the anxieties contemporary children and adults feel about gender and to portray these anxieties and uncertainties in sympathetic and complicated ways. In other words, critics have reached very different conclusions about gender in these books because the portrayal of gender in the Harry Potter series is often ambivalent and mirrors less an ideal feminist or patriarchal vision of what boys and girls ought to be and more the messy, contradictory reality of what they are. It is within these contradictions that spaces can open up to view gender, specifically masculinity, in the novels in alternative ways.

WITCHY MASCULINITIES IN THE HARRY POTTER NOVELS

Issues of masculinity in the Harry Potter novels—depictions of male characters, the structure of the Wizarding subculture, the structure of the novels as works of literature, and the relationships between boys and boys and between girls and boys—should be examined in ways that acknowledge the complexities of contemporary children's culture and current thinking about boys and masculinity. For example, over the past decade there have been many texts published, predominantly parenting advice books, about rearing and educating boys. It is unfortunate that quite a few of these books have black and red covers and seem to invoke fears about boys and violence, illiteracy, attention deficit disorder, and emotional instability. As I discuss in the prologue, one of the more prominent texts has been Dan Kindlon and Michael Thompson's book *Raising Cain: Protecting the Emotional Life of Boys*. Although the therapist authors have been accused of basing too many generalizations about all boys on a narrow population of their troubled boy patients, the book does point out some damaging cultural misconceptions about boys that are worth noting:

> It is vital that parents and teachers not take boys at face value, even though they sometimes insist, furiously, that we do so. They often present us with an apparently simple set of needs: Ninja Turtles, Nike shoes, exciting and violent video games, and support for their athletic ambitions. It may seem that every boy wants to "be like Mike." But it isn't so. Boys want different and complicated and conflicting things. (Kindlon and Thompson 1999: xii)

The authors of *Raising Cain* argue that many boys suffer because hegemonic ideals of masculinity deny them access to their emotions and to unconventional forms of masculinity. Furthermore, parents and educators who conceive of masculinity in hegemonic ways participate in denying boys a "rich emotional life" and other alternative ways of being masculine. Well-meaning educators, parents, and critics sometimes make assumptions about boys, their literature, and characters within that literature that can oversimplify boys' emotional complexity and that assume boys' complete complicity in perpetuating stereotypical gender roles: we sometimes assume that *all boys,* even those who are unconventionally masculine, always already work to perpetuate hegemonic masculinity because it keeps them in a position of privilege over girls.

For example, Heilman seems to argue that the surface of the Harry Potter books is sexist and one can read the books as feminist only if one reads against the grain of the text. She writes, "Though both feminist and poststructuralist theories tell us that text can be read from multiple, contradictory, and even transgressive positions, it is still important for criticism to reveal dominant and hegemonic traditions" (2003: 223). Although this is most definitely true and there are aspects of the Harry Potter novels that can be interpreted as supporting hegemonic and patriarchal notions about gender, there is, however, also much in the Harry Potter series that combats dominant ideology. One does not even need to read against the grain of the text because there are complex and contradictory portrayals of gender right on the surface of the text and evident to even the youngest or most literal-minded reader. Heilman writes, for example, "The girls on the Quidditch team provide another example of how token inclusion reinforces inequality" (p. 226). In this example, Rowling's depiction of coed sports teams is dismissed as tokenism, even though Rowling purposefully uses the makeup of the teams to make a point about inclusion: in *Harry Potter and the Sorcerer's Stone* (HPSS) the only house without girls on the Quidditch team is Slytherin, and that house is made up of the "bad guys." Rowling's point here is obvious even in a surface reading of the text: the Slytherins, who exclude wizards who are not of pure blood and who mock lower-class wizards, can also add sexism to their list of antisocial beliefs and practices. In the other houses at Hogwarts, boys and girls play equally together and there are several girl Quidditch players referenced in positive ways in each text of the series, sometimes as valuable and famous members of professional teams—girl and women Quidditch players are not merely tokens.

When we read with the grain of even the first and simplest novel, HPSS, which is an introduction to the Wizarding world, many such examples occur. For example, Rowling establishes marked differences between the "normal" Muggle world and the "abnormal" Wizarding world—differences that are often articulated through different portrayals of gender and different relationships between men and women. Gender in the Muggle world, as represented by the Dursleys, is portrayed as being normative, whereas gender roles in the Wizarding world are sometimes not as easily categorized. Mr. Dursley, Harry's awful uncle, defines both "normal and abnormal" for us in the opening chapters of HPSS. The Dursleys, in many ways, are like the exaggerated caricatures of villainous adults that populate so many beloved children's books—a type of character (à la Roald Dahl's aunts Sponge and Spiker) that resonates with children because they often feel powerless in the face of arbitrary adult authority. Mr. Dursley quickly comes to represent the grumpy adult who stands in the way of children's aspirations and desires: "He didn't approve of imagination" (Rowling 1997: 5). He is that sort of adult who tells children to stop daydreaming and to conform to constricting norms. In this sense, then, he also represents the voice of dominant culture. The first two sentences of HPSS set up the Dursleys as killjoys by describing them as people who "were perfectly normal, thank you very much. They were the last people you'd expect to be involved in anything strange or mysterious, because they just didn't hold with such nonsense" (p. 1). In contrast, the Wizarding world is fun and exciting, strange and mysterious, and the Dursleys are the prudes who try to keep Harry (and also the readers who identify with him) from accessing this world of adventure, this abnormal subculture. The Dursleys disapprove of anyone who dresses differently or behaves oddly: they can't tolerate Harry's untidy hair, they won't allow Harry to ask questions or to describe his dreams, and they believe that all wizards and witches are "freaks." Also, because it is not clear to the uninitiated reader in the opening chapters of the first book exactly what the Dursleys disapprove of, the reader can substitute a variety of words or phrases into the Dursleys' vague condemnations. Mr. Dursley refers to Lily Potter's associations with "her crowd" (p. 7), Harry can't ask the Dursleys any questions because "they seemed to think he might get dangerous ideas" (p. 26), and Mr. Dursley says, "I'm not having one in the house, Petunia! Didn't we swear when we took him in we'd stamp out that dangerous nonsense?" (p. 36). Because readers do not, at this point in the book, know that these statements are referring to wizards, all sorts of social transgressions—some of them gender transgressions—come to mind.

This separation between normal and abnormal (or subject and object) can have profound meaning for child readers who feel like freaks. For instance, after surveying seventy-five gay male fans of the *Wizard of Oz* stories, Dee Michel (2004) concluded that many gay men have been fans of Oz since they were very young children. Michel theorized that gay men are attracted to Oz from a very early age because of the escape from the everyday, normal world that the stories represent. Gay boys can begin to feel different or outside of the norm from as young as three to five years of age. According to Michel, with Oz, they can fantasize about leaving the ordinary world and escaping into a strange, fantastical, colorful world that welcomes them and their supposed abnormalness. Boys (heterosexual and homosexual) who do not easily conform to hegemonic versions of masculinity also may similarly find comfort in the abnormal Wizarding world of the Harry Potter novels. The Wizarding world, like Oz, is far more attractive than the mainstream culture partially because otherness is welcomed and celebrated—at least when compared to the rigid values of the Dursleys.[1]

Because the narrow-minded Dursleys are so unpleasant, readers are led to disapprove of the dreadful, abusive, normal Dursleys and, conversely, to find pleasure in the abnormal and freakish things that distress the Dursleys. The fact that Mr. and Mrs. Dursley are depicted as conventional in their gender roles becomes conflated with the other unpleasant aspects of their personalities and beliefs. Mrs. Dursley is a doting, stay-at-home mother and a gossip who spies on her neighbors. Mr. Dursley is described as "a big, beefy man with hardly any neck" who is "the director of a firm called Grunnings, which [makes] drills" (p. 1). He is successfully masculine in very conventional ways. Ian Harris, in his book *Messages Men Hear: Constructing Masculinities,* writes about various societal expectations men are expected to fulfill to succeed at hegemonic masculinity. In contemporary capitalistic society, men should make a lot of money and rise to the top of the corporate ladder. He writes, "Successful men aspire to be leaders," and they are "not happy when others control them" (Harris 1995: 109). Mr. Dursley superficially fits the contemporary mold of masculine success: he is a large man, he is the head of his household, he directs a successful business, and the company he works for produces the manliest of products: drills. Mr. Dursley also works to pass his knowledge of how to be manly on to his son, Dudley, who is a conventionally masculine boy because he is big and a bully. Furthermore, Dudley also does not participate in such "girly" activities as reading—the very thing that male readers of HPSS are doing as they learn about Dudley. The description of Dudley's extra room illustrates much about the way his character is revealed as excessively, stereotypically, and negatively masculine:

> Nearly everything in here was broken. The month-old video camera was lying on top of a small, working tank Dudley had once driven over the next door neighbor's dog; in the corner was Dudley's first-ever television set, which he'd put his foot through when his favorite program had been cancelled, there was a large birdcage, which had once held a parrot that Dudley had swapped at school for a real air rifle, which was up on the shelf with the end all bent because Dudley had sat on it. Other shelves were full of books. They were the only things in the room that looked as though they'd never been touched. (pp. 37–38)

This description of Dudley's room works to construct him as a violent boy with a nasty temper who would rather shoot animals than care for them and as a boy who never reads.

Several recent studies examining boys and literacy have reached the conclusion, among others, that many boys see reading as a feminine activity. In his book *Misreading Masculinity: Boys, Literacy, and Popular Culture,* Thomas Newkirk writes, "Boys often feel that an open show of enthusiasm for schoolwork, particularly in the language arts, can undermine their identity as a 'real boy'" (Newkirk 2002: 39), and Michael Smith and Jeffrey Wilhelm claim in their book *"Reading Don't Fix No Chevys": Literacy in the Lives of Young Men* that although boys are all different in their interests and aptitudes, overall "a variety of research shows that boys learn to read later than girls and never catch up. They trail girls in almost every literary measure in every country and culture from which data are available. They are particularly behind when it comes to reading novels and narrative fiction" (Smith and Wilhelm 2002: xix). Young male readers, however, make up a significant number of the fans who enthusiastically dive into Rowling's lengthy narratives. Because Dudley has already been established as an unlikable bully by this point in the book, readers (especially those boys who are fond of reading) can take pleasure in the fact that Dudley doesn't read books and that they do.

In the book *The Irresistible Rise of Harry Potter,* Andrew Blake claims that Mr. Dursley and Dudley represent not merely exaggerations but a disturbing norm for many men and boys. He writes:

> Harry is brought up in the world of real boys in suburban Surrey, with real, surrogate or stepfathers like Mr. Dursley, who play no part in their children's education beyond sending them to school, and never read at home themselves. In this world, boys are more interested in computer games and football than in reading and writing. But Harry becomes a willing reader as soon as he is

introduced into a world in which books and reading are important. (Blake 2002: 31)

Boy readers who are victimized by other boys because they do not easily conform to hegemonic masculinity (perhaps because they are called "bookworms" or "nerds") can take pleasure in the unflattering portrayal of a macho, semiliterate bully and in the power that Harry and his friends in the Wizarding world gain from reading. Although Harry and Ron are not as studious as Hermione, reading is central to their survival at Hogwarts, and textbooks, letters, diaries, and the Wizarding newspaper are featured prominently in each novel. There are no television sets at Hogwarts, whereas the television seems to always be on at the Dursleys' and Dudley seems even to have owned several television sets of his own.

Like his father, Dudley is also unlikable because of his excessively conventional masculinity. In HPSS, we witness this normal behavior being passed from father to son through discussions about Smeltings, Mr. Dursley's old private school, which Dudley will attend and, we assume, is not coeducational. The boys at Smeltings "carried knobbly sticks, used for hitting each other while the teachers weren't looking. This was supposed to be good training for later life" (p. 32). To become men, boys, traditionally, are often expected to go through violent rituals that build character. In his book *Proving Manhood*, Timothy Beneke argues that boys are often subjected to painful initiation rituals that prepare them for manhood. He writes, "Symbols of masculinity often contain and express a history of suffering successfully endured" (Beneke 1997: 42). Rowling is clearly mocking this mentality through her comic description of the Smeltings stick, and both Dudley and Mr. Dursley are made to look ridiculous through their rigid adherence to exaggerated and stereotypical masculinity and the character-building rituals associated with it.

It is in contrast to this normal, Muggle family that we are introduced to the Wizarding world. Much of the abnormal behavior in the Wizarding world, of which the Dursleys disapprove, is behavior that does not conform to conventional ideas of gender. In the first few pages of HPSS, Mr. Dursley is enraged to see strangely dressed people out on the street and is specifically horrified to see a "man [who] had to be older than he was, and wearing an emerald-green cloak! The nerve of him!" (p. 3). Later, Mr. Dursley is distraught when an old man, wearing a violet cloak, hugs him. "He had been hugged by a complete stranger. He also thought he had been called a Muggle, whatever that was. He was rattled" (p. 5). Mr. Dursley's disturbing encounters with the Wizarding world are often described in ways that are gendered. They specifically involve men behaving in ways that are not conventionally masculine: manly men do not wear violet, and they certainly do not hug other men. Because Mr. Dursley has been constructed as such an unsympathetic character, his negative reactions to these abnormal gender performances lead readers into the pleasure of approving of these strange characters and this odd subculture, which are able to rattle Mr. Dursley.

Once this relationship between the Muggle and Wizarding worlds is established, we meet Professor McGonagall and Professor Dumbledore. The Dursleys do not meet them at this point—they would, we assume, be horrified if they did—but we see these characters as the Dursleys might because they first appear in the Dursleys' world, on their very doorstep, with the threat of an opened door and a prudish judgment always lingering in the background of our introduction. We, as readers, understand that the Dursleys would be appalled to meet a man described in this way:

> Nothing like this man had ever been seen on Privet Drive. He was tall, thin, and very old, judging by the silver of his hair and beard, which were both long enough to tuck into his belt. He was wearing long robes, a purple cloak that swept the ground, and high-heeled buckled boots. His blue eyes were light, bright, and sparkling behind half-moon spectacles and his nose was very long and crooked, as though it had been broken at least twice. This man's name was Albus Dumbledore. (p. 8)

The purple, floor-length cloak and high-heeled boots introduce Dumbledore as a man who is in sharp contrast to Mr. Dursley. He is depicted as unconventionally masculine in his appearance—as freakish. McGonagall also is abnormal, especially when compared to the image-conscious Mrs. Dursley. In addition to first coming on the scene transformed as a cat, McGonagall is described as a severe-looking woman wearing an emerald-green cloak and looking "distinctly ruffled" (p. 9). Our first impression of these great and powerful wizards is that they are quirky folk who don't quite perform their gender properly. The fact that the Dursleys would most certainly disapprove makes us like the professors even more. Indeed in the book *Harry Potter and the Half-Blood Prince*, Rowling finally has Dumbledore and the Dursleys meet in a scene that is both funny and pleasurable because the Dursleys are as horrified and uncomfortable in Dumbledore's presence as we had hoped they would be. Dumbledore—who "looked quite extraordinarily out of place" (p. 47) in the Dursleys' living room—has a bit of fun making them feel even more uncomfortable when he playfully bounces teacups off their heads (pp. 45–56).

Our first impressions of Hogwarts's groundskeeper Rubeus Hagrid are also presented to us through the lens of Muggle normalcy. He arrives on Privet Drive astride a giant motorcycle and is holding a bunch of blankets that contain the infant Harry Potter. He is both conventionally manly—large, hairy, riding a motorcycle—and nurturing—caring for a baby. When the three wizards leave the infant on the Dursleys' doorstep, Hagrid's shoulders shake, we assume, because he is overcome by emotion: "Wiping his streaming eyes on his jacket sleeve, Hagrid swung himself onto the motorcycle" (p. 16). These layered portrayals of Hagrid are even more pronounced when we meet him a second time at the shack in the sea to which the Dursleys have escaped, and he makes a dramatic entrance brandishing a pink umbrella. Hagrid, initially, is a terrifying figure who knocks down the front door and says, "Ah, shut up, Dursley, yeh great prune" (p. 49). However, in addition to being Harry's rescuer, he is also a nurturer. When he pulls a crumpled birthday cake out of his magically abundant overcoat and he makes sausages and tea for a hungry Harry, Hagrid is both manly and motherly. Later in the book, we see Hagrid's ambiguously gendered personality again when he adopts and cares for an illegal baby dragon. "'I've decided to call him Norbert,' said Hagrid, looking at the dragon with misty eyes. 'He really knows me now, watch. Norbert! Norbert! Where's mommy?'" (p. 236). Even though Hagrid's tenderness is often portrayed, as in this scene, in ways that are comical, the seemingly incongruent combination of both traditionally masculine and unconventionally masculine traits in a man so large is what makes him such a beloved character. Boys can identify with and admire a man who is neither feminized nor excessively masculine, a man who comfortably embodies a range of masculine traits.

Harry also possesses masculine traits that are both conventional and unconventional, which work together to create a complex, imperfect boy struggling to figure out who he is. He is, as Ximena Gallardo and Jason Smith point out, a "Cinderfella" who has been feminized by the abuse he received at the hands of the Dursleys. It is sometimes difficult to differentiate the characters described in the books from the charming and handsome actors who play them in the film versions of the texts, but in the novels Harry and his friends are often described in ways that are not conventionally attractive. When we meet Harry in HPSS, he is described as "small and skinny for his age" (p. 20) and as having hair that grows "all over the place" (p. 21). His glasses are taped together because Dudley has punched him in the nose so many times, and, according to Gallardo and Smith, he "inhabits 'feminine' spaces" such as the cupboard under the stairs" (Gallardo and Smith 2003: 197). However, it is important to point out that being abused or being a victim often defines, but should not, the feminine. Furthermore, because boys are often victims of what Kindlon and Thompson call "the culture of cruelty," where boys endure physical and mental abuse from other boys, victimhood should never be defined as exclusively feminine. It is significant that even though many boys are victims of bullying, most boys do not report acts of cruelty to adults "because they know the acts are so intimate and so obviously hurtful that any teacher or parent would disapprove and there would be penalties to pay; the repercussions could be worse than the original incident" (1999: 74). Within this social context, then, Dudley and Draco may represent for many boys their own tormentors on the school playground, about whom they cannot speak for fear of being labeled a tattletale, or because they have been taught to believe that boys are not supposed to be victims. Harry's numerous encounters with bullies are not so much a feminization of his character as a realistic portrayal of the complexities of being a contemporary boy.

Perhaps better, more positive examples of Harry Potter's so-called feminine or unconventionally masculine traits can be seen in the fact that he shares treats with Ron when he first meets him, or the point that—more than anything else—Harry longs for a family and to be part of a community, or that, as the novels progress, he learns to empathize with others. Indeed, learning to understand the feelings of other characters is a key aspect of Harry's coming-of-age. In *Harry Potter and the Goblet of Fire,* for example, he learns that Neville lives with his grandmother because his parents were tortured so cruelly by Voldemort that they lost their sanity and can no longer recognize their son. "Harry shook his head, wondering, as he did so, how he could have failed to ask Neville this, in almost four years of knowing him. ... Harry sat there, horror-struck. He had never known ... never, in four years, bothered to find out" (pp. 602–3). Harry not only identifies with Neville but also chastises himself for never having thought about Neville's situation, for not caring enough about his friend. Another example of Harry's emotional growth is when, in book five of the series, *Harry Potter and the Order of the Phoenix,* Harry must struggle with strong and mixed feelings as he learns about events in the past that involved his parents and their friends. He learns, for example, that the father he has idealized and some of the adult males who have become his mentors all took great pleasure in tormenting a young Severus Snape. Harry is deeply troubled by the cruelty of his male role models and learns to develop empathy for Snape, a character he has, until then, despised and feared.[2] Empathy is conventionally viewed as a feminine trait, but Kindlon and Thompson rightfully question defining such characteristics as feminine at all and argue that *when our culture allows them to be,* boys are just as sensitive and emotional as girls.

With Harry, we see a boy who is working to understand his emotions, often within the context of hegemonic masculinity, as he grows and matures. Some critics have pointed out Harry's masculine traits and the masculine structure of the novels' narratives as being negative characteristics of the books. Harry is a boy and behaves as many boys do—he is good at and enjoys sports, he is not terribly interested in his studies, and he is, at times, insensitive. But compared to the hypermasculinity of Dudley and Mr. Dursley, Harry is not stereotypical or excessive in his gendered behavior. Of course, after completing a study of dozens of books with boy protagonists written over the past fifty years, Tami Bereska concluded, "Some variations and contradictions in masculinity are permitted" (Bereska 2003: 163) in books with male protagonists, but only when they are in the context of traditionally masculine traits. She argues, "Variations and contradictions are permissible only within a larger context of No Sissy Stuff. That is, a male can deviate from the ideal of one, or even a few components of manhood, as long as he lives up to most of the ideals. If he deviates from too many of the ideals, then he runs the risk of being labeled a sissy" (p. 164). This charge of "no sissy stuff" can apply to the novels in the Harry Potter series (and to Disney's *Tarzan, Holes,* and other texts discussed here), but it may not be fair to ask authors to create characters that deviate entirely from dominant gender expectations, especially because we must necessarily understand gender roles in relation to these dominant expectations and within current cultural contexts.

To better understand the complex masculinity embodied by Harry and some of the other male characters in the books, we need to work to understand it within the context of contemporary boy culture. For example, although it is stereotypically masculine that Harry must shake off physical injuries he suffers on the Quidditch field, he also must endure being much more sensitive than his peers in many instances. The Dementors, for instance, affect him more deeply than they affect any of the other children, both male and female. For example, in the book *Harry Potter and the Prisoner of Azkaban,* both Harry and Ron's little sister, Ginny, are distraught when a Dementor boards the Hogwarts train. Ginny was "shaking like mad," but Harry is the only student on the train who faints. "Harry didn't understand. He felt weak and shivery, as though he were recovering from a bout of flu; he also felt the beginnings of shame" (p. 86). Harry cannot exhibit behavior—fainting—that is unconventionally masculine without suffering social consequences. After the fainting spell, he must endure months of taunting from other students. Professor Lupin, who also doesn't live up to ideals of hegemonic masculinity because he is poor, shabbily dressed, and a werewolf (an Other in the Wizarding world), becomes a mentor to Harry and helps Harry to understand the despair he feels when Dementors are near. He tells Harry, "You have nothing to be ashamed of" (p. 187) and that it is OK for boys to feel and express emotions.

For many boys, expressing emotions or being seen as sensitive is complicated. William Pollack argues in his book *Real Boys: Rescuing Our Sons from the Myths of Boyhood* that many boys feel compelled to adhere to a "boy code" that limits their emotional expressions. He reports:

> Even very young boys reported that they felt they must "keep a stiff upper lip," "not show their feelings," "act real tough," "not act too nice," "be cool," "just laugh and brush it off when someone punches you." These boys were not referring to subtle suggestions about how they "might" comport themselves. Rather, they were invoking strict rules they had absorbed about how they "must" behave, rules that most of them seemed to genuinely fear breaking. (Pollack 1998: 23)

Harry often keeps a stiff upper lip when he is knocked off his Quidditch broomstick or when he is injured by a dragon and keeps on playing in the first task of the tri-wizard tournament, but he is also a boy who feels a range of emotions and who struggles with appropriately expressing these. For example, after his ordeal with Voldemort and the Death Eaters near the end of *Harry Potter and the Goblet of Fire*, Harry is overcome with emotion but still aware of the boy code. Harry is talking to Mrs. Weasley about Cedric's death and his feelings of responsibility and sadness, and he begins to cry: "Now the burning feeling was in his throat too. He wished Ron would look away" (p. 714). Hegemonic masculinity is enforced, often, through the male gaze—men and boys must perform their gender appropriately before one another. We see this when, even in a tragic moment, Harry worries that his best male friend will see him cry. It is significant, though, that there is no mention of Ron turning away as Harry sobs in Mrs. Weasley's arms, and, more important, Ron never chastises Harry for this display of emotion. Contemporary boys working to negotiate their identity must reconcile feelings they have that may sometimes be at odds with perceived norms of behavior, and they must navigate through often contradictory messages about masculinity presented to them in popular culture and enforced by their peers. It is not enough, then, simply to ask boys or male characters to be less stereotypical or more sensitive without also understanding the social contexts for masculine behavior. Rowling is able to depict Harry's emotional vulnerability within a realistic context that makes it believable enough for many boys to relate to.

Harry is also unconventionally masculine in his choice of best friends. Public schools are often coeducational, and girls and boys have many opportunities to interact in the classroom or in after-school activities. However, when they are not required to socialize together, most boys and girls do not choose to do so. In her essay "Boys and Girls Together … but Mostly Apart," Barrie Thorne reports, "In nearly every study of school situations where kids from age three through junior high are given the opportunity to choose companions of the same age, girls have shown a strong preference to be with girls, and boys with boys" (Thorne 1998: 331). In the Harry Potter novels, Harry, Ron, and Hermione, although their individual performances of gender and their interactions with one another may not always be ideal, are friends who spend most of their time with one another. The simple fact that they are friends—and best friends at that—is an example of gendered behavior that is unconventional. In the book *Harry Potter and the Goblet of Fire*, for example, rumors circulate that Harry and Hermione are boyfriend and girlfriend. The two insist they are not dating and are just friends, and despite the teasing they endure from other children, they remain friends and do not end their close relationship. In their essay "Playing in the Gender Transgression Zone: Race, Class, and Hegemonic Masculinity in Middle Childhood," C. Shawn McGuffey and B. Lindsay Rich find that social spaces that involved heterosocial interactions were those most likely to be sites of patrolling and stigmatizing behaviors. "High-status boys maximize the influence of hegemonic masculinity and minimize gender transgressions by identifying social deviants and labeling them as outcasts" (McGuffey and Rich 1999: 618). We see this over and over in each book of the Harry Potter series, as Draco, Crabbe, and Goyle taunt Harry, Ron, and Hermione. These scenes function as a criticism of the social enforcement of hegemonic masculinity because readers are meant to identify with the protagonists being taunted, not with the stereotypically masculine bullies doing the taunting. Furthermore, readers witness the unconventional, heterosocial friendship among the three main characters as it endures, strengthens, and evolves over the years in each book.

This aspect of the books is especially significant when discussing the books as examples of fantasies that use motifs of the hero myth. In her book *Deconstructing the Hero: Literary Theory and Children's Literature*,

Margery Hourihan convincingly argues, "As Ursula Le Guin points out heroes are traditionally male and the hero myth inscribes male dominance and the primacy of male enterprises" (Hourihan 1997: 68). This is indeed often the case with the Harry Potter novels because Harry is a boy, most of his mentors are men, and most of his enemies are men. Hourihan writes, "If he does not travel alone the hero travels with a band of brothers, as Jason did with the Argonauts, or with a devoted male companion who is usually his inferior in some way" (p. 77). By the end of *Harry Potter and the Half-Blood Prince*, Harry is indeed beginning to follow the more conventional path of the heroic quest: "he simply knew that the task of discovering the truth about the real Horcrux had to be completed before he could move a little farther down the dark and winding path stretching ahead of him, the path that he and Dumbledore had set out upon together, and which he now knew he would have to journey alone" (pp. 635–6). However, although Harry feels alone at the end of *Harry Potter and the Half-Blood Prince*, Rowling does not seem to advocate the idea of the lone hero. For instance, there are several instances in the book when Voldemort is portrayed as evil precisely because he is a loner. Dumbledore, in explaining why Voldemort made Horcruxes to preserve parts of his soul, explains that Voldemort does not want to be dependent on others. "Voldemort likes to operate alone, remember. I believe that he would have found the thought of being dependent, even on the Elixir, intolerable" (p. 502). Harry and Dumbledore, conversely, seek out the help of others and see themselves as part of a community.

Even though Harry feels, near the end of the sixth book, that he must journey alone, his friends probably will not allow him to do this. Ron says of himself and Hermione, "We're with you whatever happens" (p. 651), and Harry seems ready to accept their offer of help and companionship. This is both like and unlike friendships in traditional heroic narratives. Hourihan writes:

> In stories in which the hero travels with a band of comrades the bonds between the members of the group are stronger than any friendships with outsiders, especially with women, and are represented as somehow "higher," more pure and more intense than any relationships involving sex. In this way they function as romantic images of the boys' gang, the sporting team, or the group of men who work and drink together and share a special camaraderie, which in Australia has been given almost mystical status in the concept of "mateship"—something no mere woman can understand. (1997: 83)

Harry has a band of comrades, but his comrades are not exclusively male. Hermione will clearly be by his side in the seventh book, and, from what we've seen in the first six books of the series, it would not be surprising to see Ginny and Luna included in on his quest as well. Harry's romantic involvement with Ginny, whom he likes, in part, because she is outspoken, smart, and a good Quidditch player, further complicates the tradition of the male band of comrades. Harry wants to protect Ginny from harm, but she has shown on several occasions an unwillingness to be protected and an ability to fight her own battles. Harry sometimes has stereotypical misconceptions about girls, but the girls in his life as part of a community of friends function to dispel some of these misconceptions: his heterosocial relationships with Hermione, Luna, and Ginny set him apart from the traditional heroic male with his male sidekick(s). It is significant, in fact, that the only exclusively male bands of comrades we see in the books are groups of bullies: Dudley and his gang of thugs, and Malfoy, Crabbe, and Goyle. The books' male villains—Voldemort, the Dursleys, and Draco—are mostly portrayed as excessively masculine bullies.

It is interesting that Draco Malfoy, who is portrayed as conventionally and negatively masculine for much of the series, is drawn sympathetically for the first time near the end of *Harry Potter and the Half-Blood Prince*. Both Harry and the reader learn that Draco, who is miserable about the horrible task Voldemort is forcing him to attempt, confides in Moaning Myrtle and cries in front of her. Myrtle says of him, "I mean he's sensitive, people bully him too, and he feels lonely and hasn't got anybody to talk to, and he's not afraid to show his feelings and cry" (p. 462). In a pivotal scene, Harry is shocked to see Draco crying, and Draco becomes enraged when he realizes Harry has witnessed this show of emotion, when he has been exposed as unconventionally masculine before the gaze of a male peer. "Malfoy gasped and gulped and then, with a great shudder, looked up into the cracked mirror and saw Harry staring at him over his shoulder. Malfoy wheeled around drawing his wand" (p. 522). Draco, always one-dimensionally cruel, is depicted here as a victim of Voldemort: he is a terrified boy whose father is imprisoned and who must kill his headmaster or be killed. By the end of the sixth book, Harry has hardened toward Snape, Dumbledore's murderer, but he has learned to see Draco, his enemy for six years, in ways that are more ambiguous, more sympathetic: "Where, Harry wondered, was Malfoy now, and what was Voldemort making him do under threat of killing him and his parents?" (p. 640). This new understanding for Draco Malfoy is due in part to Draco's demonstration of behavior that is not stereotypically masculine and in part to Harry's increasing maturity and ability to feel empathy.

Although several critics discuss some of the male characters in the novels as being feminine, I have purposely avoided using the terms *feminine* or *feminized* in this chapter to describe unconventional relationships or behaviors on the part of male characters to raise a particular point: these unconventional forms of masculinity are masculine characteristics, not feminine, even if they do not fit the mold of hegemonic masculinity. In her essay "Welcome to the Men's Club: Homosociality and the Maintenance of Hegemonic Masculinity," Sharon Bird argues that when we view nonconventional forms of masculinity as feminine, we deny men and boys access to aspects of their masculinity that are not hegemonic. She argues, "The presumption that hegemonic masculinity meanings are the only mutually accepted and legitimate masculinity meanings helps to reify hegemonic norms while suppressing meanings that might otherwise create a foundation for the subversion of the existing hegemony" (Bird 1996: 122). In other words, when Hagrid is nurturing or emotional, he is not being feminine, he is expressing an aspect of masculinity that is at odds with hegemonic masculinity. Furthermore, we sometimes see these expressions of unconventional masculinity policed throughout the books because that is what, realistically, happens to boys and men. Harry often, for example, polices himself by holding back tears and by restraining other expressions of emotion. It is significant that Rowling does not negatively portray unconventionally masculine behaviors. In fact, she paints sympathetic characterizations of boys and men who often have experiences and emotions at odds with perceived norms and who struggle to understand them.

Bird writes that even though many boys and men struggle with fitting into the mold of dominant masculinity, "masculinities that differ from the norm of hegemonic masculinity, however, are generally experienced as 'private dissatisfactions' rather than foundations for questioning the social construction of gender" (1996: 123). The varied depictions of Harry, Hagrid, Neville, Ron, Dumbledore, Lupin, Malfoy, and other male characters in the Harry Potter novels show us that unconventional versions of masculinity are quite prevalent—not merely private dissatisfactions—and these depictions show boys that they are not alone in their difficult negotiations with, on the margins of, and against hegemonic masculinity. By portraying a cast of boys and men performing a range of masculine characteristics and doing so in negotiation with hegemonic masculinity, Rowling's novels open up more possibilities for boys, portray broader definitions of what it means to be masculine, acknowledge a readership able to grapple with contradictions, and give readers characters and situations that test and contest the constructed borders of gender.

CONCLUSION
Marking Masculinity

> For it seems impossible to alter what has long not been altered. We are always coming on things that are too obvious for us to bother to understand them.
>
> —**Brecht (1964: 192)**

> The currently sanctioned appearance of maleness remains more or less what it always was: not a matter of wearing a costume, but instead, supposedly, a matter of not having one on. Masculinity is taken to be somehow natural and free—the state one achieves by resisting societal norms and being one's true self.
>
> —**Nodelman (2002: 2)**

When Bertolt Brecht wrote in his famous essay "A Short Organum for the Theatre" that some things are "too obvious for us to bother to understand them," he meant that some things seem so obvious that we do not work to understand them; we (mis)take them for common sense or assume that they are the natural way of things—permanent, unalterable, determined by nature and with fixed borders. Although femininity has long been understood by theorists to be largely a social construction, masculinity has undergone less scrutiny and is still often uninterrogated, seen as something not worthy of inquiry because it is often unmarked. If, as Nodelman states, masculinity is perceived as being "one's true self," then being a man still means being human, not being gendered, just as whiteness is seen as not being raced and heterosexuals do not need to "come out." To be unmarked is to be perceived as the norm against which the abnormal must define itself. There is great power and privilege in being unmarked: someone can be described in a newspaper as being a "police officer," not as a "black, female police officer"; someone can be an "actor," not a "gay actor"; and someone can see his or her experience of the world as universal, not as culturally specific. Indeed, attempts by marginalized groups to mark the unmarked by labeling people or characters as white or male or heterosexual are sometimes met with hostility because becoming marked destabilizes the norm by making it visible; it takes away the illusion of universality, and it takes away a position of privilege characterized by not having to work to understand one's position within a culture. Changing the ways our culture perceives dominant masculinity, and the hierarchal systems constructed in relation to it, must first begin with marking masculinity as a gender, making visible the ways it is both socially constructed and evolving, and creating spaces for child readers to see themselves as agents of change. This would involve less focus on what children are reading and increased emphasis on how they are reading and less focus on what a narrative depicts and increased emphasis on how narratives depict and on the ways narratives interact with readers within culture(s).

Prescriptions for texts that avoid gender stereotypes and positively depict counterhegemonic masculinity are only part of a solution, then. First, most male characters—Disney's Tarzan, Stanley and Zero, George and Harold, Harry Potter and friends—represent a combination of gendered traits that can be characterized as both stereotypical and nonstereotypical. Only the most one-dimensional characters are entirely stereotypically masculine, and these—Clayton in Disney's *Tarzan*, Mr. Sir, and Mr. Dursley—are marked as being so excessively macho that they present easy opportunities to critique an exaggerated version of dominant masculinity without having to interrogate it, without having to move into spaces that are below a surface reading of a text. Indeed, the excessive masculinity of many contemporary villainous manly men is almost too easy a target and often creates a dichotomy that works to smooth over the more complex, contradictory versions of dominant masculinity portrayed by popular male protagonists. Second, advocating didactic texts that model the ways we believe boys and men ought to behave is a problematic dictate because some of these texts—Disney's *Tarzan* and *Holes,* for example—are not as counterhegemonic as they may initially appear to be. Furthermore, Stephens argues that even if some texts are beginning to depict more versions of a "new man," "the constitution of an alternative hegemonic masculine paradigm may not in itself be a cause for celebration if all it achieves is the idealization of another model of masculinity" (Stephens 2002: xi). As long as subjectivity is part of a hierarchical binary, dominant versions of masculinity will be oppressive to people not granted full access to these. Stephens argues, "To degender social relations requires the resignification of masculinity and femininity so that they are not bounded and oppositional concepts. This remains a matter of unfinished business for children's literature" (p. xiv). The binaries we use to construct gender should be further destabilized, and I have worked to do this by exploring various ways dominant masculinity is constructed most often in opposition to an other or an abjection.

Of course, entirely resignifying masculinity and femininity is a difficult (perhaps utopian) goal partially because gendered subjectivity most often works to conceal the ways in which it is constructed, works *precisely because* it conceals its construction. Furthermore, so much of subject formation occurs in minutia, in an accretion of details that build on one another through repetition—innumerable insignificant moments join together to create the seamless-seeming narratives that shape our sense of self. In my introduction, I cited Peter Hollindale, who argues, "Ideology is not something which is transferred to children as if they were empty receptacles. It is something which they already possess, having drawn it from a mass of experiences far more powerful than literature" (Hollindale 1988: 17). And it is significant that most of these experiences, accumulated since birth, are largely unexamined.

For example, Michael Messner wrote an article based on his observations of his son's experience playing soccer in a league for four- and five-year-olds—an age he notes many sociologists point to as being a time when gender roles are beginning to become more solidified for many children. Teams in this soccer league were segregated by gender, and the children chose what to name their teams; the boys chose names such as the "Sea Monsters," and girls chose names such as the "Barbie Girls." As he observed both the children and the parents involved in the league, Messner began to notice a pattern: when children behaved in ways appropriate for their gender, parents would nod and say such things as, "They [boys and girls] are SO different!" and would discuss the obvious naturalness of their children's gender-appropriate behavior. Often, however, when the children behaved in ways that did not conform to expectations for their gender, the parents ignored this behavior or, in some cases, actively discouraged it. Indeed, even though the boys and girls often shared many behaviors—they all played soccer, they all cried over injuries, they all occasionally ignored their coaches—the many ways boys and girls were alike were not noticed, not commented on, and not marked. "In the entire subsequent season of weekly games and practices, I never once saw adults point to a moment in which boy and girl soccer players were doing the *same* thing and exclaim to each other, 'Look at them! They are so *similar!*'" (Messner 2000: 770). It is as if the parents needed to convince themselves that their sons and daughters were opposites and that all we have in common as humans, all the players had in common as children, is less significant than the differences we use to define ourselves. And it is ironic that the parents who so heartily insisted on the naturalness of their children's gendered behaviors were actually actively contributing to the socialization of their children by reinforcing what was appropriate and by ignoring or dissuading what was not. As Kenneth Kidd notes when discussing the discourse of boyology, we want to teach boys how to naturally be boys, but we seem to be unaware of the paradox inherent in this.

Indeed, this paradox of constructed naturalness is vital to the maintenance of hegemonic masculinity. In her book *Critical Practice*, Catherine Belsey argues that ideology "is apparent in all that is 'obvious' to us" (Belsey 1980: 57). She continues:

> Ideology obscures the real conditions of existence by presenting partial truths. It is a set of omissions, gaps rather than lies, smoothing over contradictions, appearing to provide answers to questions which in reality it evades, and masquerading as coherence in the interests of the social relations generated by and necessary to the reproduction of the existing mode of production. (Belsey 1980: 58)

Therefore, texts and readings of texts that work to make visible the gaps and contradictions necessary to construct and reify gendered subjectivity can aid in reimagining gender in ways that are more fluid and inclusive. Highlighting the ways abjection functions in narratives for and about boys is one way to mark those spaces where borders are formed, a way to make visible the gaps, contradictions, and paradoxes that work to smooth over the unanswered questions and anxieties about shifting gender roles that trouble both child and adult readers.

My analysis of the evolving icon of Tarzan is an attempt to make visible the ways dominant masculinity in the United States is constructed through an intricate web of social relations in which race, nation, colonialism, class, individualism, bodies, and freedom of movement work together, sometimes in contradictory ways, to define the fantasy of the ideal American man. My analyses of Disney's *Tarzan, Holes,* Captain Underpants, and *Dragon Ball Z* all focus on the contradictions inherent in the ways masculinity is currently being constructed in these popular texts and the gaps that these contradictions make visible. My final chapter on the Harry Potter series is an attempt to account for texts within the context of a culture many boys in the United States inhabit.

Within the confines of contemporary boy culture, I tried to reimagine an analysis of gender in the series in a manner that moves beyond discussing stereotypes or the binary of gender roles into a space that allows for more fluid definitions of gender, and I tried to do so in ways that account for the limits of the everyday lives of boys, who are not empty receptacles and who already have gender defined for them in myriad ways. This chapter is also an attempt to highlight those potential moments of affinity between genders that are possible only with portrayals of complex, multifaceted subjectivity.

In each chapter, I wanted to analyze texts in ways that did not discount boys as agents, readers, and thinkers and that simultaneously did not assume that boys are empty receptacles or blank slates. "It is important to consider how boys are influenced by cultural messages and social pressures but also how boys draw on their continually evolving self-knowledge and conceptions of reality as they develop an understanding of who they are and what they are like" (Way and Chu 2004: 79). Perhaps the best texts for boy readers (and girl readers), both popular and literary, are those that envision the child reader as capable of understanding and acting, those texts that work to engage child readers in some of the discussions we usually reserve for adults, and those texts that avoid didactically prescribing a predetermined path toward adulthood, a definitive childhood's end where identity is finally discovered as always already bounded. In other words, there are resistant ways of reading hegemonic texts, but there are also texts that lend themselves more to resistant readings, even some of the texts or some portions of texts that make up popular culture. Representation can be a tool of repression but also can be a means of resistance, especially when it highlights seams of ideology and makes gaps visible instead of merely filling them in. Stephens writes that, "Children's literature can make a significant contribution to whether or not child readers understand the conflict between the possibilities of forging new subjective agency and the propensity of a hegemonic social structure to represent itself as always already given and inevitable" (Stephens 2002: xiii).

Because many, perhaps most, children's texts fall into the latter category Stephens describes, our job as literary critics, parents, and educators is to not only give boys and girls the opportunity to read texts that portray alternative ways of being male but also give them the critical tools they need to read and interrogate all the texts that surround them in their daily lives, including those popular texts that are sometimes dismissed as not worthy of critical attention or sometimes benignly described as "just entertainment" but that function—perhaps, through sheer repetition, even more so than many literary texts—as cultural artifacts working to shape ideology, culture, and subjectivity. We need to carefully examine and teach our children to carefully examine those popular texts that often have gone underneath the radar of literary critics because they seem beneath consideration or seem to be fads that are too short-lived to bother with in the slow-paced world of academic publishing or because we may feel we do not always have the critical language to discuss texts that seem so foreign to us because they are speaking to another generation.

Understanding and making visible the ways masculinity functions in popular, commercially successful texts are vital to ultimately beginning to understand the broad array of texts that make up contemporary children's culture. If we listen to our boys and read along with them the same texts they are reading, viewing, and consuming, we may better be able to understand the difficult negotiations they currently must make as they form their gendered identities within, against, or on the margins of hegemonic masculinity. Quite a few of the popular texts adults dismiss as being violent, stereotypical, less than literary, or silly actually portray for boy readers the anxieties that boys (both male protagonists and male readers) feel about the conflicting messages they receive about what it means to be a boy in the contemporary United States. Instead of working to censor and control the texts boys choose to read, we would do boys a far greater service by carefully working to understand contemporary children's culture and by helping them to become critical readers of all of the texts they enjoy.

NOTES

PROLOGUE

1. "In 1970, 43 percent of degrees were awarded to women; by 1997, the percentage had increased to 56 percent, effectively reversing the ratio from 1970. Nationwide, this split is now about 55:45 and is expected to approach 60:40 by the year 2010" (p. 37). Thomas Newkirk, 2002, *Misreading Masculinity: Boys, Literacy, and Popular Culture*.
2. For more detailed discussions of these studies see, for example, Kenneth Kidd's *Making American Boys: Boyology and the Feral Tale* (2004), Thomas Newkirk's *Misreading Masculinity: Boys, Literacy, and Popular Culture* (2002), Michael Smith and Jeffrey Wilhelm's *"Reading Don't Fix No Chevys": Literacy in the Lives of Young Men* (2002), Bruce Pirie's *Teenage Boys and High School English* (2002), Dan Kindlon and Michael Thompson's *Raising Cain: Protecting the Emotional Life of Boys* (1999), and a collection edited by Niobe Way and Judy Y. Chu titled *Adolescent Boys: Exploring Diverse Cultures of Boyhood* (2004).
3. The American Library Association notes in its annual report of the top ten most challenged and censored books a recent increase in challenges to books that portray gay characters: "Three of the 10 books on the 'Ten Most Challenged Books of 2004' were cited for homosexual themes—which is the highest number in a decade." Those three books are *The Perks of Being a Wallflower* by Stephen Chbosky, *King & King* by Linda de Haan and Stern Nijland, and *I Know Why the Caged Bird Sings* by Maya Angelou. It is interesting to note, as well, that with the exception of Angelou's book and Sonya Sones's *What My Mother Doesn't Know*, most of the books that made the ALA's most censored list for 2004 are books that many would consider as being texts for and about boys: *The Chocolate War* by Robert Cormier, *Fallen Angels* by Walter Dean Myers, *Arming America: The Origins of a National Gun Culture* by Michael A. Bellesiles, the Captain Underpants series by Dav Pilkey, *In the Night Kitchen* by Maurice Sendak, and *Of Mice and Men* by John Steinbeck.

"*The Chocolate War* tops 2004 most challenged book list." American Library Association, 2005, http://www.ala.org/ala/pressreleases2005/februarya/2004mostchallengedbook.htm (accessed June 3, 2005).

4. Researchers are just recently beginning to pay more attention to boys in the United States who are immigrants, or homosexual, or bisexual, or working class, or poor, or from various cultural, racial, or ethnic backgrounds. What some are finding is that although there is a dominant version of masculinity in the United States that privileges white, heterosexual, middle-class boys, boys from other groups must conform to definitions of masculinity that are also influenced by their subcultures. These boys must make complex negotiations to bridge the expectations of dominant culture and the different expectations of their own culture, and they often must do so while battling against racism, homophobia, or class barriers. See, especially, *Adolescent Boys: Exploring Diverse Cultures of Boyhood* (2004), edited by Niobe Way and Judy Y. Chu.

5. They report:

> On average, they [white, middle-class boys] are not dropping out of school, avoiding college or lacking in verbal skills. Although we have been hearing that boys are virtually disappearing from college classrooms, the truth is that among whites, the gender composition of colleges is pretty balanced: 51 percent female and 49 percent male, according to the National Education Association. In Ivy League colleges, men still outnumber women.
>
> One group of studies found that although poor and working-class boys lag behind girls in reading when they get to middle school, boys in the wealthiest schools do not fall behind, either in middle school or in high school. University of Michigan education professor Valerie Lee reports that gender differences in academic performance are "small to moderate."
>
> When it comes to academic achievement, race and class completely swamp gender. The Urban Institute reports that 76 percent of students who live in middle- to higher-income areas are likely to graduate from high school, while only 56 percent of students who live in lower-income areas are likely to do so. Among whites in Boston public schools, for every 100 males who graduate, 104 females do. A tiny gap. (Rivers and Barnett 2006: B01)

INTRODUCTION

1. I decided, to limit the focus of this project, to look mainly at popular fictional texts, but the nonfiction texts that boys enjoy also need to be written about and analyzed more than they have been to date by literary scholars.

CHAPTER 1

1. In her doctoral dissertation titled *Edgar Rice Burroughs, Tarzan, and Pulp Fiction: The Making of Modern American Manhood,* Jean De Silva writes of Tarzan's impact on American culture:

   > Let us consider these statistics: twenty-four Tarzan novels published between 1914 and 1965, drawn from twenty-five pulp magazine stories published between 1912 and 1941; two additional Tarzan novels written for children within that same period; eight silent films, released between 1918 and 1930, followed by thirty-two more films in sound (and eventually color) from the thirties through the late sixties. The Tarzan character populated other media as they rose to prominence, too. Since 1929, a Tarzan comic strip has been in continuous production. In the late 1930s, the character aired on radio; in the 60s, he was featured in a primetime TV series, and in the 70s, Tarzan joined the Saturday morning line-up of children's cartoons. Over the next two decades, the character returned to the movie screen in three quite different films aimed at teen and adult audiences, and also in an animated Disney production for children. In the 1990s, too, a cable series, *The New Adventures of Tarzan,* ran for a few seasons, offering sword-and-sorcery plots similar to those of the popular *Xena: The Warrior Princess.* Finally, Tarzan and Edgar Rice Burroughs have a number of websites devoted to them; one even publishes a weekly electronic fan magazine on the author and his characters. (pp. 98–99)

2. See, for example, Rolf Romören's essay "The Light of Knowledge—In the Midst of the Jungle: How Tarzan Became a Man." *CREArTA* 2, no. 2 (2001–2): 60–67, which discusses various versions of the story as following the pattern of the traditional Bildungsroman.
3. "Pulp magazines were so called because of the inexpensive, porous paper on which they were printed. They specialized in stories that were formulaic concoctions, long on twisting plot, offered in double-columned monthly installments to a mass readership. Tales of adventure, mystery, war, the Wild West, and science fiction were their stock-in-trade. These attracted a predominantly male following of adolescent boys and both blue- and white-collar men, as well as a significant number of women, as readers' letters attest" (Kasson 2001: 167).
4. Burroughs knew very little about Africa, and his books have been criticized for representing more a colonial fantasy than an attempt to accurately depict Africa: "He would have grown up reading accounts of romantic European explorers, even though he was aware that in the years since his birth, Africa had quickly passed from being the object of the most lofty professions of philanthropy to being the target of the most rapacious imperial greed. More particularly, he would have read extensive newspaper accounts of one of the first modern mass atrocities, the enslavement and death of millions in the Congo Free State under the aegis of King Leopold II of Belgium" (Kasson 2001: 184). Kasson continues, pointing out that, "despite Conrad's searing depiction of

evil at the core of the 'civilizing' enterprise, tropical Africa remained in Burroughs's and the public's imagination a great arena for white male adventure, one of the last wild places on earth" (p. 184).

5. Like many authors, Burroughs relies on descriptions of physical features to reveal character, but his descriptions are tied directly to dubious late-nineteenth-century and early-twentieth-century theories about the science of race. In his book *Against Race: Imagining Political Culture beyond the Color Line,* Paul Gilroy argues that anatomizations of the body were key to scientific discourse at the turn of the century that attempted to create clear, biological borders between races and that this "science" was key to reifying race as a category. He writes:

> The enduring power of the best-known visual material—depictions of Caucasian and Nordic heads or of the various skulls to be measured, drawn, and classified—was more than an iconic counterpoint to the inscription of respectable racial science. It raises the interesting possibility that cognition of "race" was never an exclusively linguistic process and involved from its inception a distinctive visual and optical imaginary. (Gilroy 2000: 35)

Burroughs's *Tarzan of the Apes* is indeed visual (which is why, perhaps, it has translated so well into film, television, and comic books). Physical descriptions in Burroughs's books are more than just imagery though; they are based on very specific cultural assumptions and work to establish clearly defined racial boundaries. Tarzan's father is described as having features that are "regular and strong" (p. 2), and Tarzan inherits his father's "superior" genetic makeup. In a chapter appropriately titled "Heredity," Jane admires the jungle god who rescues her from a brutal ape. As Tarzan swings through the trees, holding her in his strong arms, she looks up and sees that "the face above her was one of extraordinary beauty" and that it is "a perfect type of the strongly masculine" (p. 181). Burroughs, indeed, devotes pages to physical descriptions of the "godlike" Tarzan with a perfect body and a "well-shaped head upon his broad shoulders": "What a perfect creature!" Jane exclaims (p. 183).

6. Most historians estimate that about three thousand people, most of them black men, were lynched in the American South between around 1880 and 1930. Lynchings were often gruesome public spectacles that were publicized and attended by sometimes hundreds or even thousands of onlookers. Postcards of lynchings were sold and mailed around the country, and sometimes fingers and toes of victims were collected as souvenirs.

7. Just as depictions of dangerous Africans or African Americans are necessary to constructions of white dominance (they work to justify acts of violence), so is the construction of the safe, controlled African American or native African key to the maintenance of a racist system. The domesticated, asexual, nonthreatening servant, happy in his or her subservient role, is a common trope in American texts of the

late nineteenth and early twentieth centuries and represents the white supremacists' fantasized end result of violence and repression: a content, docile labor force. The slave or servant who takes joy in servitude, and who often functions in literature and film as comic relief, is just as dehumanizing as the stereotype of the evil, dangerous black man or woman. Esmeralda, Jane's obese, African American servant, serves this function in the text. For example, in the following scene she is being attacked by a wild animal:

> With a horrified scream the poor woman rose to her hands and knees and in this position scurried across the room, shrieking: "O Gaberelle! O Gaberelle!" at the top of her lungs. Esmeralda weighed some two hundred and eighty pounds, and her extreme haste, added to her extreme corpulancy, produced a most amazing result when Esmeralda elected to travel on all fours. (p. 131)

When Jane is attacked, it is depicted as a violation; when Esmeralda is attacked, it is funny. Esmeralda, modeled after the mammy stereotype, is loyal to Jane, asexual, uneducated, silly, and nonthreatening. For example, Tarzan, without any knowledge of Western culture, sizes up the group of explorers who have landed on the shore of his jungle immediately: he dislikes the coarse sailors, he likes the upper-class white explorers, and "as for the big black woman, she was evidently connected in some way to the girl, and so he liked her, also" (p. 124). Esmeralda represents a safe, domesticated blackness because she is connected to the girl; her identity is established in relation to the white woman she serves. The character of Esmeralda serves as a foil to the native Africans, who are not subservient and not under the control of white men, who govern themselves in their own village, who are not Christian, and who have not been stripped of their culture. She represents not a fully realized character but a caricature and the fantasized end result of successful colonization and domination.

8. Burroughs briefly mentions the exploitation of native Africans in the novel: John Clayton, Tarzan's father, is sent to Africa to investigate the abuses of "another European power" (p. 2). In other words, he has been sent by the British Empire to police the actions of another (presumably lesser and less moral) European power, which is going about colonizing in inappropriate ways. Clayton is depicted as upright in his role as a moral and paternalistic colonizer protecting the natives from the corruption of others: the text implies that there are wrong and right ways to colonize a country but never implicates colonization as a practice.
9. The violence is also justified because the Africans are carefully portrayed not as natives protecting their land from intruders but as intruders invading Tarzan's jungle. The cabin Lord Greystoke builds is on a deserted beach but then is invaded by wild animals and apes from the jungle. Tarzan lives in an uninhabited jungle until native Africans move into

his territory and kill his adoptive ape mother, at which point he is put into the position of having to defend his space. At the time when *Tarzan of the Apes* was written, many white Americans felt America was being invaded by foreign others. Catherine Jurca, in her book *White Diaspora: The Suburb and the Twentieth-Century American Novel*, writes, "While Tarzan was busy making the African Jungle safe for civilized white people, native-born white Americans watched with dismay as a flood of foreign-looking immigrants from southern and eastern Europe and the beginnings of black migration cityward created an urban jungle within the United States" (Jurca 2001: 22). Tarzan's ability to terrorize and control the invading native Africans and his ability to protect middle- and upper-class white Americans and northern Europeans (the "higher white races") work to make him a champion for his race and class but also make visible the anxieties felt by these groups during this time: a fear that the foreign Other would cross our borders and become us.

10. For example, the son of Lord Greystoke naturally becomes lord of the jungle. However, in the original text, as Jurca points out, Tarzan's upbringing is not entirely that of a feral jungle child. Tarzan, as a boy, discovers the cabin his father built on the beach, which is filled with ingenious inventions, books, journals, pictures, and other trappings of British civilization. Jurca writes:

> The handsome, distinguished gentleman that Tarzan becomes is Burroughs's tribute to the indomitable blood of Anglo-Saxon aristocrats, but it is not the case that heredity simply triumphs over environment. Rather, Tarzan's inherent nobility must be cultivated in the right environment. The house that one gentleman has naturally built becomes the site where another gentleman is naturally constructed, where the primitive virility produced by Tarzan's jungle training is refined by the recuperative influence of his Anglo-Saxon heritage. (Jurca 2001: 33)

It is significant that by studying the books left behind by his parents, Tarzan inherits the language of the Father and is able to name himself and Others. As he looks through a child's picture dictionary and matches signifier to signified, he learns, for instance, that "he was M-A-N, they were A-P-E-S" (Burroughs 1912/1963: 57). In this scene, both self and Other are constructed for him through language, and he enters into the Symbolic Order through words left to him by his father. After this point in the novel, he begins to distance himself from the apes and eventually gains a mastery over them by killing the alpha males. Such oedipal struggles—often portrayed as necessary for coming into autonomous manhood—are common in heroic narratives.

11. De Silva uses Janice Radway's work on romance novels to argue that the original Tarzan texts were read by and appealed to women readers partially because they followed the formula of the romance. Viewed in this light, then, this scene could be read as being part of a "bodice-ripper" romance, which appealed to female fans of the stories.
12. Kasson also argues that Tarzan and other popular figures in the early twentieth century "contributed to a new popular interest in the male nude as a symbol of ideals in peril and a promise of their supremacy, as a monument to strength and a symbol of vulnerability, as an emblem of discipline and an invitation to erotic fantasy" (Kasson 2001: 8).

CHAPTER 2

1. In the film adaptation of *Holes* (directed by Andrew Davis, Walt Disney Pictures, 2003), Mr. Sir's real name is revealed to be Marion at the end of the film. A camper says, "That's not a man's name," to which Mr. Sir replies, "It's not." Mr. Sir's macho behavior is explained in the film as being compensation for having a feminine name. He is ridiculed at the film's end when his performance of masculinity is revealed as a performance.
2. See, for example, Michael Smith and Jeffrey Wilhelm, *"Reading Don't Fix No Chevys": Literacy and the Lives of Young Men* (Portsmouth, NH: Heinemann, 2002). The authors claim, "More personally, both of us have taken on very different gender roles than those of our fathers, and what we found out during this research project itself emphasized to us that boys today experience different cultural expectations than we did as young men thirty years ago. For instance, the boys in this study expressed radically more liberal attitudes toward homosexuality and feminism than we expected and that our social groups possessed in the late sixties and early seventies" (p. 7).
3. In the film adaptation of the novel, the nail polish is no longer red. It is instead a shade of pink or purple, and it no longer matches the blood on Mr. Sir's face. The Warden's makeup box is brass, not flowered, and there is no mention that it resembles anything that belongs to Stanley's mother. This is one of several scenes in the film that is not as surreal or as disturbing as is depicted in the book.
4. The most frightening teacher in Sachar's wonderfully surreal series of books about the Wayside School is the reptilian Mrs. Gorf, who is pictured in the illustrations as having a forked tongue. In *Sideways Stories from Wayside School* (New York: HarperCollins, 1985), Mrs. Gorf wiggles her pointed ears and—in a creepy conflation of Eve and the serpent—she turns helpless school children into apples. She is vanquished when the students manage to turn her into an apple and she is eaten.
5. It is interesting to note that this scene was entirely cut from the film adaptation of the book.

6. Sachar has written a sequel to *Holes* titled *Small Steps* (2006), which does not contain the surreal imagery or folktale elements of the original novel. Critical reception of the sequel has been lukewarm.

CHAPTER 3

1. The boys' repeated persecution by uptight adults can be read in two very different ways. Boys may identify with George and Harold because boys have recently become the topic of scrutiny by adults and because boys are indeed unfairly labeled and criticized. However, George and Harold often are in trouble for vandalizing school property, disrupting class, and destroying the work of their peers. The author sometimes seems to imply that "boys will be boys" and George and Harold should be entitled to behave badly without consequences. In this sense, then, the books can be encouraging boy readers to feel a sense of male entitlement.
2. The author's affinity with the naughty characters in his books marks the books in the Captain Underpants series as belonging to a tradition Kenneth Kidd calls the "bad boy genre." Kidd argues that in such books the "boy subject is the author's young self in thin disguise, which implies that the boy will grow (has already grown) into a special kind of man, the man of letters" (2004: 53). This clearly is the case with the Captain Underpants books and the accompanying narrative the author has created about himself. Like the two boys in the books, the author was a disruptive student but was smart. His teachers predicted he would accomplish little in life, but he proved them wrong. The assumption is that George and Harold are just mischievous little boys who will eventually grow up to be smart, literate adults like the author. This assumption, however, is one based on entitlement. As Kidd points out, "The Bad Boy's delinquency is safely middle-class" (p. 54). The boys in such narratives can afford to be naughty and disruptive because they can count on inheriting a position of privilege when they grow into men—their "boys will be boys" antics are tolerated because we believe they will become safe, middle-class adults.
3. In its winter 2003–4 online newsletter at ncac.org, the National Coalition against Censorship (NCAC) listed several recent cases as examples:

    > In October in Atlanta, Georgia, 14-year-old honors student Robin Boim was expelled from Roswell High School for writing in her personal journal about a student who fell asleep in class and dreamed that she had killed a teacher. A hearing, in which the state poet laureate and a literary magazine publisher testified to Robin's creativity and the nonthreatening nature of her writing, failed to lift her expulsion, but, after press reports, the Board of Education allowed her to return to school, pending a future hearing.
    >
    > In San Jose, California, a 15-year-old spent 90 days in detention and was expelled from Santa Teresa High School for writing poetry school

officials considered too violent. In 2001, "Julius" was prosecuted for showing two classmates his "dark" poem including one with the line "I can be the next kid to bring guns to kill students at school." In an amicus brief filed in the California Supreme Court opposing criminal charges against him, Nobel and Pulitzer literary prize winners J.M. Coetzee and Michael Chabon wrote, "Poetry is an artistic medium particularly well suited for the examination of one's own potential for depravity. The developing genre of 'dark poetry,' as practiced by 'Julius,' is merely a continuation of this literary tradition." NCAC joined the free speech and literary groups' brief.

Eleven-year-old Dylan Finkle, a student at H.B. Thompson Middle School in Syosset, New York, was subjected to psychological testing in November, without parental permission, and suspended after he read aloud in class a novel from his journal based on the teenage slasher movie, *Halloween*.

Dylan had discussed his novel with his parents who agreed that he could use his own name as the fictional killer and his friends' names as victims if they gave permission. He was suspended by school officials for more than six weeks for making "threats of violence." Moreover, school administrators telephoned parents of students who were named in the novel to tell them that Dylan had threatened their children without explaining it was just a story. Appeals to the School Board to lift the suspension were unsuccessful. The case is under review by the State Education Commissioner and is being watched closely by the New York Civil Liberties Union and others. (NCAC 2003-4)

4. I have heard several anecdotes from parents and teachers who tell me they have noticed there are quite a few girls who do not like the books in the Captain Underpants series. A student, for example, told me that her younger sister hated the books and complained to her family when her second-grade teacher read one of them aloud to her class. I could find no quantitative research to support these anecdotes, but I find them interesting and relevant: girls, perhaps, are not too pleased to read books that routinely depict the feminine as Other or as abjection.

CHAPTER 5

1. Giselle Liza Anatol problematizes the otherness of the Wizarding world in her essay titled "The Fallen Empire: Exploring Ethnic Otherness in the World of Harry Potter." She writes, "Rowling employs a discourse of difference—one that appears to embrace the landscape of the foreign and the situation of the outsider, heightening the books' appeal to children who remain outside of positions of power and agency in society" (p. 164). However, she goes on to complicate this reading: "Beneath this aspect of foreignness, however, lies the fact that the excursions to Hogwarts are not away from the homeland and to a symbolic colonial outpost, but

rather journeys back to Harry's true homespace" (p. 167), a homespace that is marked as imperialist, for example, by colonialism in the form of Bill and Charlie's colonial enterprises in far-off lands.
2. At the end of *Harry Potter and the Half-Blood Prince,* Snape has become an even more mysterious, ambiguous character. There is much debate among fans about Snape's role as Dumbledore's murderer, about Harry's interpretations or misinterpretations of Snape's actions, and about the future of their relationship.

BIBLIOGRAPHY

FICTION, FILM, AND VIDEO GAME TEXTS

Anderson, M.T. *Feed.* Cambridge, MA: Candlewick, 2002.
Angelou, Maya. *I Know Why the Caged Bird Sings.* New York: Random House, 1970.
Beauty and the Beast. Directed by Gary Trousdale. Walt Disney Pictures, 1991.
Bellesiles, Michael. *Arming America: The Origins of a National Gun Culture.* Brooklyn, NY: Soft Skull Press, 2000.
Burroughs, Edgar Rice. *Tarzan of the Apes.* 1912. New York: Del Rey, 1963.
Carroll, Lewis. *Alice's Adventures in Wonderland and Through the Looking Glass.* 1866. New York: Signet, 2000.
Chbosky, Stephen. *The Perks of Being a Wallflower.* New York: Pocket Books, 1999.
Conrad, Joseph. *Heart of Darkness.* 1902. New York: Penguin, 1995.
Cormier, Robert. *The Chocolate War.* New York: Random House, 1974.
_____. *Tenderness.* New York: Delacorte, 1997.
Crutcher, Chris. *Staying Fat for Sarah Byrnes.* New York: Harper Tempest, 1994.
_____. *Whale Talk.* New York: HarperCollins, 2001.
Dahl, Roald. *Matilda.* New York: Puffin Books, 1988.
Defoe, Daniel. *Robinson Crusoe.* 1719. New York: Alfred A. Knopf, Everyman's Library, 1993.
De Haan, Linda, and Stern Nijland. *King & King.* Berkeley, CA: Tricycle Press, 2000.
Dinosaur. Directed by Eric Leighton. Walt Disney Pictures, 2000.
Farmer, Nancy. *The House of the Scorpion.* New York: Antheneum, 2002.
Finding Nemo. Directed by Andrew Stanton. Walt Disney Pictures, 2003.
Frank, E.R. *America.* New York: Simon and Schuster, 2002.
Gantos, Jack. *Jack's New Power.* New York: Farrar, Straus, and Giroux, 1995.
Greystoke: The Legend of Tarzan, Lord of the Apes. Directed by Hugh Hudson. Warner Bros., 1984.
Hartinger, Brent. *Geography Club.* New York: HarperCollins, 2003.
Hercules. Directed by Ron Clements. Walt Disney Pictures, 1997.

Holes. Directed by Andrew Davis. Walt Disney Pictures, 2003.
The Iron Giant. Directed by Brad Bird. Warner Bros., 1999.
Jimenez, Francisco. *The Circuit: Stories from the Life of a Migrant Child*. Albuquerque: University of New Mexico Press, 1997.
The Lion King. Directed by Roger Allers and Rob Minkoff. Walt Disney Pictures, 1994.
Lowry, Lois. *The Giver*. Boston: Houghton Mifflin, 1993.
Mulan. Directed by Barry Cook and Tony Bancroft. Walt Disney Pictures, 1998.
Myers, Walter Dean. *Scorpions*. New York: HarperCollins, 1988.
_____. *Monster*. New York: HarperCollins, 1999.
_____. *Bad Boy: A Memoir*. New York: HarperCollins, 2001.
Pilkey, Dav. *The Adventures of Captain Underpants*. New York: Scholastic, 1997.
_____. *Captain Underpants and the Attack of the Talking Toilets*. New York: Scholastic, 1999a.
_____. *Captain Underpants and the Invasion of the Incredibly Naughty Cafeteria Ladies from Outer Space (and the Subsequent Assault of the Equally Evil Lunchroom Zombie Nerds)*. New York: Scholastic, 1999b.
_____. *Captain Underpants and the Perilous Plot of Professor Poopypants*. New York: Scholastic, 2000.
_____. *Captain Underpants and the Wrath of the Wicked Wedgie Woman*. New York: Scholastic, 2001.
_____. *The Adventures of Super Diaper Baby*. New York: Scholastic, 2002.
_____. *Captain Underpants and the Big, Bad Battle of the Bionic Booger Boy, Part 1: The Night of the Nasty Nostril Nuggets*. New York: Scholastic, 2003a.
_____. *Captain Underpants and the Big, Bad Battle of the Bionic Booger Boy, Part 2: The Revenge of the Ridiculous Robo-Boogers*. New York: Scholastic, 2003b.
Rowling, J.K. *Harry Potter and the Sorcerer's Stone*. New York: Scholastic, 1997.
_____. *Harry Potter and the Chamber of Secrets*. New York: Scholastic, 1999a.
_____. *Harry Potter and the Prisoner of Azkaban*. New York: Scholastic, 1999b.
_____. *Harry Potter and the Goblet of Fire*. New York: Scholastic, 2000.
_____. *Harry Potter and the Order of the Phoenix*. New York: Scholastic, 2003.
_____. *Harry Potter and the Half-Blood Prince*. New York: Scholastic, 2005.
Sachar, Louis. *Sideways Stories from Wayside School*. New York: HarperCollins, 1985.
_____. *Holes*. New York: Dell Yearling, 1998.
_____. *Small Steps*. New York: Delacorte, 2006.
Sendak, Maurice. *In the Night Kitchen*. New York: Harper & Row, 1970.
Sones, Sonya. *What My Mother Doesn't Know*. New York: Simon and Schuster, 2001.

Spinelli, Jerry. *Maniac Magee.* New York: Little, Brown, 1990.
_____. *Crash.* New York: Knopf, 1996.
_____. *Wringer.* New York: HarperCollins, 1997.
Steinbeck, John. *Of Mice and Men.* 1937. New York: Penguin, 1993.
Tarzan. Directed by Kevin Lima and Chris Buck. Walt Disney Pictures, 1999.
Tarzan II. Directed by Brian Smith. Walt Disney Video, 2005.
Tarzan, the Ape Man. Directed by W.S. Van Dyke. Metro-Goldwyn-Mayer, 1932.
Tarzan Untamed. Playstation II video game. Ubi Soft, 2001.
Tashjian, Janet. *The Gospel According to Larry.* New York: Henry Holt, 2001.
Toy Story. Directed by John Lasseter. Walt Disney Pictures and Pixar Animation Studios, 1995.
Wallace, Rich. *Wrestling Sturbridge.* New York: Knopf, 1996.
Walter, Virginia, and Katrina Roeckelein. *Making Up Megaboy.* New York: Delacorte, 1999.
Wieler, Diana. *Bad Boy.* Toronto and Vancouver: Groundwood Books, Douglas & McIntyre, 1989.

SECONDARY SOURCES

Allison, Anne. "Cuteness as Japan's Millennial Product." In *Pikachu's Global Adventure: The Rise and Fall of Pokémon,* edited by Joseph Tobin, 34–52. Durham, NC: Duke University Press, 2004.
American Library Association Web site. December 1, 2005, http://ala.org.
Anatol, Giselle Liza. "The Fallen Empire: Exploring Ethnic Otherness in the World of Harry Potter." In *Reading Harry Potter: Critical Essays,* edited by Giselle Liza Anatol, 163–78. Westport, CT: Praeger, 2003.
Bakhtin, Mikhail. *Rabelais and His World.* Translated by Helene Iswolsky. Bloomington: Indiana University Press, 1984.
Bauerline, Mark, and Sandra Stotsky. "Why Johnny Won't Read." *Washington Post,* January 25, 2005, A15.
Belsey, Catherine. *Critical Practice.* London: Methuen, 1980.
Beneke, Timothy. *Proving Manhood: Reflections on Men and Sexism.* Berkeley: University of California Press, 1997.
Bereska, Tami. "The Changing Boys' World in the 20th Century: Reality and 'Fiction.'" *Journal of Men's Studies* 11, no. 2 (2003): 157–74.
Bilz, Rachelle Lasky. *Life Is Tough: Guys, Growing Up, and Young Adult Literature.* Lanham, MD: Scarecrow Press, 2004.
Bird, Sharon R. "Welcome to the Men's Club: Homosociality and the Maintenance of Hegemonic Masculinity." *Gender and Society* 10, no. 2 (1996): 120–32.
Blake, Andrew. *The Irresistible Rise of Harry Potter.* New York: Verso, 2002.

Bloomberg, Simon. "It's Rubbish, but It Keeps Them Quiet." *Nelson Mail* (New Zealand), April 19, 2003, 144. Lexis-Nexis Database. Eastern Michigan University Library, Ypsilanti, MI. http://www.lexisnexis.com (accessed April 7, 2004).

Bosmajian, Hamida. "Reading the Unconscious: Psychoanalytical Criticism." In *Understanding Children's Literature: Key Essays from the International Companion Encyclopedia of Children's Literature,* edited by Peter Hunt, 100–11. London: Routledge, 1999.

Brecht, Bertolt. *Brecht on Theatre*. Edited and translated by John Willett. New York: Hill and Wang, 1964.

Brians, Paul. "Common Errors in English." February 21, 2004. Washington State University. www.wsu.edu/~brians/errors/index.html (accessed January 8, 2005).

Brozo, William G. *To Be a Boy, To Be a Reader: Engaging Teen and Preteen Boys in Active Literacy*. Knoxville: University of Tennessee Press, 2002.

Business Wire. "Funmation's Dragonball Still at the Top on Lycos; Popular Television Series in Top 10 on the Lycos 50 for 200 Weeks." June 26, 2003. Lexis-Nexis Database. Eastern Michigan University Library, Ypsilanti, MI. http://www.lexisnexis.com (accessed April 7, 2004).

Butler, Judith. *Bodies That Matter: On the Discursive Limits of "Sex."* New York: Routledge, 1993.

Cheyfitz, Eric. "Tarzan of the Apes: US Foreign Policy in the Twentieth Century." *American Literary History* 1, no. 2 (1989): 339–60. Eastern Michigan University Library, Ypsilanti, MI. www.jstor.org (accessed May 17, 2004).

Coats, Karen. *Looking Glasses and Neverlands: Lacan, Desire, and Subjectivity in Children's Literature*. Iowa City: University of Iowa Press, 2004.

Creed, Barbara. *The Monstrous Feminine: Film, Feminism, Psychoanalysis*. New York: Routledge, 1993.

Darwin, Charles. *The Descent of Man, and Selection in Relation to Sex*. 1871. Princeton, NJ: Princeton University Press, 1981.

De Castell, Suzanne, and Mary Bryson. "Retooling Play: Dystopia, Dysphoria, and Difference." In *From Barbie to Mortal Combat: Gender and Computer Games,* edited by Justine Cassell and Henry Jenkins, 232–61. Cambridge, MA: MIT Press, 1998.

Derrida, Jacques. *Of Grammatology*. Translated by Gayatri Chakravorty Spivak. Baltimore, MD: Johns Hopkins University Press, 1976.

De Silva, Jean. "Edgar Rice Burroughs, Tarzan, and Pulp Fiction: The Making of Modern American Manhood." PhD diss., Emory University, 2004.

Doughty, Terri. "Locating Harry Potter in the 'Boys' Book' Market." In *The Ivory Tower and Harry Potter: Perspectives on a Literary Phenomenon,* edited by Lana A. Whited, 243–57. Columbia: University of Missouri Press, 2002.

Dresang, Eliza T. "Hermione Granger and the Heritage of Gender." In *The Ivory Tower and Harry Potter: Perspectives on a Literary Phenomenon*, edited by Lana A. Whited, 211–42. Columbia: University of Missouri Press, 2002.

Elliott, Jane. "Stepping on the Harry Potter Buzz." 2001, http://www.bitchmagazine.com (accessed December 12, 2003).

Faludi, Susan. *Stiffed: The Betrayal of the American Man*. New York: Harper Perennial, 1999.

Gallardo C., Ximena, and C. Jason Smith. "Cinderfella: J.K. Rowling's Wily Web of Gender." In *Reading Harry Potter: Critical Essays*, edited by Giselle Liza Anatol, 191–205. Westport, CT: Praeger, 2003.

Gilroy, Paul. *Against Race: Imagining Political Culture Beyond the Color Line*. Cambridge, MA: Harvard University Press, 2000.

Giroux, Henry A. "White Noise: Toward a Pedagogy of Whiteness." In *Race-ing Representation: Voice, History, and Sexuality*, edited by Kostas Myrsiades and Linda Myrsiades, 42–76. New York: Rowman & Littlefield, 1998.

Gravett, Paul. *Manga: Sixty Years of Japanese Comics*. New York: HarperCollins Design, 2004.

Gurian, Michael, and Terry Trueman. *What Stories Does My Son Need? A Guide to Books and Movies That Build Character in Boys*. New York: Penguin Putnam, 2000.

Harris, Ian M. *Messages Men Hear: Constructing Masculinites*. Bristol, PA: Taylor & Francis, 1995.

Heilman, Elizabeth E. "Blue Wizards and Pink Witches: Representations of Gender, Identity and Power." In *Harry Potter's World: Multidisciplinary Critical Perspectives*, edited by Elizabeth E. Heilman, 221–39. New York: Routledge Falmer, 2003.

Hipple, Ted, and Amy B. Maupin. "What's Good About the Best?" *English Journal* 90, no. 3 (2001): 40–42.

Hollindale, Peter. "Ideology and the Children's Book." *Signal* 55 (1988): 3–22.

Hourihan, Margery. *Deconstructing the Hero: Literary Theory and Children's Literature*. New York: Routledge, 1997.

Isocrates. "Antidosis." In *The Rhetorical Tradition: Readings from Classical Times to the Present*, edited by Patricia Bizzell and Bruce Herzberg. Boston: Bedford Books of St. Martin's Press, 1990.

Iwabuchi, Koichi. "How 'Japanese' is Pokémon?" In *Pikachu's Global Adventure: The Rise and Fall of Pokémon*, edited by Joseph Tobin, 53–79. Durham, NC: Duke University Press, 2004.

Jenkins, Henry. "'Complete Freedom of Movement': Video Games as Gendered Play Spaces." In *From Barbie to Mortal Combat: Gender and Computer Games*, edited by Justine Cassell and Henry Jenkins, 262–97. Cambridge, MA: MIT Press, 1998a.

———. "Introduction: Childhood Innocence and Other Modern Myths." In *The Children's Culture Reader,* edited by Henry Jenkins, 1–37. New York: New York University Press, 1998b.

Johnston, Ingrid, and Jyoti Mangat. "Making the Invisible Visible: Stereotypes of Masculinity in Canonized High School Literature." In *Ways of Being Male: Representing Masculinities in Children's Literature and Film,* edited by John Stephens, 133–49. New York: Routledge, 2002.

Jurca, Catherine. *White Diaspora: The Suburb and the Twentieth-Century American Novel.* Princeton, NJ: Princeton University Press, 2001.

Kasson, John F. *Houdini, Tarzan, and the Perfect Man: The White Male Body and the Challenge of Modernity in America.* New York: Hill and Wang, 2001.

Katsuno, Hirofumi, and Jeffrey Maret. "Localizing the Pokémon TV Series for the American Market." In *Pikachu's Global Adventure: The Rise and Fall of Pokémon,* edited by Joseph Tobin, 80–107. Durham, NC: Duke University Press, 2004.

Kidd, Kenneth. *Making American Boys: Boyology and the Feral Tale.* Minneapolis: University of Minnesota Press, 2004.

Kimmel, Michael S. "Masculinity as Homophobia: Fear, Shame, and Silence in the Construction of Gender Identity." In *Construction of Difference and Inequality,* edited by Tracy E. Ore, 119–36. New York: McGraw-Hill, 2003.

———. "Foreword." In *Adolescent Boys: Exploring Diverse Cultures of Boyhood,* edited by Niobe Way and Judy Y. Chu, xi–xiii. New York: New York University Press, 2004.

Kindlon, Dan, and Michael Thompson. *Raising Cain: Protecting the Emotional Life of Boys.* New York: Ballantine Books, 1999.

Kirkham, Pat, and Janet Thumim. "You Tarzan." In *You Tarzan: Masculinity, Movies and Men,* edited by Pat Kirkham and Janet Thumim, 11–26. New York: St. Martin's Press, 1993.

Kristeva, Julia. *Powers of Horror: An Essay on Abjection.* Translated by Leon Roudiez. New York: Columbia University Press, 1982.

Lee, Stacey J. "Hmong American Masculinities: Creating New Identities in the United States." In *Adolescent Boys: Exploring Diverse Cultures of Boyhood,* edited by Niobe Way and Judy Y. Chu, 13–30. New York: New York University Press, 2004.

Lind, Michael. "*Tarzan:* Disney Turns Burroughs' Ape-Man into a Momma's Boy." *Slate,* June 25, 1999, http://slate.msn.com/id/31081 (accessed September 8, 2005).

Madden, Ed. "Introduction." In *The Emergence of Man into the 21st Century,* edited by Patricia L. Munhall, Ed Madden, and Virginia Fitzsimons, xxvii–xxxvi. Boston: Jones and Bartlett Publishers, 2002.

Markovitz, Jonathan. *Legacies of Lynching: Racial Violence and Memory.* Minneapolis: University of Minnesota Press, 2004.

McCallum, Robyn. "Masculinity as Social Semiotic: Identity Politics and Gender in Disney Animated Films." In *Ways of Being Male: Representing Masculinities in Children's Literature and Film,* edited by John Stephens, 116–32. New York: Routledge, 2002.

McCloud, Scott. *Understanding Comics: The Invisible Art.* New York: Harper Perennial, 1994.

McGuffey, C. Shawn, and B. Lindsay Rich. "Playing in the Gender Transgression Zone: Race, Class, and Hegemonic Masculinity in Middle Childhood." *Gender and Society* 13, no. 5 (1999): 608–27.

Melnz, Barbara. "Child Caring: Legislation Would Target Violence in Video Games." *Boston Globe,* May 22, 2003, H1.

Messner, Michael. "Barbie Girls Versus Sea Monsters: Children Constructing Gender." *Gender and Society* 14, no. 6 (2000): 765–84.

Michel, Dee. "*The Wizard of Oz:* Fantasy, Gay Men, Escape." Paper presented at the Fantastic Genres Conference, State University of New York, New Paltz, May 1, 2004.

Morton, Walt. "Tracking the Sign of Tarzan: Trans-media Representation of a Pop-Culture Icon." In *You Tarzan: Masculinity, Movies and Men,* edited by Pat Kirkham and Janet Thumim, 106–25. New York: St. Martin's Press, 1993.

National Coalition Against Censorship. "Does Censorship Make Schools Safe?" *Censorship News* 92 (Winter 2003–4), http://www.ncac.org/cen_news/cn92schools.htm (accessed December 1, 2005).

Newkirk, Thomas. *Misreading Masculinity: Boys, Literacy, and Popular Culture.* Portsmouth, NH: Heinemann, 2002.

Nodelman, Perry. "Making Boys Appear: The Masculinity of Children's Fiction." In *Ways of Being Male: Representing Masculinities in Children's Literature and Film,* edited by John Stephens, 1–14. New York: Routledge, 2002.

———. "Blank Slates." Child_Lit: Theory and Criticism of Children's Literature Listserv, September 2, 2005, https://email.rutgers.edu/pipermail/child_lit (accessed September 2, 2005).

Nodelman, Perry, and Mavis Reimer. *The Pleasures of Children's Literature.* 3rd ed. New York: Allyn and Bacon, 2003.

Osgerby, Bill. *Youth Media.* New York and London: Routledge, 2004.

Ostry, Elaine. "Accepting Mudbloods: The Ambivalent Social Vision of J.K. Rowling's Fairy Tales." In *Reading Harry Potter: Critical Essays,* edited by Giselle Liza Anatol, 89–102. Westport, CT: Praeger, 2003.

Perkinson, Jim. "The Body of White Space: Beyond Stiff Voices, Flaccid Feelings, and Silent Cells." In *Revealing Male Bodies,* edited by Nancy Tuana, William Cowling, Maurice Hamington, Greg Johnson, and Terrance MacMullan, 173–97. Bloomington: Indiana University Press, 2002.

Pilkey, Dav. "Dav Pilkey's Extra Crunchy Web Site o' Fun." 2003c, http://www.pilkey.com/index.php.

Pinsent, Pat. "Fate and Fortune in a Modern Fairy Tale: Louis Sachar's *Holes.*" *Children's Literature in Education* 33, no. 3 (2002): 203–12.

Pipher, Mary. *Reviving Ophelia: Saving the Selves of Adolescent Girls.* New York: Ballantine Books, 1994.

Pirie, Bruce. *Teenage Boys and High School English.* Portsmouth, NH: Boynton/Cook, 2002.

Pleck, Joseph H. "Men's Power with Women, Other Men, and Society: A Men's Movement Analysis." In *Men's Lives,* edited by Michael Kimmel and Michael A. Messner, 19–27. New York: Macmillan, 1992.

Pollack, William. *Real Boys: Rescuing Our Sons from the Myths of Boyhood.* New York: Henry Holt, 1998.

Reimer, Mavis. "Making Princesses, Re-making *A Little Princess.*" In *Voices of the Other: Children's Literature and the Postcolonial Context,* edited by Roderick McGillis, 111–34. New York: Garland, 1999.

Reynolds, Kimberley. "Come Lads and Ladettes: Gendering Bodies and Gendering Behaviors." In *Ways of Being Male: Representing Masculinities in Children's Literature and Film,* edited by John Stephens, 96–115. New York: Routledge, 2002.

Rivers, Caryl, and Rosalind Chait Barnett. "The Myth of 'The Boy Crisis'." *Washington Post,* April 9, 2006, B01. http://www.washingtonpost.com (accessed April 10, 2006).

Rollin, Lucy, and Mark West. *Psychoanalytic Responses to Children's Literature.* Jefferson, NC: McFarland, 1999.

Romören, Rolf. "The Light of Knowledge—In the Midst of the Jungle: How Tarzan Became a Man." *CREArTA* 2, no. 2 (2001–2): 60–67.

Rose, Jacqueline. *The Case of Peter Pan; or, the Impossibility of Children's Fiction.* London: Macmillan, 1984.

Sabo, Don. "Pigskin, Patriarchy, and Pain." In *Men's Lives,* edited by Michael Kimmel and Michael A. Messner, 184–90. New York: Macmillan, 1992.

"*Sailor Moon* Petition." June 24, 2004, www.petitiononline.com.

Schoefer, Christine. "Harry Potter's Girl Trouble." January 13, 2000, http://www.salon.com (accessed December 12, 2003).

Sedgwick, Eve Kosofsky. "How to Bring Your Kids Up Gay." In *The Children's Culture Reader,* edited by Henry Jenkins, 231–40. New York: New York University Press, 1998.

Seiter, Ellen. *Sold Separately: Children and Parents in Consumer Culture.* New Brunswick, NJ: Rutgers University Press, 1993.

———. "Children's Desires/Mothers' Dilemmas: The Social Contexts of Consumption." In *The Children's Culture Reader,* ed. Henry Jenkins, 297–317. New York: New York University Press, 1998.

Smith, Michael W., and Jeffrey Wilhelm. *"Reading Don't Fix No Chevys": Literacy in the Lives of Young Men.* Portsmouth, NH: Heinemann, 2002.

Sommers, Christina Hoff. *The War Against Boys: How Misguided Feminism Is Harming Our Young Men.* New York: Simon and Schuster, 2000.

Stephens, John. "Preface." In *Ways of Being Male: Representing Masculinities in Children's Literature and Film,* edited by John Stephens, ix–xiv. New York: Routledge, 2002.

Sugar Quill. "Gender in Harry Potter." Harry Potter fan discussion forum, September 11 to December 3, 2003, http://www.sugarquill.net (accessed December 12, 2003).

Talsorian Games. January 28, 2004, www.talsorian.com.

Thacker, Deborah. "Disdain or Ignorance? Literary Theory and the Absence of Children's Literature." *The Lion and the Unicorn* 24, no. 1 (2000): 1–17.

Theweleit, Klaus. *Male Fantasies: Volume 1: Women, Floods, Bodies, History.* Translated by Stephen Conway. Minneapolis: University of Minnesota Press, 1987.

Thorne, Barrie. "Boys and Girls Together … but Mostly Apart." In *The Children's Culture Reader,* edited by Henry Jenkins, 318–36. New York: New York University Press, 1998.

Tobin, Joseph. "Introduction." In *Pikachu's Global Adventure: The Rise and Fall of Pokémon,* edited by Joseph Tobin, 3–11. Durham, NC: Duke University Press, 2004.

Trelease, Jim. "Captain Underpants Tremors." *Trelease on Reading,* 2003, http://www.trelease-on-reading.com (accessed December 20, 2004).

Warner, Charles Dudley. *Being a Boy.* Boston: James R. Osgood, 1877.

Way, Niobe, and Judy Y. Chu, eds. *Adolescent Boys: Exploring Diverse Cultures of Boyhood.* New York: New York University Press, 2004.

Winik, Lyric Wallwork. "We Need to Pay More Attention to Boys." *Parade,* January 16, 2005, http://www.parade.com/archive.jsp (accessed January 28, 2005).

Wojcik-Andrews, Ian. *Children's Films: History, Ideology, Pedagogy, Theory.* New York: Garland, 2000.

Wu, Mei-Ying. "'What Fantastic Creatures Boys Are': Ideology, Discourse, and the Construction of Boyhood in Selected Juvenile Fiction." PhD diss., University of Idaho, 2005.

Xie, Shaobo. "Rethinking the Identity of Cultural Otherness: The Discourse of the Difference as an Unfinished Project." In *Voices of the Other: Children's Literature and the Postcolonial Context,* edited by Roderick McGillis, 1–16. New York: Garland, 1999.

Yano, Christine R. "Panic Attacks: Anti-Pokémon Voices in Global Markets." In *Pikachu's Global Adventure: The Rise and Fall of Pokémon,* edited by Joseph Tobin, 108–40. Durham, NC: Duke University Press, 2004.

Yearwood, Stephenie. "Popular Postmodernism for Young Readers: *Walk Two Moons, Holes,* and *Monster.*" *ALAN Review* 29, no. 3 (2002): 50–53.

Zipes, Jack. "Once Upon a Time Beyond Disney: Contemporary Fairy-Tale Films for Children." In *In Front of the Children: Screen Entertainment and Young Audiences,* edited by Cary Bazalgette and David Buckingham, 109–26. London: British Film Institute, 1995.

———. *Sticks and Stones: The Troublesome Success of Children's Literature from Slovenly Peter to Harry Potter.* New York: Routledge, 2002.

INDEX

A

Abjection
    adult repulsion by, 30
    and ambiguity, 29
    association with feminine and homosexuality, 113
    and bounded/gendered identity, 35
    in Captain Underpants series, 34, 85–87
    as central focus of literature, 28
    constructing dominant masculinity in opposition to, 149
    as crucial to gender identity and performance, 128
    food loathing as, 98
    and formation of boundaries, 150
    and gender performance, 95–101
    and masculine body in *Dragon Ball Z,* 104–105
    and normative masculinity, 95–101
    in *Peter Pan,* 31
    in Tarzan myth, 38, 50
    threat of, 29
Action stories, as traditional boys' favorites, 15
Adult readers, vs. boy readers, 18, 21
Adventure stories, as traditional boys' favorites, 16
Adventures of Super Diaper Baby, 98–99
All-male communities, 70
Alternative masculinity, 20
American Library Association
    Best Book for Young Adults award, 68
    and censorship of books on gay characters, 153
    critique of Captain Underpants series, 90
American Men's Studies Association, 20
Anime, 35, 104
    popularity with boys, 16, 103
Aristocracy, in Tarzan story, 41
Attention deficit/hyperactivity disorder, 130
    in Captain Underpants series, 89
    predominance among boys, 2
Authority
    masculine need to defy, 71, 73
    ridicule of adult, 91
    subversion in Captain Underpants series, 85–95
Award committees, choice of children's literature, 18

B

Bakersfield City School District, banning of Captain Underpants series by, 91
Bibliotherapy, 3
Black males, as sexual predators in Tarzan myth, 48
Blank slates
    assumption of children as, 23
    children as other than, 27–28
    and debates over Harry Potter novels, 121
    use of boys as, 7–8
Bodily borders, 128
    in Captain Underpants series, 85–87
    disruption of, 92, 95, 98
    in *Dragon Ball Z,* 105
    and Majin Buu, 113

use of grotesque, 92
Bodily humor. *See also* Bodily borders
 in coming-of-age narratives, 31
Body
 as both natural and constructed, 27
 complexities of being born into
 defined, 28
 in Disney's version of *Tarzan*, 62–63
 and gendered subjectivity, 27
 masculine, in *Dragon Ball Z*, 104
 as open and leaky with shifting
  borders, 93
 parental control over, 94
 in Tarzan myth, 56
Boundaries
 between child and adult, 30
 and literature of the abject, 29, 35
 vs. abjection, 35
Boy crisis, 123
 rhetoric of, 1–11
Boyology, 33, 37, 150
 as conservative American ideology, 6
 and feral tale, 153
Boys
 attraction to Captain Underpants
  series, 86
 damage by social expectations of
  stifled emotions, 116
 inability to identify with female
  protagonists, 86–87
 as natural savages, 37
 and social pressures to stifle
  emotions, 123
 U.S. fixation with, 3
"Boys will be boys" theory, 30, 38, 122, 160
 and invisible masculinity, 24–25
Bullying, in Harry Potter novels, 138
Burroughs, Edgar Rice, 38
 self-liberation through Tarzan
  stories, 43

C

Camp Green Lake, 69
Captain Underpants and the Attack of the Talking Toilets, 97
Captain Underpants and the Big, Bad Battle of the Bionic Booger Boy, 92, 99–100
Captain Underpants and the Perilous Plot of Professor Poopypants, 89
Captain Underpants series, 21, 160
 abjection in, 34
 banning by Bakersfield City School
  District, 91
 as cultural artifact, 86, 87
 lowbrow origin, 88, 92
Carnival
 parallels to Captain Underpants
  humor, 93–94, 95
 as parody and festive laughter, 96–97
Childhood
 conflation with wild and primitive
  nature, 45
 social construction of, 3
Children, as dupes of media, 24
Children's literature
 and adult desires, 23
 as cultural artifact, 69
 as legitimate academic discipline, 22
 as maternal literature, 18
 Tarzan's absence from canons of, 38
 as women's domain, 18
Chivalry, in Tarzan myth, 47
Class privilege
 and characterizations of Tarzan, 33
 in Tarzan myth, 38
Clayton, 148
 as male antihero in Disney, 39, 59, 63
College attendance, among boys vs.
  girls, 2
Colonization, 157
 in Tarzan myth, 49–53
Columbine shootings
 and gender identity, 119
 and suspicion of aggressive play, 118
Comic books, as traditional boys'
  favorites, 16
Comics Code, 9
Coming-of-age narratives, 69
 bodily humor and the grotesque
  in, 31
 confirming stereotypical constructs
  of masculinity in, 70
 negating the feminine in, 72
 Sachar's *Holes,* 68–69
Conrad, Joseph, 50
Consumerism, shielding of children
 from, 106

Creative role play, and *Dragon Ball Z*, 110–112
Cultural odor, 114
Cultural studies, views of children's literature in, 24
Culturally relevant literature, 4
Cyclical art, in Asian traditions, 107

D

Delinquency, debate over media influence on, 9
Dementors, 139–140
Digimon, 103
Disney films
    bowdlerized version of Tarzan in, 38
    characterization of Tarzan in, 34
    conflicting ideas of contemporary masculinity in, 58–66
    free market goals of, 61
    popularity with boys, 16
    and reinforcement of dominant social structures, 61
    sanitizing of colonialism in *Tarzan*, 58
    and Tarzan as modernized male, 39
    watered-down hero narrative of *Tarzan*, 60
Draco Malfoy, 143, 144
Dragon Ball Z, 35, 103, 150
    creative role-play in, 110–111
    debate over contributions to violent behavior, 111
    editing of violence in, 109
    as international franchise, 108
    popularity with American boys, 104, 112
Dropout rate, among boys vs. girls, 2
Dursleys, 148
    as disturbing norm for boys, 133–135

E

Economic class, and boy crisis, 7
Elite education, hierarchy of reading in, 13
Emasculating female characters, in Sacher's *Holes*, 81
Emotional suppression
    as cultural construction, 139
    and Harry Potter novels, 130–131
    pressures on boys, 123
Empathy
    in Harry Potter novels, 143–144
    as nonhegemonic masculine trait, 138
Eugenics, in Tarzan story, 46

F

Fainting, in Harry Potter novels, 140
Fantasy, as traditional boys' favorites, 16
Femininity
    boy's need to distance self from, 69
    construction as Other, 124, 161
    as emasculating, 81
    as frightening/disgusting, 71
    as inhuman or abject, 99
    negating to become masculine, 70, 71, 76
    personification in horror films, 77
    as poisonous, 79, 82
    and stigmas against boys with feminine traits, 76
Feminism
    debate about effects on boys, 2–3
    debate over J.K. Rowling and, 121
    as emasculating force, 123
    in Harry Potter novels, 125
    and politicization of boy crisis debates, 5
    suspicions about boys in crisis, 6
    use of boys as foil to critique, 5
Feral boy myth, 37, 41, 50, 65, 153
    and chivalrous masculinity, 51
    in Disney's *Tarzan*, 61
    in Tarzan story, 158
Fictional child
    adult perceptions of, 30
    as cultural artifact, 16
    as projection of adult desire, 1
Food loathing, as abjection, 98
Frankfurt School, 24
Freudian Child, 117

G

Gender
    as alterable, 87

as both fixed and tenuous, 32
changing expectations of, 33
children's and adults' anxieties about, 130
in children's literature, 25
construction through exclusionary means, 100
cultural anxieties about instability of, 101
fluid construction of, 128
as foundation of subjectivity, 26
in Harry Potter novels, 124–130
nuanced portrayal in Harry Potter novels, 35
as socially constructed, 5, 26, 125, 127
and subjectivity, 27
in Tarzan myth, 52–53
testosterone-driven portrayals in *Dragon Ball Z*, 112
Gender differences, in reading habits, 16
Gender identity
conflict resolution in Captain Underpants series, 86
cultural anxieties about, 10
Gender performance
abjection and, 96, 128
in Captain Underpants series, 95–101
Gender roles
adult investments in, 14
complexity in Wizarding world, 132
nonstereotypical in Harry Potter novels, 124
reinforcement by parents, 149–150
Gender studies, as domain of women, 20
Gendered identity, nuances of, 8
Girl readers, identification with male and female protagonists by, 86
Global capitalism, 117–118
God's Thumb, 82–83
Grand Theft Auto game, 9
Greystoke: The Legend of Tarzan, Lord of the Apes, 42
Grotesqueness
boys' enjoyment of parents' horror of, 118
in Captain Underpants series, 92, 95
in children's literature, 94
in *Dragon Ball Z*, 108–109

H

Harry Potter, 150
empathy in, 138
heterosocial friendships and unconventional masculinity in, 141
nonhegemonic masculinity in, 137–138
Harry Potter and the Half-Blood Prince, 124, 136, 162
Harry Potter and the Order of the Phoenix, 138
Harry Potter and the Prisoner of Azkaban, 139
Harry Potter novels, 35
and debates over gendered behavior, 124–130
nonhegemonic masculinity in, 137
witchy masculinities in, 121, 130–145
Heart of Darkness, 50
Hegemonic masculinity
assumption of harm to boys by, 14
categories of, 33
Clayton as representative of undesirable, 63–64
cultural basis of, 32
difficulty of defining, 21
failure to conform in Harry Potter novels, 122
intrinsic contradictions in Disney's *Tarzan*, 66
potential damage to boys and men, 20
as problem in Disney's *Tarzan*, 39
and scrutiny by other males, 73
separation from mother to achieve, 79–80
slow change in images of, 40
in Tarzan myth, 50
unflattering portrayals in Harry Potter novels, 133–135
Hermione, 126
critique by radical feminists, 129
in Harry Potter novels, 122
and heterosocial friendships, 141–143
as role model for girls, 124
Hero tales, 4

Heterosexuality
  discourse to maintain superiority of, 8
  reinforcement by Tarzan myth, 56–57
  in Sachar's *Holes*, 68
  as site of privilege, 32
Heterosocial friendships, in Harry Potter novels, 141–143
Hobby literature, as traditional boys' favorites, 16
Holes, 34, 67
  film adaptation, 159
Homosexual traits
  association with abjection, 113–114
  censorship of books featuring, 153
  literary intolerance for, 76
  and *Wizard of Oz*, 133
Horror films, monstrous feminine in, 77
Hudson, Hugh, 42
Humor, 16
  bodily-oriented, 87–95
  in Captain Underpants series, 86
  as traditional boys' favorites, 15

I

Identity formation, 23
Immigration fears, in Tarzan story, 45
Imperialism, in Tarzan myth, 38, 45, 49
Individuality, and characterizations of Tarzan, 33
Information books, 16
  as traditional boys' favorites, 15
Innocent child myth, 109
  and debates over Harry Potter novels, 121
Invisibility
  of gay, poor, minority boys, 8
  of masculinity concepts, 147, 148

J

Japanese cultural exports, 35, 103. *See also* Anime; Manga

K

Kissin' Kate Barlow, 77–78, 82

L

Liberal educators, 4
Literacy levels, 159
  and boys' view of reading as feminine activity, 134
  decline among boys, 2
  Holes as antidote to low boys', 68
  narrow definition of, 21
Literary canon, 14
  children's literature within, 22
  debate about, 4
Literary merit
  differing adult perceptions of, 14
  links to issues of gender and childhood, 13
Literature of quality, boys' disdain for, 16
Lord Greystoke, 41
  and fantasy of empire, 50
Lower class
  depictions as Other in Tarzan myth, 53–55
  in Tarzan story, 44
Lynchings, 48, 156
  and Tarzan myth, 47–49

M

Magical realism, in Sachar's *Holes*, 67
Majin Buu, 103, 115
  and frustrations of global capitalism coming-of-age, 117
  grotesque bodily transformations of, 113–114
Manga, 35
  American xenophobic reactions to, 107
  illustrative and narrative techniques in, 107, 108
  popularity with boys, 16, 103
  prevalence at bookstores, 104
Manifest destiny, in Tarzan myth, 50
Marginalization, and critique of dominant masculinity, 19

178 • Index

Masculinity
    and abjection in Captain Underpants series, 95–101
    ambivalence about contemporary, 66
    complicated portrayal in contemporary texts, 10
    conflicts inherent in Disney's version of Tarzan, 62, 66
    conforming to culturally dominant versions of, 71
    continuous need to prove, 84
    contradictions in current constructs, 150
    critique of assumptions by recommended literature, 19
    deep cultural anxiety about contemporary, 35
    in Disney's *Tarzan*, 39
    dominant versions of, 154
    as fascistic in *Dragon Ball Z*, 115
    fluid nature of, 24
    inherent contradictions in Tarzan myth, 55
    invisibility in natural theory of, 25
    marginalization by dominant versions of, 20
    marking, 147–152
    as natural development, 147
    need for critical language of discourse, 25
    offer of antidotes to negative images of, 15
    proving through physical endurance, 72
    rescuing boys from, 1
    and rites of passage in Sacher's *Holes*, 75
    and sensitivity in Disney's *Tarzan*, 64
    slow historical change in depictions of, 40
    as social construct, 19, 24, 70, 148
    stereotypical traits in U.S., 71
    ties to whiteness in Tarzan story, 43
Mateship, 142
Media influence
    as factor in delinquency, 9
    per Frankfurt School of cultural studies, 24
Men's studies, 24

Middle-class boys
    discourse of superiority, 8
    in Tarzan myth, 43, 63
Miscegenation, fears of, in Tarzan myth, 48, 49
Monolithic Boy, 17
Monstrous feminine
    in horror films, 77
    in Sacher's *Holes*, 77–81
    symbolic triumph over, 83
    Warden as, 80–81
Moral education, texts as, 14–15
Moral panics, and reactions to Japanese cultural imports, 106
Mother
    boy's need to distance self from, 69, 79
    gaining independence from, 99
    motif of overcoming bad, 70
    in Sacher's *Holes*, 75
Mother domination theory, 81
Mrs. Gorf, 159
Muggle world, normative nature of, 132

N

National Book Award, 68
National Coalition against Censorship, 160–161
Nature, restoring connection with, 70
Neville Longbottom, 138
    gender in, 126
Newberry Medal, 67

O

Other
    and abjection, 29
    boy as, 31
    construction of femininity as, 124
    lower class in Tarzan myth as, 53–55
    need for responsibility to, 74
    in Tarzan myth, 37–40, 44
    and Western colonialism ethic, 52

P

Pain, masculine need to endure, 71–72

Parody, in Captain Underpants series, 86
Patriarchy, damage to boys by, 123
Peter Pan, 31
Pilkey, Dav, 85, 89
Poetry, as traditional girls' favorites, 16
Pokémon, 103
　parental critiques of, 106
Politically correct literature, 4, 129
Popular texts
　attraction to amoral and violent, 18
　as cultural artifacts, 23, 69, 151–152
　depiction of white, heterosexual, middle-class boys in, 32
　disconnect with recommended texts, 13
　dismissal as garbage, 21
　disregard by academia, 21
　history of criticism, 35
　perceptions of adult readers as threatening, 31
　as space filled with anxiety, 29
　as subliterature, 15
　subversive and liberatory potential in, 24
　and threat of abjection, 29
　vs. choices of award committees, 18
　vs. literature of quality, 16
　vs. recommended texts, 9, 15
Power fantasies
　in Captain Underpants series, 91
　and *Dragon Ball Z,* 118
Privilege, 32
　taking responsibility for, 74
　white denial of, 73
Problem novels, 4, 14
Professor Dumbledore, 136
Professor McGonagall, 122, 136
Protagonist gender, and gender reading preferences, 10
Pulp literature, Tarzan's origins in, 40–42, 155
Pure white woman, in Tarzan myth, 48

R

Racial differences
　in Sachar's *Holes,* 73–75
　in Tarzan myth, 45–46
　vs. boy crisis, 7

Rage, in *Dragon Ball Z,* 113
Reading, as feminine activity in boys' view, 134
Reading habits, gender differences in, 16
Reading lists
　for girls vs. boys, 10
　as remedies to social ills, 14
Realistic fiction, as traditional girls' favorites, 16
Recommended texts
　and critique of assumptions about masculinity, 19
　vs. popular texts, 9, 13, 15
Right wing, 6
　and politicization of boy crisis discourse, 5
Robinson Crusoe, 44
Role models, 14
　beyond, 13
　and Harry Potter novels, 127
　recommendation of texts containing male, 10
　troubling cruelty of Harry Potter's, 138
　for whiteness, 74
Rowling, J.K., 121
Rubeus Hagrid, and unconventional masculinity, 137

S

Sachar, Louis, 34
Small Steps, 160
Sailor Moon, girls' preference for, 112
Saiyans
　and cultural odor, 114
　similarities to Nordic cultures, 115
Scatological texts. *See also* Bodily humor
　boys' fascination with, 34
　Captain Underpants series, 88, 93
School Library Journal, Best Book of the Year award, 68
Science fiction, 16
　as traditional boys' favorites, 15
Sensitivity
　in Disney's *Tarzan,* 64
　in Harry Potter novels, 139–140
Series books, as traditional boys' favorites, 16
Single-sex education, 3

Slytherins, sexist portrayal of, 131–132
Social construction
    of childhood, 3
    of gendered behavior, 5
    of masculinity, 24
Sports books, as traditional boys' favorites, 16
Stanley Yelnats, 78
    as subject of *Bildungsroman*, 69
Stereotypes, beyond, 13
Strong character, debate over defining, 10
Subjectivity, 28
    and abjection, 28
    complexities of formation, 8, 17
    defined, 26
    dominant cultural understandings of, 32
    gender as foundation of, 26
    never-ending journey toward, 31
    and requirement of internalizing social norms, 68–69
    threat to, in children's literature, 29
    via taking responsibility for white privilege, 74
Subversion, in Captain Underpants series, 87–95
Surrealism, in Sachar's *Holes*, 68

T

Tarzan, 148
    Americanization of, 42
    aristocratic origins of, 42, 52, 54
    changing characterizations in 20th century, 33, 34
    as colonizer, 49–53
    and conflicting ideals of masculinity, 58–66
    contradictions in Disney version, 39, 63
    differences between Disney and Burroughs, 59
    and dubious science of race, 45–46, 156
    as environmentalist in Disney version, 64
    evolution of icon, 37–40
    heterosexual orientation of, 56–58
    and history of lynching, 47–49
    Hugh Hudson's alternative telling, 42
    impact on American culture, 155
    as impossible ideal of American masculinity, 38
    individualism of, 43
    and Jim Crow mythologies, 47–49
    lowbrow origins of myth, 40–42
    and lower class as Other, 53–55
    as master of environment, 43
    as mother's boy in Disney, 58–66
    as object of female desire, 56–58
    as object of modern male fantasies, 43–45
    origins in pulp fiction, 40–42
    representation of both democracy and aristocracy in, 55
    rite of passage into manhood, 59
    as sensitive modern male, 59
    as vegetarian in Disney version, 59
Tarzan of the Apes, 38, 44, 47
Television programs
    anxieties based on class bias, 110
    critiques of links to violence, 110
    popularity with boys, 16
Text–child reader relationships, 23
Text–reader–culture relationship, 23, 26
    continuous negotiation in, 124
Title IX, challenge from boy crisis, 5
Top-down socialization theories, 17

V

Vagina Dentata, 77, 83
    the Warden as, 78
Video games
    Disney's *Tarzan*, 61–62
    as Japanese cultural imports, 103
    as traditional boys' favorites, 16
    violence in, 9
Violence
    boys' perceived propensity to, 21
    concerns about boys and, 130
    critiques of studies linking television to, 110
    and editing in Japanese cartoons, 109
    in Japanese cultural exports, 104
    justification in Tarzan stories, 157
    and rites of passage, 135

school bans on writing about, 90
in Tarzan story, 41
in video games, 9

W

Warden, the, 78–81
    as monstrous feminine, 77
White boys
    and characterizations of Tarzan, 33
    discourse of ensuring superiority of, 8
    Sachar's role model for, 74
    as site of privilege, 32
    in Tarzan myth, 43
White supremacy, in Tarzan myth, 46
Witchy masculinities, in Harry Potter novels, 121, 130–145
Wizard of Oz stories, appeal to gay men and boys, 133
Wizarding world
    appeal to nonconforming males, 133
    complex gender roles in, 132
    otherness of, 161–162
Women's Educational Equity Act, 6
Women's studies, 24

X

Xenophobia
    in American reactions to manga, 107
    in Tarzan myth, 45

Lightning Source UK Ltd.
Milton Keynes UK
UKOW03f0346101213

222683UK00018B/343/P